Lord Jesus, I Want To See...

Adult Edition

Reverend Peter G. Vu

To

Thank you for your kind support. May this book keep you close to Jesus & bring you His love, joy, & peace when you pray it.

☺ Fr. Peter

First published by Dog Ear Publishing
4011 Vincennes Rd
Indianapolis, IN 46268
www.dogearpublishing.net

ISBN: 978-1-4575-5490-2

This book is printed on acid-free paper.

Printed in the United States of America

I dedicate this book to the following people:

- My Family: Grandparents, Parents, Uncles, and Aunts who first taught me how to pray and laid the foundation for me to build a strong and faithful prayer life.
- My Teachers: Priests, Religious Brothers and Sisters, Deacons, Catechists, and Laypeople who lifted my prayer life to a higher level and gave it some depth and tradition, but also challenged me to pray often.
- My Parishioners: Families and individual members who have let me be a part of their lives and faith journey to see their daily struggles have added real flavor to my prayer life as I try to remember them often in my daily prayers.
- My Friends: These Dear Souls have helped and encouraged me with this project.

Thank you and God bless you all! You are in my thoughts often and my prayers always.

Introduction

This project transpired thanks to a combination of these factors.

First, I have seen how the science and technology sectors have put much time and resources into research and development to devise with new ways to improve and advance their businesses and our modern way of life. Following their thinking, I want to do the same for our spirituality sector. I want to come up with a new way of prayer that is simple, personal, relatable, character-building, and suitable to the busy way of life for a twenty-first-century Christian.

Second, I have looked at various ways we have dealt with exercises for our bodies. Most of them involve running, stretching, or weight lifting. Some of these physical exercises are designed for specific functions such as Zumba, Yoga, or Abs work. These specific exercises inspire me to come up with a spiritual exercise that could give people a sense of prayer and simultaneously help them work on specific attributes such as faith, kindness, caring, gentleness, generosity, peacefulness, and so on. Hence, I have chosen the format of this Prayer Book with a specific word or issue for each day and a practical exercise at the end throughout the year.

Third, each day we see on the news and through various personal encounters how the public is in desperate need of character-building and moral guidance to help create good citizens and a healthy society. Unfortunately, due to political correctness and other social trends, moral character and great personal attributes have taken the back seat to other qualities such as appearances, charm, glamor, fame, social status, and possessions. We must demand and encourage our citizens of this great nation and future generations to work on and acquire these qualities and other moral characteristics for the sake of their well-being and happiness.

Finally, some of my dear friends have introduced and encouraged me to look at other forms of prayer besides the traditional way of praying, namely, reciting memorized prayers.

After putting all the factors above together and after twenty years of serving God's people in parishes and ten years of seminary training, I have designed a format of praying that is rooted in Holy Scriptures, daily issues, personal experiences, character-building, and practical spiritual exercises. The format is designed to be self-reflecting and easy reading, and, I hope, will help each person work on essential qualities while spending some quiet time in the presence of Jesus.

I chose the title of the book "**Lord Jesus, I want to see…**" after prayerful reflection on the miracles that Jesus did for the public during His ministry, as well as all the problems our world is facing right now. Like a blind man, our world does not seem to see what is wrong or know how to deal with its current problems. Furthermore, in the course of delivering my homilies, many children have told me that blindness is much more difficult to endure compared to other problems such as being deaf, mute, paralyzed, or having leprosy.

My hope is that our Lord Jesus will heal the spiritual blindness of our world and allow you see things in your life with a better vision. May you also grow closer to Him and accumulate many great personal qualities each day as you try to become a better Christian in this challenging world.

Fr. Peter G. Vu

January

Lord Jesus,
I Want to See...

January 1

<u>Issue:</u> **Acceptance**
"Listen to counsel and accept instruction that you may eventually become wise." (Proverbs 19:20)

<u>Reflection</u>
It is difficult for us to accept ourselves—our strengths and weaknesses along with the situations in which we find ourselves. We tend to hate who we are and the way we look. Or, we become covetous and desire what our neighbors have. We curse our current situations and do not make good use of what God has given us. Worse yet, we become destructive and destroy our neighbors. That is what Cain did to Abel. That is what King David did to his General Uriah.

<u>Lord Jesus, I want to see</u>
Loving God, help me learn to give thanks often and accept the good and the bad, who I am, how I look, and whatever situation in which I might find myself today, with a smile. Make me realize that cursing my misfortunes or forcing a solution out of envy for my neighbor will not bring me true happiness. Help me remember that you will always love me for who I am and that you have a plan for my life.

<u>Resolution</u>
Today, I will welcome whatever God might send my way during the day with a smile and a quick prayer.

January 2

Issue: **Appreciation**
"In all circumstances give thanks, for this is the will of God for you in Christ Jesus." (1 Thessalonians 5:18)

Reflection
We live in an age that is all about me and my accomplishments. We take for granted what God and everyone around us has done for us and contributed to our successes. We criticize others freely, but hesitate to say thank you to all our benefactors. Like the crowd that Jesus healed and fed in thousands later that did not hesitate to condemn him to death, we might not have any problem biting the hand of God that feeds us.

Lord Jesus, I want to see
Gracious God, I thank you for creating me and continuing to bless me each day. Open my eyes to see that all I have now, and all I have ever accomplished comes from you. Move me to express my appreciation for you and all my benefactors often. Help me never take you, or anyone, or anything for granted.

Resolution
Today, I will try to find as many things and people for which I can say thank you or give appreciation.

January 3

Issue: **Belief**

"These signs will accompany those who believe: in my name they will drive out demons, they will speak new languages." (Mark 16:17)

Reflection

One of the complaints we often hear about our politicians is that they do not have any conviction and go with whatever way the wind blows. We like people who have a backbone and who are willing to stand up for something despite its consequences. But, politicians are not the only ones who have this problem. Many people, including me, are afraid to take a stand or show a strong conviction about something. Worse yet, many people these days find it difficult to believe in God or have a relationship with the divine.

Lord Jesus, I want to see

Heavenly Father, give me the courage to believe in something and have the conviction to see it through despite the cost. Help me put my trust and hope in you in good times and in bad and know that you will be there to protect and guide me.

Resolution

Today, I will find someone or some idea that I truly believe in and can count on for protection and guidance through all the ups and downs of my life.

January 4

Issue: **Birth**

"Blessed be the God and Father of our Lord Jesus Christ, who in His great mercy gave us a new birth to a living hope through the resurrection of Jesus Christ from the dead." (1Peter 1-3)

Reflection

We often hear about the miracle of child birth and the joy a baby brings into our lives. We can see the joy and smile on the face of the parent or grandparent when he/she holds a baby in his/her arms. A baby, or a new birth, can bring about all sorts of mixed emotions and a complete transformation in one's life. That's why Jesus suggested to Nicodemus that he be born again if he wanted to enter the Kingdom of God. For that Kingdom belongs to anyone who has child-like faith.

Lord Jesus, I want to see

Lord Jesus, you entered our world in the form of a baby to bring me joy and wonderful promises of the Kingdom of God. Help me welcome and embrace every child as I would embrace you. Teach me to change my old ways and be open to new thinking and adventures that you might show me today, and every day, for this reflects the spirit of a child.

Resolution

Today, I will do something different and be open to all the adventures the Lord might send my way, for this is the "new me."

January 5

<u>Issue:</u> **Blindness**

"Two blind men were sitting by the roadside and when they heard that Jesus was passing by, they cried out, 'Lord, Son of David, have pity on us!'...Jesus stopped, called them and said: 'What do you want me to do for you'...They answered, 'Lord, I want to see'". (Matthew 20:30-33)

<u>Reflection</u>

Jesus did a lot of healing during His years of ministry on earth. But, what He healed quite a few times was blindness. Once, He asked one of the blind men what he wanted the miracle worker to do for him. The blind man answered, "Lord, I want to see!" Not being able to see is probably one of the toughest impediments a person must endure. Ironically, our world has suffered from a terrible problem of spiritual blindness, which has reached the level of pandemic. More and more people suffer from depression and run into a spiritual dead end. This has caused all sorts of violent outbursts in society and has caused people to make wrong decisions in their lives.

Lord Jesus, I want to see

Jesus the Healer, I want to see what I must do in this life to enter your Kingdom. Help me find my life mission here on earth and continue your healing work in our spiritually blind world. Open my heart to welcome you and your messages in good times and in bad.

<u>Resolution</u>

Today, I'll call out to Jesus for help in prayer and search for His presence in everything I do, for He is my vision and guide in this life.

January 6

Issue: **Celebrations**
"Therefore, it is in this month that you must celebrate this rite, after the Lord, your God, has brought you into the land of the Canaanites, Hittites, Amorites, Hivites and Jebusites, which He swore to your Fathers He would give you, a land flowing with milk and honey." (Exodus 13:5)

Reflection

In these last few months, we have celebrated Thanksgiving, Christmas, and a New Year besides birthdays, anniversaries, and other fun occasions. Most people enjoy those celebrations and love to be a part of them so that they can be with their families and friends. How about inviting Jesus, the lost, and the outcast? Do we include and invite them to our celebrations? Often, we forget to invite, and we exclude Jesus and these folks from our celebrations. We need to have Jesus and all the lowly people be a part of our lives.

Lord Jesus, I want to see

Humble Jesus, you told us in the Scriptures to invite the lowly and unimportant people to our banquets and celebrations, even though they have no way to pay us back. Help me to keep that advice in mind and include you as part of all my celebrations and also in every day of my life. Make me realize that, by inviting you to my life events, you will bring me a lot of blessings and miracles like you did to the newlywed couple at their wedding party in Cana.

Resolution

Today, I will think about Jesus and make Him an important part of all my decisions and activities of my day, especially giving thanks and praise to Him often in my prayers.

January 7

Issue: **Choice**

"I have set before you life and death, the blessing and the curse. Choose life, then, that you and your descendants may live, by loving the Lord your God and heeding His voice, and holding fast to him." (Deuteronomy 30:19-20)

Reflection

Our lives are all about choosing and making choices. If we make a wrong choice, we will pay a dear price later for it. If we pick the right things, our lives will be blessed and we will not feel regret when looking back. Adam and Eve made wrong choices and picked something else over their faithful and loving God. Their wrong choice affected not only them but also many generations after them. Judas chose twenty pieces of silver over his master, and that choice hurt Jesus deeply; but it did not bring Judas any happiness in the end. On the other hand, eleven other disciples chose Jesus over everything else, and that choice was confidently supported as Peter professed, "Lord, to whom shall we go? You have the words of everlasting life."

Lord Jesus, I want to see

Lord Jesus, help me make the right choices each day by coming to you for wisdom and guidance for all my decisions. Open my eyes to see your will for me in my daily life and seek you above all things. For you are the source of true happiness and peace.

Resolution

Today, I will choose things that will bring glory to God and result in long-lasting happiness for me and everyone around me.

January 8

Issue: **Complacency**

"Woe to the complacent in Zion, to the overconfident on the mount of Samaria... Now they shall be the first to go into exile and their wanton revelry shall be done away with." (Amos 6:1-7)

Reflection

The opposite of complacency is to be alert, awake, or vigilant. We usually fall into the state of complacency when everything becomes boring and routine in our lives. We do not feel any excitement or have any goal to look forward to. We simply sit back and let the world go by without worrying one way or another. We also take for granted everything in our lives. Of course, spiritual complacency is a dangerous state for any Christian to fall into. For we Christians might get caught unprepared at the Second Coming of Jesus. Worse yet, the Prince of Darkness might sneak up on us when we least expect it and cause us permanent harm.

Lord Jesus, I want to see

Lord Jesus, you constantly challenged your disciples to stay alert by continuing to pray. Help me not to take for granted my relationship with you or neglect my spiritual life. For without you, I can do nothing. Open my senses to feel your presence and search for you always. For you are the joy of my life and the reason I wake up each day.

Resolution

Today, I will search for God's presence in everything I do and find ways to build my spiritual life. Perhaps I will motivate myself to pray for one of my family members or friends each day.

January 9

<u>Issue:</u> **Contribution**

"All the princes and the people rejoiced; they brought what was asked and cast into the chest until it was filled." (2Chronicles 24:10)

<u>Reflection</u>

We live in a world that is obsessed with wealth, fame, and vain glory. The rich, famous, and powerful feel that they contribute more to the world and assume they have more influence and control over it. But, from the story of the poor widow, Jesus reminds us that she contributed to the Temple and to God a lot more than the rich and powerful. The rich all contributed from their surplus, but the poor widow did it from her own livelihood. Similarly, each one of us is called to contribute in our own ways and make a difference in our world. Keep in mind that when we contribute to God, we'll be repaid a hundredfold in this life and the next.

Lord Jesus, I want to see

Generous God, I know that my contributions to you and to the world might not be as significant as the rich and powerful. But, all my little acts of kindness, caring, and compassion not only make a difference in our world but also add up over time and will make you proud of me on the Last Day.

<u>Resolution</u>

Today, I will begin my contribution to God and society by helping someone in need or giving a hand around my home on a regular basis.

January 10

Issue: **Courage**
"Be courageous and steadfast; have no fear for it is the Lord, your God, who marches with you; he will never fail you or forsake you." (Deuteronomy 31:6)

Reflection
Our world is facing two serious problems in the modern age: not enough courage to stand up for what is right and lack of humility to beg the high power for help. Our secular society tries to convince us that there is no God, no accountability, and no right or wrong. But, all the laws and regulations in our lives tell us that there are rights and wrongs. Most of those laws derive from natural law and point us to a higher power. We just need to have the courage to do what is right despite our personal cost and ask God for help when needed.

Lord Jesus, I want to see
Judge of the living and the dead, I thank you for giving me a conscience to know right from wrong. Give me courage not only to seek that knowledge but also to stand up for what is right regardless of my personal cost. Also, give me the humility to ask you for help in times of need instead of relying on myself or other worldly powers.

Resolution
Today, I will speak up for what is right or come out to defend the weak and the lowly no matter of the price I must pay for it.

January 11

<u>Issue:</u> **Decisions**
"Each must do as already decided, without sadness or compulsion, for God loves a cheerful giver. Moreover, God is able to make every grace abundant for you." (2Corinthians 9:7-8)

<u>Reflection</u>
Our lives are full of decisions. Every day we must face one decision after another. Some decisions are more serious compared to others. There is nothing we might regret more than making a wrong decision. Adam and Eve committed the first sin, and their mistake caused them to be kicked out of the Garden of Eden. Their decision affected their family and future generations. On the other hand, the decision of Jesus to enter our world and die for us on the Cross helped Him carry out the will of God the Father and brought us all salvation and promise of eternal life. The best source of help for us to make the right decisions is certainly the wisdom of God.

Lord Jesus, I want to see
Wise Counselor, I come to you for wisdom and guidance as I must confront all kinds of decisions every day. Some of them make me fearful, whereas others cause me to be anxious and worried. I do not know where to turn in moments like that. But, with you by my side, I have nothing to worry about. I know that you will help me make the right decisions.

<u>Resolution</u>
Today, I will consult the wisdom of God in prayers before I do something. I will make that a habit for all my future decisions.

January 12

Issue: **Desire**

"The eyes of all look hopefully to you, and you give them their food in due season...You fulfill the desire of those who fear you." (Psalms 145:15-19)

Reflection

The Bible is full of stories about human desires. Some were honorable, whereas most were selfish and wicked. Abraham desired to make it to the Promised Land, and Moses wished to see the Lord in the burning bush. Unfortunately, the rest of God's people simply desired worldly things such as the golden calf. Even after God freed them from the yoke of slavery, they wished that they were back in Egypt with the pot of meat next to them.

Lord Jesus, I want to see

Kind and loving God, you always wish good things for me. Sadly, my heart is filled with selfish and wicked desires. Some of them are harmful to my soul and my relationship with you. Help me avoid those harmful wishes and only desire you and the Kingdom of Heaven above everything else. For being with you for a short moment can bring joy, peace, and other blessings to my weary soul. Other worldly things will come and go, but you and the Kingdom of Heaven will last beyond time.

Resolution

Today, I will spend some time in prayer to be with God and imagine how it feels to be in the Kingdom of Heaven with God.

January 13

<u>Issue:</u> **Direction**

"I, the Lord your God, teach you what is for your good and lead you on the way you should go." (Isaiah 48:17)

<u>Reflection</u>
Today,, we have GPS, Garmin devices, MapQuest, or Google to tell us exactly wherever we'd like to go. There's no way we can ever get lost with that much help! It took the people of God more than forty years to search for right directions before they made it to the Promised Land. Yet, many people in our time continue to feel lost or do not know where they should go with their lives. They are not sure which way they should turn with all the confusing signs, distracting allurements, and misguiding temptations around them. Standing at the intersection of a fork road, they do not know if they should go right or left with their lives.

Lord Jesus, I want to see
Lord Jesus, my Teacher and Guide, you once told Thomas, who asked you about the way to Heaven, "I am the way, the truth, and the life." Help me stay close to you as I try to find my way to Heaven. Lead me when I am lost among worldly things or feel overwhelmed by the mundane things of my life. Hold my hand so that I may not stray too far from you and Heaven. Show me what I need to do each day so that I might make it to Heaven someday.

<u>Resolution</u>
Today, I will look for ways to stay close to Jesus, either spending time in prayer or doing an act of kindness for someone.

January 14

<u>Issue:</u> **The Dove**

"Behold, I am sending you like sheep in the midst of wolves; so be shrewd as serpents and simple as doves." (Matthew 10:16)

<u>Reflection</u>
A dove is one of God's beautiful creatures in God's wonderful creation. Doves are released at social events as a symbol of peace and life, as this gentle creature flies freely and soars in the open sky above us. Noah sent out a dove to check on the flood level. The last time he sent it out, it did not return, signaling that the water had receded. A dove takes on many important roles in our lives.

<u>Lord Jesus, I want to see</u>
Gentle and Loving Jesus, you once gave this advice to your disciples on how to survive in this world as your followers, "Be as cunning as a snake and simple or innocent as a dove." It's not easy to have a pure heart and a simple faith in a world full of tricks and temptations. We're constantly bombarded by negative attitudes, bad language, and all sorts of cheating and deceptions. Many people do not hesitate to stab another in the back and take from one's neighbors what they want. But, as your follower, I am called to have a clean heart and a pure conscience, like an innocent dove, for that is how we deserve to be your disciple.

<u>Resolution</u>
Today, I will avoid any thoughts or actions that might taint my conscience or make me callous to sins and wickedness.

January 15

The Ears

"For the eyes of the Lord are on the righteous and His ears turned to their prayer, but the face of the Lord is against evildoers." (1Peter 3:12)

Reflection

We are told that a voice cried out in the desert, "Prepare the way of the Lord." Another place in the Bible reads, "Hear, O Israel, the Lord your God is Lord alone. Thou shall love the Lord…" Meanwhile, we recall the story of the ten virgins who were called at midnight to go out and welcome the groom. We are also reminded in the Book of Revelation that on the Last Day the Archangel Michael will sound the trumpet to call the dead to life for the judgment of the Lord. Only with a good set of ears or an ability to listen well will we hear the messengers above and their messages.

Lord Jesus, I want to see

Jesus the Medicine Man, you healed all sorts of problems and illnesses in your ministry. But, you also healed more than one deaf man. For you know that listening ability is so crucial to be your followers and to make it through the Gate of Heaven. Help me listen more attentively to your teachings and guidance so that I might know when to go out to welcome you upon your Second Coming and how to live a good Christian life here on earth.

Resolution

Today, I will listen more and speak less. In fact, I'll sit in silence and let you, Jesus, talk to me so that I may sharpen my listening skills a little better.

January 16

Issue: **Eternity**
"These will go off to eternal punishment, but the righteous to eternal life."
(Matthew 25:46)

Reflection
We would love to have services and products that come with a lifetime warranty. For that would free us from all sorts of worries and save us a ton of future expenses. Otherwise, we must buy one insurance policy after another to cover the value of our possessions. But, we do not have an insurance policy or a warranty in this life, which is eternal. So, we should hold tight to anything that can promise us eternal value. The last time we checked on things that have such a value they were our soul and spirit.

Lord Jesus, I want to see
Loving and Eternal God, you sent your Son Jesus to remind us of the value of our Soul and the world of Spirit and to point us to the promise of eternal life and the Kingdom of Heaven. I might not have seen all of that when I was first introduced to Jesus, because I was too preoccupied with worldly things and pleasure. But, over time I've come closer to Him, and now I really want everything that has eternal value. Worldly things do not matter to me that much anymore. All I want is eternal life.

Resolution
Today, I will imagine how it feels to enjoy eternal life in Heaven with Jesus.

January 17

<u>Issue:</u> **Follow**

"Jesus says, 'I am the Light of the World. Whoever follows me will not walk in darkness, but will have the Light of Life.'" (John 8:12)

<u>Reflection</u>

If you have ever followed a tour guide or a troop leader, you realize that in order to be save and not get lost, you need to pay attention to his/her instructions. You should do what the guide or leader tells you, and everything will be fine. On the other hand, if you do not do what you were told or wander off in your own way, chances are you will get lost. Worse yet, you might even get hurt. Unfortunately, this is what we see many folks fall victim to today.

<u>Lord Jesus, I want to see</u>

Jesus, Guide and Leader of the Christian community, I thank you for showing me how to make it to the Kingdom of Heaven in this uncertain world. Help me listen to your teachings and follow your way even though the world might try to distract or convince me otherwise. Give me your hand to lift me up when I fall and wave to me when I wander far from you. For without you, I will be lost in this confusing world.

<u>Resolution</u>

Today, I will think through our Christian traditions and read the Gospels to remind myself what Jesus wants me to do as His follower.

January 18

Issue: **Head**

"There are many parts, yet one body. The eye cannot say to the hand, 'I do not need you,' nor again the head to the feet, 'I do not need you.'" *(1Corinthians 12:20-21)*

Reflection

We often hear someone being referred to as the head of an institution, of an office, or of an organization. These people are considered important and powerful. They usually have many individuals work for them, and they tell others what to do. It is difficult to see these folks perform a humbling act or reach out to do something nice for people below them for change. These folks in high positions often think only about themselves and use their power or position to benefit them and their ambition.

Lord Jesus, I want to see

Lord Jesus, Son of God, you once told your disciples if they want to be the greatest or the head of everyone else, they need to be the servant of all. Help me learn to be the servant of others and reach out to the least among us. Teach me to be humble in my thoughts and actions so that I will bring glory to you and not myself. Open my eyes to see that if I am only "the head" without other parts of my body, I do not have a complete picture of myself. Only by working in concert with others will I bring about the fruitful result that you have intended for your disciples.

Resolution

Today, if I am the head of a household or an organization, I will humble myself and reach out to people below and around me and help them with an act of kindness and care.

January 19

Issue: **Ignorance**

"Ignorance of Scripture is ignorance of Christ." (St. Jerome)

Reflection

There is nothing worse than finding ourselves not knowing anything at all. That's why we are encouraged to stay in school and keep reading and learning every day. Unfortunately, as we advance in computers and technology, many people stop getting to know history, appreciating tradition, and searching for the mystery of life and God in religion. For some reason, we no longer challenge ourselves and the younger generations to have a holistic approach to learning and maturing.

Lord Jesus, I want to see

Jesus, Wise Counselor, you came to enlighten us with knowledge of eternal life and mesmerize our world with your Good News. Thousands of people find comfort and hope in your teachings like the Beatitudes. Help me fight the trend of being ignorant and lazy in our modern time and learn to search for you in Scripture and every place you might be found. Enlighten me with your words of wisdom. I do not want to be ignorant of you and the spiritual world any more.

Resolution

Today, I will pick up the Bible and start reading one of the Gospels until something intriguing makes me stop and reflect for a while.

January 20

Issue: **Indifference**

"I know your works…I wish you were either cold or hot. So, because you are indifferent, neither hot nor cold, I'll spit you out of my mouth." (Revelation 3: 15-16)

Reflection

There are so many challenges in our modern times. One of these is indifference toward God and religion. Many people do not seem to care about morality and a good spiritual life. All they focus on is instant self-gratification and materialistic possessions. They spend very little time and effort on God and spiritual life. But, when things go wrong in their lives, they call on God for help or blame it on a mental problem. Our modern society does not seem to recognize the importance of God and spirituality in its life. But, it does attribute all its social problems to mental illness.

Lord Jesus, I want to see

Creator and Faithful God, I thank you for creating me and continuing to sustain me with every new day. You are always there for me whether I realize and appreciate it or not. Help fill my heart with burning love for you and my mind with fascinating thoughts for your awesome plan of creation. Help me learn to appreciate your care and love for me. Help me learn to appreciate your care and love for me. Awake in me the sense of your divine goodness. Help me yearn to make a difference in this world and someday achieve a share in the eternal life of Heaven with you.

Resolution

Today, I will find something in my life that I should appreciate and be motivated to do good for some misfortunate folks around me.

January 21

Issue: **Jesus**

"At the name of Jesus every knee should bend, of those in Heaven and on earth and under the earth, and every tongue confess that Jesus Christ is Lord." (Philippians 2:10-11)

Reflection

Jesus is the name that all creatures on earth know about one way or another. Unfortunately, some misuse it in derogatory ways, whereas many ignore it completely. But, for faithful Christians, the name of Jesus is always on their lips and minds. For they call on that Holy Name often, especially in this day and age or in times of danger. Some realize its great benefits and make it a habit to start their day by calling on the name of Jesus or end their day by giving thanks to that same name.

Lord Jesus, I want to see

Lord Jesus, your name is praised in Heaven and brought life and salvation to all creatures on earth. Yet, I might not have given it the respect and attention it deserves. Open my ears to hear your name and my heart to welcome you throughout my day. Give me courage to proclaim your name with joy and conviction daily and call on it in times of need and danger. For your name is what brought fear to evil spirits and healing to the afflicted during your years of ministry.

Resolution

Today, I will call upon the name of Jesus as often as I can, from blessing my food to making sure all my decisions are the right ones.

January 22

"You shall not violate the rights of the alien or of the orphan, nor take the clothing of a widow as a pledge. For you were once slaves in Egypt."
(Deuteronomy 24:17-18)

Reflection
Pledges are special oaths that people make for different causes and on various occasions. Some people take a solemn oath when they take over an official office or position. Others make a special pledge to donate to charities or causes. We make the pledge of allegiance to the United States flag to show our commitment and loyalty to this nation. Similarly, we Christians made a pledge on the day of our baptism to commit ourselves to Jesus and follow His teachings. Unfortunately, we have often forgotten about that special oath and failed to live up to it.

Lord Jesus, I want to see
Lord Jesus, you made a special pledge to God the Father to bring us salvation, and you followed through with it. I have made a similar pledge about my baptism and promised to follow you and be your witness to the world. Sadly, I have not taken that oath seriously and have failed to live up to it or completely ignoring it. Give me a sincere appreciation for my baptismal pledge and courage to live out every moment of my life despite all the hurdles around me. For that pledge will help ensure your Good News will carry on for many generations to come.

Resolution
Today, I will think of a pledge or an oath I have made to God or someone and try to follow through with it.

January 23

<u>Issue:</u> **Rest**

"My soul rests in God alone, from whom comes my salvation." (Psalms 62:2)

<u>Reflection</u>
Resting is essential for our well-being and sanity. We routinely rest and recharge to stay healthy and deal with the challenges of tomorrow. That is how we try to take care of our physical and mental health. What about our spiritual health? Have we looked for ways to rest our spirit and make it strong? Unfortunately, we often neglect our spirit and fail to take care of it. That is one of the biggest problems of our secular and modern age.

<u>Lord Jesus, I want to see</u>
Heavenly Father, I learn in the Bible that you rested on the seventh day after you completed your wonderful creation. The busy pace of modern life makes me tired easily, and I often forget to rest, especially my spirit. Help me realize the value of rest and learn to spend more time with you in prayer, especially on the Sabbath day, so that my spirit may have some time for rest and relaxation in this fast-paced world. For rest is the best medicine you bring for my weary soul and tiresome spirit.

<u>Resolution</u>
Today, I will take some time out of my busy schedule to pray, read the Bible, or take a walk with Jesus.

January 24

Issue: **Reveal**

"Beloved, we are God's children now; what we shall be has not yet been revealed. We do know that when it is revealed we shall be like Him."
(1John 3:2)

Reflection

The whole Universe is full of secrets, and it is the eureka moment when one of these secrets is revealed to us. In fact, our whole life is about searching for meaning and discovering things about ourselves, others around us, and the universe. Some of these discoveries might reveal things that we like, whereas others scare us to death. Imagine if you learned that you came from a royal bloodline! It would definitely be a proud and happy revelation for you. However, if you have found that you have some sort of cancer, that revelation will not be a happy moment for you.

Lord Jesus, I want to see

Creator God, thank you for revealing yourself to me on the day of Christmas and continuing to do so every new day. Open my heart and mind to welcome your new revelations to me each day with joy and thanksgiving. Help me understand your plan for me in this life and the courage to see it through without regrets or complaints.

Resolution

Today, I will stop during my day to see what God might want to reveal to me and try to make a connection with God through that.

January 25

"I the Lord alone searches the mind and tests the heart, to reward every-one according to one's ways, according to the merit of one's deeds." (Jere-miah 17:10)

Reflection
You might think we only begin to search when we lose something. But, the truth is that we start searching for various things, particularly how to achieve happiness, from the moment of our birth. Some of us get caught up in the search for money, fame, pleasure, or some vain glory and forget what matters most in this life. Others let daily worries or mundane things overwhelm and sidetrack them from the most important focus in this life, namely, to find true peace and happiness for their lives.

Lord Jesus, I want to see
Lord Jesus, you once said to Thomas and the other disciples, "I am the way, the truth, and the life." The reason you said this is because you knew your followers wouldn't stop searching for the way to true peace and happiness and might be lost in this world. However, like a Good Shepherd, you continue to search for me and other lost sheep. I am so thankful and happy for your bountiful love and mercy for me. Help me to look for you daily and put you above other worldly things. That way, I will truly have peace and happiness in my life.

Resolution
Today, I will search for a sign of God's presence in my day and give thanks for it.

January 26

Issue: **Sow**
"Those who plow for mischief and sow trouble, reap the same." (Job 4:8)

Reflection
When we hear the word "sow," we often associate it with gardening or farming. But, Jesus used this word a few times in the Gospels to explain to us about how to share the words of God and the Kingdom of Heaven. For God has sown the Word of God in the hearts of the faithful, especially Christians, since the day of their baptism. Still, God continues to sow God's love and blessings upon us with every passing day. Unfortunately, we often do not recognize it and do not let the Word of God take root in our hearts and minds. Consequently, we end up not being productive and joyful as Christians.

Lord Jesus, I want to see
Jesus, Word made flesh among us, you never stopped sowing good deeds and hopeful messages, while trying to put an end to hatred and fighting during your years of ministry on earth. Help me sow only joy, peace, love, kindness, compassion, and unity wherever I go. Give me the strength and courage to prepare my heart and soul to welcome your messages with joy and humility, so that I can produce abundantly for your Kingdom.

Resolution
Today, I will sow good seed by doing something nice for someone or expressing my gratitude to someone.

January 27

<u>Issue:</u> **Spiritual**

"Pursue love, but strive eagerly for the Spiritual gifts, above all that you may prophesy." (1Corinthians 14:1)

<u>Reflection</u>

We live in a time that focuses a lot on our bodies and the physical world, but very little on our minds and the spiritual world. We don't take care of our mind and spirit or put much effort into coming up with new and effective ways to strengthen our spirit. Yet, without a strong spirit, everything we put into a body will be useless, and we will end up dead. Moreover, without a healthy and morally-right spirit, we will get totally messed up and end up hurting ourselves and everyone around us. Sadly, that is the tragedy we see in our world these days.

<u>Lord Jesus, I want to see</u>

Jesus, Great Spiritual Master of all time, you've shown us how important it is for us to have a healthy and morally-right spirit by driving out demons and healing the sick, not only in body but also in spirit. Help me realize the importance of the spiritual world and make it a priority to take good care of my spirit by spending more time in prayer, at church, or with some charity cause.

<u>Resolution</u>

Today, I will spend about ten minutes reading the Bible and try to repeat this habit for at least a week.

January 28

Issue: **Truth**
"In every wicked deceit for those who are perishing because they have not accepted the love of truth so that they may be saved." (2Thessalonians 2:10)

Reflection
Standing in front of Jesus, Pontius Pilate asked, "What is the truth?" But, Pilate is not the only human being or politician who wants to know the truth. Most people would love to see the truth or be near it. For the truth will bring them confidence, reassurance, guidance, clarification, comfort, and peace. However, the truth also challenges people and points out things they need to change. This causes many people to be afraid of the truth. In turn, they run away from the truth and God altogether.

Lord Jesus, I want to see
Jesus, Son of God, you alone hold the truth. You also have the words of everlasting life. Give me courage and humility to embrace the truth and be near its source so that I may know what I need to avoid, change, or do more of in my life. Open my eyes to the way of the truth that will bring me peace and contentment in this life and eventually eternal life in your kingdom.

Resolution
Today, I will confront the truth about something and try to resolve it without fearing its consequences.

January 29

Virtuous
"If you were raised with Christ, seek what is above...Over all these virtues, put on love, that is the bond of perfection."
(Col 3:1-14)

Reflection
If there is one word we rarely hear these days, it is "virtuous." If there is one thing our rich and modern society still needs every day, it is "virtue." Everyone chases after material things, vanity, glamour, fame, or pleasure. But, what every home needs the most is virtue. For virtue is one of the best ways for our world to deal with its current social problems. It holds a person accountable for his/her actions and challenges him/her to act and live by a higher code of conduct. This is how we can build character and create a respectful and loving society.

Lord Jesus, I want to see
Jesus, Virtuous Master of all times, thank you for showing us why and how a virtuous way of life is the way a person and a society should pursue. I want to live a virtuous life for all the benefits listed above, especially training myself to become like you. Help me search for and desire virtues above everything so that you may be glorified daily in this sinful world of mine.

Resolution
Today, I will find during my day the virtuous way to deal with a tough issue that happened recently or has been troubling my life.

January 30

Issue: **Vocation**
"Anyone who does not teach one's son or daughter a useful trade is bringing him or her up to be a thief." (A Jewish sage's saying)

Reflection
We all have our own interests and daily jobs. But, a vocation is more than a job or a personal interest. It is a calling, because a person has discovered what he/she would like to do with his/her life and what will give life some meaning. Vocation is not about earning a living or making as much money as one can like a career. Rather, it is about finding something meaningful in life that we can serve with joy and commitment. In fact, the more people who know their own vocations, the better and more peaceful our society will be.

Lord Jesus, I want to see
Lord Jesus, you knew your own vocation after the day of your baptism and were whole-heartedly committed to it throughout your years of ministry. I thank you for your example of living out faithfully the vocation that God the Father called you to do. I ask you to show me my own vocation in this life and give me the courage and strength to follow through with it. For I know that is what brings joy and meaning to my life.

Resolution
Today,, with the help of the Holy Spirit, I will try to figure out my vocation in this life or what Jesus is calling me to do. I will then commit myself to follow through with that calling.

January 31

"Happy is the one who finds wisdom, the one who gains understanding! For her profit is better than profit in silver and better than gold is her revenue." *(Proverbs 3:13-14)*

Reflection

Throughout history, we humans, especially our leaders, have longed to possess the gift of wisdom. In fact, King Solomon asked God for a gift, and he simply prayed for wisdom. As you can see, wisdom is the most desired gift on the planet. For a wise person knows what the best choice is or what makes the right choice. No one in this world can fool or dupe a wise person. Nothing can tempt a wise person from his/her life mission. For wisdom will show us how to have a happy and meaningful life on earth while preparing for an eternal life in Heaven.

Lord Jesus, I want to see

Lord Jesus, God's Wisdom made flesh, I am grateful for all your wise counsel and wonderful teaching to help me deal with my life here on earth. When I stray from the right path, wisdom will bring me back. When I try to do something hurtful and destructive, wisdom will help me avoid it. Most importantly, wisdom will help me succeed in this life and the next. Wisdom is the best companion I can ask for.

Resolution

Today, I will ask God to let wisdom help me make the right choice in my daily decisions.

February

Lord Jesus,
I Want to See...

February 1

Issue: **Altruism**
"The just always lend generously, and their children become a blessing. Turn from evil and do good, that you may inherit the land forever."
(Psalms 37:26-27)

Reflection
Altruism is one of those words we rarely see or hear these days. All we hear in our modern time is me, my success, my fun, or my fame. We seldom hear people talk about doing good for others or trying to do the right things because that is the noble thing. Everyone tends to act on the principle of "quid pro quo," or worse yet, tries to exploit others for one's own benefits/interests. However, history tells us that ancient prophets, our forefathers, saints, and missionaries in our Christian tradition always put noble goals, the common good, or service above self-interests or material gain. Because of this ideal, altruism or benevolence was the main goal for these folks; our human society had benefited a great deal from their great sacrifices. Our world will surely be a lot better if many more people would believe in and work for altruism like those special folks noted above.

Lord Jesus, I want to see
Jesus, Generous and Kind Giver of all times, your whole life was about doing good for others and promoting the idea of service to the community by sending out disciples two by two. Help me to grow into the spirit of service and doing good for everyone around me like you did throughout your life.

Resolution
Today, I will reach out and try to help someone around me without expecting anything in return.

February 2

Issue: **Apology**

"Bearing with one another and forgiving one another, if one has a grievance against another; as the Lord has forgiven you, so must you also do."
(Colossians 3:13)

Reflection

Saying "I'm sorry" is never easy. Today, blaming a mistake on someone or something else is usually the way people go. We have seen how Adam and Eve blamed someone or something else after they violated God's Commandments. Thankfully, we have had some brave and humble folks over the years— although they might be rare—who dared to admit their wrongdoings and ask for forgiveness. Some of them were tax collectors like Zacchaeus, who apologized to Jesus for his past sins and promised to make up for them. Others were saints in our Christian tradition who realized their wrongdoing and decided to turn their lives over to Jesus. Indeed, apology is the first step for someone to grow closer to Jesus.

Lord Jesus, I want to see

Merciful Jesus, you never condemned or humiliated a repentant sinner in your years of ministry. Help me trust in your compassion and humbly apologize to you as I try to find my way back. Give me courage to admit my faults and search for ways to improve myself each day.

Resolution

Today, I will figure out one thing I did wrong to God or someone else and apologize for it without delay.

February 3

Issue: **Arrogant**
"For you, O God, delight not in wickedness; no evil one remains with you; the arrogant may not stand in your sight. You hate all evildoers." (Psalms 5:5-6)

Reflection
No one likes a person with an arrogant attitude. For this person usually considers him/herself to be "God" and looks down on everyone around him/her. There is no accountability or collaboration with an arrogant person. He/she does not care about anyone except him/herself. So, he/she would not need God or anyone else. Certainly, this is a big mistake. There are many examples in the Bible that show us how God humbled an arrogant person, from Lucifer (The Prince of Darkness) to Goliath (the giant leader of the Philistines).

Lord Jesus, I want to see
Humble Jesus, you took on our human form to save us even though you are our God. You also never hesitated to mingle with sinners or reach out to help the poor and the outcast during your time of ministry on earth. I thank you for giving me such a great example of humble service with your own life. Help me have a humble attitude in my daily life by giving proper respect to you, my God, and being willing to serve others around me.

Resolution
Today, I will look for a humble act that I can do to help someone and bring glory to God.

February 4

<u>Issue:</u> **Avoid**
"It is honorable for a person to avoid strife, while every fool starts a quarrel." (Proverbs 20:3)

<u>Reflection</u>
We humans often avoid the right paths and our duties and flock to bad alleys and other-worldly distractions. St. Paul once wrote, "…Things that I'm supposed to do I don't do. Things I'm not supposed to do I do." This dichotomy within us, often called our internal struggle, is what causes us to avoid wrong things and gets us into significant trouble. The only way to correct this is to have the right guidance, which comes from our moral compass. To have the right guidance, which comes from our moral compass, will tell us what to avoid and encourage us what to do.

<u>Lord Jesus, I want to see</u>
Lord Jesus, our source of guidance and encouragement, help me know what to avoid in my daily life so that I will not hurt myself and will do what I am supposed to do. Give me the wisdom to know what is right and wrong and the courage to flow through with my daily duties. With you by my side, I am sure I will be able to pass through this tough journey here on earth and make it safely to the Gate of Heaven.

<u>Resolution</u>
Today, I will think about something that is difficult for me to avoid and determine ways to achieve my goal for a week.

February 5

<u>Issue:</u> **Change**
"Jesus said, '...Unless you change and become like children, you will not enter the Kingdom of Heaven.'" (Matthew 18:3)

<u>Reflection</u>
Change is difficult whether it is a little thing like how things are arranged around the house or a big thing like a career switch. Change often makes us feel vulnerable and pushes us to ask for help from above and around us. Yet, all these things are difficult for a proud person to accept. And yet, change is all around us and an essential part of our circle of life. We can see changes clearly in nature, particularly changes in the four seasons. These changes bring about death and uncertainty but also life and transformation.

<u>**Lord Jesus, I want to see**</u>
Lord Jesus, your life is full of changes from the beginning to the end. You had no control over many of life's uncertainties except putting your total trust in God's love and plan for you. Help me embrace changes and uncertainties in my life with the same resolve and trust in God the Father as you did. Also, give me the wisdom to see that changes are an important part of my life here on earth and are designed to prepare me for eternal life in Heaven with you.

<u>Resolution</u>
Today, I will name a change I recently encountered and try to embrace it with some openness and hope that something great will happen.

February 6

Issue: **Clean**

"A person whose hands are sinless, whose heart is clean, who desires not what is vain, nor swears deceitfully to one's neighbor shall receive a blessing from the Lord." (Psalms 24:4-5)

Reflection
We all want to live in a clean home and environment, partly for good hygiene and partly because cleanliness is a great prevention measure to help us avoid sickness and stay healthy. However, in the Jewish faith tradition, cleanliness plays a very important role with its rituals and beliefs. If someone is found impure in any way, that person needs to be purified and prevented from celebrating any public liturgy. Hence, cleanliness is more than just personal hygiene; it is also about one's spiritual worthiness before God.

Lord Jesus, I want to see
Lord Jesus, you once said in the Beatitudes, "…Blessed are the clean of heart, for they shall see God." That is not only a promise but also an encouragement for us on our earthly journey. It is difficult to keep ourselves clean when we are surrounded daily by filthy language and the dirty acts of a sinful world. Help me have a clean heart and a pure conscience so that I can be worthy for your presence always.

Resolution
Today, I am committed not to say or do something that might make my heart or conscience unclean.

February 7

Issue: **Conscience**
"... The testimony of our conscience is that we have conducted ourselves in the world with simplicity and sincerity of God, not by human wisdom but by the grace of God." (2Corinthians 1:12)

Reflection

Most people don't know that they have a conscience. But, the truth is that we all have been given a conscience. It is more than our mind, heart, and spirit combined. A conscience is often compared to a moral compass that helps us know right from wrong and guides us through some of the tough decisions of our daily lives. Hence, it is important to give that compass a good formatting and careful update with the right teachings and ethical standards. Imagine if you have the best computer running on some bad or old software. That is what many folks face in our day and age. Their conscience is not formatted correctly or not updated with the right morals.

Lord Jesus, I want to see

Lord Jesus, source of good teachings and right conduct, you have helped clean my conscience with your blood on the Cross and the holy water of my baptism. Since then, I might not have received the correct software updates. Give me the wisdom and courage to find the right teachings to update my conscience and keep it from endangering me and others with wrongful thoughts and actions.

Resolution

Today, I will thoroughly examine my conscience with Jesus' Two Commandments of Love (Mark 12:28-34) and see what I must do to heal and correct my conscience.

February 8

"My sacrifice, O Lord, is a contrite Spirit, a heart contrite and humbled, O God, you will not spurn." (Psalms 52:19)

Reflection
We often hear in the Bible that God desires a contrite heart. A contrite heart is open to God's messages and allows God to work wonders with it. A contrite person turns away from one's dark past and commits oneself totally to God. God is the last hope for a contrite person, the light that will bring guidance and a new day for someone who has been lost in the jungle of life for a while. In the end, both God and a contrite person are happy to embrace one another.

Lord Jesus, I want to see
Lord Jesus, you once said, "I am the way, the truth, and the life." Anyone who follows you faithfully finds this saying quite true. A contrite person who has been lost for some time hears this saying as a call to come home. I pray that I will have a contrite spirit and see the value of your words above. That way, I will always find my way back to you and experience life fully in your presence.

Resolution
Today, I will show a contrite heart by turning away from some bad habits and replacing them with something good.

February 9

Issue: **Conversion**

"…God raised up this servant and sent Him to bless you by turning each of you from your evil ways." (Acts 3:26)

Reflection

Everyone is fascinated by a big conversion like that of St. Paul or St. Augustine. But, small, daily conversions are as important as the big ones. For a conversion demands a change of heart and a total commitment to God. But, it takes a lot of soul-searching and humility for a person to turn one's life around. A converted person ultimately finds his/her way back to God and is on the same path with God. What a great feeling of joy and peace it must be for a converted soul and all the Heavenly hosts!

Lord Jesus, I want to see

Lord Jesus, you once said, "…Heaven rejoices when a sinner is converted back to God." The reason for this is because God constantly searches for a converted soul. Realizing this, I need to convert my life and move it a bit closer to you with every passing day. Only in this way can I be found again and bring joy to Heaven. This is a reunion that you have been waiting for since the first day of your ministry.

Resolution

Today, I will determine what area of my life might be keeping me from a total conversion to God and try to work on it.

February 10

<u>Issue:</u> **Correction**

"Anyone who loves correction loves knowledge, but anyone who hates reproof is stupid." (Proverbs 12:1)

<u>Reflection</u>

Everyone wants to be correct, but it is not easy to be corrected. It is our human tendency to desire to be right and be praised. When we say, "I stand corrected," we feel humiliated and lose control over a situation or a part of our lives. Hence, most of us do not say this phrase easily or try to avoid saying it at all costs. God has a way to help us stay humbled and call us back to the fold with various ways of correction in our lives. The challenge for us is to be humble enough to welcome God's corrective ways in our daily lives.

<u>Lord Jesus, I want to see</u>

Jesus, Master, you always tried to show the public the right way to come home to God and never hesitated to correct the scribes and Pharisees when they veered far away from your teachings. Open my eyes to find your way as the correct one in my daily life. Give me courage and humility to embrace your way and all the corrections you might send my way so that I can be on the right path home with you.

<u>Resolution</u>

Today, I will welcome something that might appear as a correction in my life without any defensiveness.

February 11

<u>Issue:</u> **Detachment**

"No one can serve two masters. One will either hate one and love the other, or be devoted to one and despise the other. One cannot serve both God and wealth." (Luke 16:13)

<u>Reflection</u>
One of the most important messages Jesus often preached during His ministry was detaching oneself from the earthly world and attaching oneself to the Heavenly one. He called on His followers to make good use of earthly things to gain lasting things in Heaven like eternal life. In fact, many early Christians like the Fathers and Mothers of the desert took this teaching of detachment seriously by leaving all their possessions behind and entering the desert to live a simple life and heighten their spiritual senses for a life in Heaven.

<u>Lord Jesus, I want to see</u>
Lord Jesus, you know how it must have felt to detach oneself from a cozy world. This makes us feel scared and insecure, because we like to surround ourselves with earthly possessions and consider those our life blood. Help me learn to attach to you and the Kingdom of Heaven instead of earthly things. For everything in this world will pass away except you and Heaven.

<u>Resolution</u>
Today, I will see those things to which I am most attached—money, fame, or vanity—and try to detach myself from them every day.

February 12

Issue: **Devil**
"Jesus was led by the Spirit into the desert to be tempted by the Devil."
(Matthew 4:1)

Reflection
Whenever we think about the Devil, we often associate it with the Power of Darkness and source of bad temptations. Most people are scared of it and try to stay away from it. Some, however, do not take the Devil seriously. Nevertheless, the Devil and its bad influences are real. They often bring about death and destruction. Unfortunately, our current world continues to follow its ways and subjects itself to the Devil's yoke and allurements.

Lord Jesus, I want to see
Jesus, Light of the World, you came to shine your Light of hope and love into our world of darkness. One of the regular miracles you performed was to drive out evil and unclean spirits in the life of God's people and bring them peace and new life. Those spirits and the Devil knew your identity and were very fearful of you. I am thankful for your presence here on earth and the difference it has made in my life. Help me stay committed to you and stay away from the ways of the Devil and all its empty promises.

Resolution
Today, I will identify some evil influence or temptation in my life and devise a plan to avoid it or rid it from my life.

February 13

Discord
"The Spirits of prophets are under the prophets' control, since He is not the God of discord but of peace." (1Corinthians 14:32-33)

Reflection
Discord happens every day and continues throughout our lives. We all differ from one another in various ways and usually want to be right. Arguments and discord often occur for some selfish reason. Everyone simply cares for and intensely focuses on one's own interests instead of trying to build the common good. No one wants to compromise or make sacrifices for the good of the whole. Individualistic desires can and do take over the harmonious and sacrificing life of a community. Of course, discord thrives in that kind of environment.

Lord Jesus, I want to see
Loving Jesus, you entered our world of darkness and discord to help us reconcile with God the Father and one another. You know that by not focusing on God the Father, we will turn on each other and fight. Help me keep my eyes focused on Him always and learn to put the common good before my own interests. In this way, I can bring peace and harmony wherever I go.

Resolution
Today, I will see what discord I might have with someone around me and try to put it away.

February 14

Issue: **Evil**
"For the love of money is the root of all evils; and some people, in their desire for it, have strayed from the faith and have pierced themselves with many pains." (1 Timothy 6:10)

Reflection
Evil is all around us, whether we want to admit it or not. Since the beginning of Creation, evil has been here. It took on the form of a tempting snake and the killing of Cain over his brother Abel. It brings death and destruction while luring its victims with all kinds of empty promises. Common sense warns us to stay away from anything evil. Unfortunately, our world does not seem to take that caution seriously or pay attention to the wise source of counsel like the Bible. The tragic consequence is that evil not only roams free but also thrives in our time.

Lord Jesus, I want to see
Lord Jesus, one of the main things you did during your ministry was to drive out evil spirits. I know they are real and harmful to my spiritual and daily life. They also knew who you were. You made it your priority to keep evil spirits in check and maintained an upper hand on them with prayers and kind acts. Help me realize the threat and harm that evil spirits might bring to my soul. Strengthen me with your grace and prayers so that I will always resist evil things.

Resolution
Today, I will identify an evil influence around me and try to avoid it or get rid of it.

February 15

Issue: **Fault**

"If your brother or sister sins against you, go and tell him/her his/her fault between you and him or her alone. If he or she listens to you, you have won over your brother or sister." (Matthew 18:15)

Reflection

None of us wants to be associated with fault or wrongdoing. Do so would show our vulnerabilities and need for repentance or help from a high power. It also means everyone around us might lose respect for us, and our enemies might exploit our faults for their own interests. This is why many people have lived in denial about their own faults and do not know how to deal with them. Over time, a few faults can spread and consume one's life totally.

Lord Jesus, I want to see

Rabbi Jesus, you once said, "Let anyone who is without fault throw a stone about her [an accused sinner]." You did not excuse the alleged sinful woman in any way. You simply wanted the public to realize that we all have faults, and we need to ask for God's mercy and forgiveness. I know that I am not fault-free, but it is difficult for me to admit this and face my own faults. Give me humility and courage to commit myself to change and be a better Christian with every passing day.

Resolution

Today, I will name a fault of mine that has bothered me for a while and try to change it.

February 16

Issue: **Hypocrisy**

"When you give alms, do not blow as trumpet before you as hypocrites do in the synagogues and in the streets to win the praise of others." (Matthew 6:2)

Reflection

If there is a term that often came up during Jesus' ministry, it is hypocrite. Jesus did not like hypocrites because they talked and demanded that others follow a strict set of rules, but would not practice those same rules themselves. Worse yet, a hypocrite might set a bad example for others with that kind of double standard. But, the world is full of hypocrites and most people, including Jesus, do not like a hypocrite.

Lord Jesus, I want to see

Lord Jesus, you constantly reminded your disciples to avoid the yeast of hypocrisy because of its double lifestyle and untruthfulness. You certainly want your followers to have one lifestyle only—the one that is dedicated to the truth and your Commandments of Love. Unfortunately, I could be affected by the same yeast and follow the same double lifestyle. If that is the case, I will not have peace and happiness. All I do is simply hide from the truth and cause more trouble for others.

Resolution

Today, I will examine my thoughts and actions to see if I am affected by the yeast of hypocrisy and try to practice what I preach in my daily life.

February 17

Issue: **Inquisitive**

"When people say to you, 'Inquire of mediums and fortune tellers; shouldn't a people inquire of their gods?' – then this document will furnish its instruction." (Isaiah 8:19-20)

Reflection
We ask questions and become worried over many issues in our lives. But, we rarely inquire about our soul and the spiritual realm. We spend an enormous amount of time, effort, and resources to advance our physical world and try to make it better. But, we seldom make any time to learn more about the spiritual world or commit any effort to protect our soul. Yet, our body will not survive a second if our spirit is all messed up. Of course, with all the talk of mental illness these days, we can see how crucial our spirit/soul is to the well-being of our body right here on earth.

Lord Jesus, I want to see
Lord Jesus, you continuously point people to the spiritual world and take care of their souls. You even said, "What good is it for one to win the whole world, but lose one's soul in the end?" Help me to have the right focus in this life and inquire more about different ways to enhance my spiritual life. Get me to be curious about my soul, the eternal life, and the Kingdom of Heaven.

Resolution
Today, I will read the Bible and inquire a lot more about my spiritual life to see what I need to do to improve my relationship with Jesus and enrich my prayer life.

February 18

Issue: **Lies**

"The person tells the truth who states what one is sure of, but a lying witness speaks deceitfully." (Proverbs 12:17)

Reflection

In the Bible, lies and empty promises are often associated with the Prince of Darkness. We have seen how the snake, which represented the power of darkness, lied to Adam and Eve about what they would get by defying God. But, that is not difficult for us to see, especially when we must deal with people who lie to us daily. We would naturally consider these folks as agents of darkness and slowly lose any trust and respect for them. Indeed, they can bring us all sorts of harm and bad influences over time.

Lord Jesus, I want to see

Gentle Jesus, you once said, "If you say yes, then mean yes. If you say no, then mean no." This will keep us on the right path and keep our conscience clean. Unfortunately, we live in a time when a person may pay a dear price to stick with the truth. Worse yet, many of our leaders do not set a good example and tell us the truth regardless of the consequences. Give me courage and strength to be true to myself, my God, and everyone around me despite any personal cost.

Resolution

Today, I will practice telling the truth and avoid saying any lie that might bring harm to others and less glory to my God.

February 19

<u>Issue:</u> **Obedience**
"Christ humbled himself, becoming obedient to death, even death on the Cross." (Philippians 2:8)

<u>Reflection</u>
Obedience is a rare term we hear in modern times. Instead, we hear a lot about revolt or contrarians. No one wants to obey and follow the law. People find it more convenient to do what they like and follow whatever makes them feel good. But, obedience helps a person practice humility and helps a community find harmony and peace. Everyone should put away their differences and learn to follow a certain order without much resistance.

<u>Lord Jesus, I want to see</u>
Lord Jesus, you obediently carried out the saving plan of God the Father and offered your life on the Cross for us. The result of your obedience was our salvation and the promise of the eternal life for us. Help me see your example of obedience as an inspiring source of strength and courage in my daily life. Make me realize that it does not make me less of a person by being obedient, especially to your Laws.

<u>Resolution</u>
Today, I will learn to obey authorities and commit myself to follow God's Laws even though I might find it difficult to do at times.

February 20

<u>Issue:</u> **Right**

"Go and learn the meaning of the words 'I desire mercy, not sacrifice.' I did not come to call the righteous but sinners." (Matthew 9:13)

Reflection

Most of us want to be right. No one likes to admit that they are wrong on certain issues. Everyone is so fascinated by the whole idea of being right that they fight, argue, and hurt one another just to be right. This struggle is played out around the world all day long. Ironically, the best source of "being right" is God, and yet people do not want to be close to Him or use Him as the standard measure in their lives.

Lord Jesus, I want to see

Lord Jesus, after being slapped by a soldier in front of the religious leader Caiaphas, you said, "…If I testified it wrong, point it out to me. If I did it right, why did you slap me?" Clearly, Jesus was correct in front of that kangaroo court. But, the soldier and court officials could not admit that and insisted otherwise. This is the struggle and battle that I see around me every day. Help me avoid being stuck in the battle and the whole idea of being right that I forget to be caring, considerate, peaceful, compromising, kind, and forgiving to others around me.

Resolution

Today, I will look back on the times I insisted on being right and promise to be open to other possibilities with the guidance of God's grace.

February 21

<u>Issue:</u> **Sabbath**
"You must keep the Sabbath as something sacred. Whoever desecrates it shall be put to death." (Exodus 31:14)

<u>Reflection</u>
The Sabbath is a sacred day in the lives of God's people. It is the day they spend with God. This day has its origin in the Creation story as the seventh day when God finished all the work and decided to rest. Thence, the Sabbath is often considered not only the day of worship, but also as the day of rest. The idea of working 24/7 is simply a modern idea and an American way. By not honoring the Sabbath, we cut ourselves off from the divine and tradition. That will eventually end up hurting us.

<u>Lord Jesus, I want to see</u>
Jesus, Lord of the Sabbath, you always tried to honor the Sabbath by visiting the Temple and helping people see that it is the day to do good and enhance life. Help me to make good use of this day as a time to be with my God and faith community and a time to give thanks and renew my spirit. By keeping the Sabbath, I honor my God and help nourish my spirit with the Word of God and the Sacraments.

<u>Resolution</u>
Today, I will commit myself to keep the Sabbath and use this time in prayer to nurture my spirit.

February 22

<u>Issue:</u> **Self-Examination**
"Let us stand and examine our ways that we may return to the Lord!"
(Lamentations 3:40)

<u>Reflection</u>
We take in our car for an annual tune-up. We visit our family physician for a checkup once a year. But, do we ever examine our soul to see if it needs any care or attention? When we do that examination regularly, we will catch a problem right away and give our soul the care it needs. Hence, it has been suggested that we do self-examination daily so that we can take good care of our soul and have a right relationship with God.

<u>Lord Jesus, I want to see</u>
Lord Jesus, you warned your followers to be prepared and stay in a good relationship with God the Father. We do not know when or where we might be called home. The best way for me to be prepared for that day is to do a self-examination regularly with the help of God's Commandments. By checking on my Soul and examining my life often, I will know what I need to change and can fix it before things get out of control.

<u>Resolution</u>
Today, I will review what is going on in my life, where I am heading, and how I can improve my spiritual life. I will practice this exercise weekly or daily.

February 23

"I shall get up and go to my Father and say to him, 'Father, I have sinned against Heaven and against you.'" (Luke 15:18)

Reflection
Sin is often considered a wrong doing that we humans commit. It violates a set of commandments, rules, and regulations. It also harms our relationship with God and has the potential to destroy our souls and spiritual life. Like deadly viruses and bacteria, sin attacks our spiritual senses and renders our souls lifeless over time. Gradually, its bad influence reaches beyond our soul and conscience and affects all aspects of family life and society. Surely, sin is worse than the deadly Ebola or Zika virus.

Lord Jesus, I want to see
Compassionate Jesus, you hate sins but not sinners. You practiced that philosophy faithfully throughout your ministry. While asking everyone to avoid sin, you never stopped searching for sinners and bringing them back to the fold. I am certainly not sin-free and thankful to have a merciful and loving God. Help me learn to resist sin and avoid anything that might lead me away from my God.

Resolution
Today, I will commit myself to stay away from sin and have compassion toward sinners or anyone who might be stuck in darkness.

February 24

Issue: **Snake**
"I am sending you like sheep in the midst of wolves; so be shrewd as snakes and simple as doves." (Matthew 10:16)

Reflection
Snakes have always been considered slimy, dangerous creatures. In the Old Testament, God sent out poisonous snakes to punish God's people for their sins. The snake was also used as a symbol of the power of darkness to tempt us humans, beginning with Adam and Eve. Gradually, the concept of snake has taken on the symbolic meaning of "cunning, deceptive, or sneaky" in the popular culture to describe parts of our human nature. This nature certainly goes contrary to everything that righteous folks usually live by.

Lord Jesus, I want to see
Lord Jesus, you are the anti-venom vaccine that keeps us safe from harmful toxins that the snake might cause. You also advised your disciples, "Be as cunning as a snake and as pure/simple as a dove." Your advice does not tell us to be either a snake or a dove. Rather, it calls us to be flexible and wise in dealing with the world. Open my mind to know which occasion is meant for me to be as sneaky as a snake and which one is meant for me to be as pure as a dove during my days.

Resolution
Today, I will try to be open-minded and figure out how to deal with the world, even if I must be as cunning as a snake.

February 25

Stubborn

"Happy the one who is always on one's guard; but anyone who hardens one's heart will fall into evil." (Proverbs 28:14)

Reflection
In the Bible, the phrase "stubborn heart" or "hardness of heart" is used to describe how God's people refused to follow God's Law and guidance despite God's relentless revelation to them. Certainly this frustrated God and delayed God's work and transformation in their lives. They erected a hurdle between God and themselves with such an attitude. They refused to let God guide them and show them the way. They lacked any trust in God. Faith in God is the condition for God's work and miracles to happen in one's life.

Lord Jesus, I want to see
Jesus, Son of God, you frowned on the scribes and Pharisees for their stubborn attitude and opposition to your Good News. They refused to listen to your preaching and constantly prevented others from coming close to you. Open my mind and heart to your teachings and message of life. Help me put my trust and hope in you alone so that I may live my life to the fullest.

Resolution
Today, I will try to remove any hurdle between me and Jesus and me and allow God's grace to work its magic in my daily life.

February 26

Issue: **Sunshine**

"I [Jesus] say to you, love your enemies, and pray for those who persecute you, that you may be children of your Heavenly Father, for He makes the Sun rise on the bad and the good, and causes rain to fall on the just and the unjust." (Matthew 5:44-45)

Reflection

We can only imagine what our lives would be like without sunlight. A ray of sunshine warms our heart and makes us feel upbeat. Hence, anyone with the sunshine attitude has a hopeful and positive outlook on life. All of us are honored and enjoy being around someone with the sunshine attitude. Our world would certainly be different if there were more positive people. They would lift us up from the negative, gloom, and doom outlook that we often see around us daily.

Lord Jesus, I want to see

Jesus, the Shining Star of Bethlehem, you not only brought the divine light to our dark world on that Holy Night but continue to shine the light of hope and love onto our broken world with your Good News. You certainly brought life and hope to many people during your ministry. Help me to be a ray of sunshine to our broken world and try to bring hope and joy to others wherever I go.

Resolution

Today, I will stop being negative and complaining about my daily life. Instead, I will try to be hopeful and positive in my outlook.

February 27

Issue: **Temple**
"Do you not know that you are the Temple of God, and that the Spirit of God dwells in you? If anyone destroys God's Temple, God will destroy that person. For the Temple of God, which you are, is holy." (1Corinthians 3:16-17)

Reflection
Like a church, a temple is considered the place where God resides. Hence, it is a sacred space. It is also a place for God's people to gather and worship. They come together in this spiritual home to be with God, to find peace and comfort for their souls, to ask God for help and guidance, to give thanks for God's blessings in their lives, or to simply have a sense of belonging to a faith community. Like a public rest area, a temple/church gives all pilgrims a spiritual shelter to rest and be refreshed.

Lord Jesus, I want to see
Lord Jesus, you visited the Temple regularly and spent time with spiritual leaders to discuss the Scriptures. The Temple was surely a special place for you. Help me have the same thinking and view of the Temple as my spiritual home, where I can find peace, comfort, guidance, nourishment, and encouragement for my daily life.

Resolution
This weekend I will try to visit a temple or church and spend some time there in prayer with God and the community of faith.

February 28

<u>Issue:</u> **Weakness**

"I am content with weaknesses, insults, hardships, persecutions, and constraints, for the sake of Christ. For when I am weak, then I am strong."
(2Corinthians 12:10)

<u>Reflection</u>

We all have our own strengths and weaknesses. We certainly have no problem bragging about our strengths. But, we often find it difficult to admit our weaknesses, for that would put us in bad light with the world. Yet, without knowing what we need to change and tend to, it is difficult for us to move forward and find success. Also, by realizing our own weaknesses we can control all the temptations that the Prince of Darkness might dangle in front of us every day.

Lord Jesus, I want to see

Lord Jesus, even you were tempted by the Devil in the desert as you tried to prepare for your death and resurrection. The Devil tried to probe and test you in various ways to find any weakness in you. But, he found none and left you. Help me know my own weaknesses and learn to make necessary changes in my life. This will give the Devil fewer chances to tempt me, and I can enjoy a life of joy and peace with you.

<u>Resolution</u>

Today, I will try to figure out some of my weaknesses and see what I can do to change as many of them as possible.

February 29

<u>Issue:</u> **Wrong**
"See that no one returns wrong for wrong; rather, always seek what is good for each other and for all." (1 Thessalonians 5:15)

<u>Reflection</u>
None of us wants to be wrong, for that will make us look bad and potentially humiliate us. Certainly, it requires humility and courage for us to admit that we are wrong and try to make amends. Furthermore, in our litigious society, admitting that we're wrong might imply admitting our guilt and locking in our sentence. Hence, everyone vehemently tries to deny their wrongdoing, even though all the evidence points squarely at them.

<u>Lord Jesus, I want to see</u>
Lord Jesus, during your ministry, you often praised and rewarded anyone who dared to admit they were wrong. Even your stories like the Prodigal Son were about realizing that one can be wrong and return to God. Indeed, you are more interested in one's repentance than God's punishment. Help me have the courage and humility to admit my misconduct and see the need for God's grace to change and become more like you, Jesus, each day.

<u>Resolution</u>
Today, I will say I am sorry to God or someone about something I did and try to amend or change my wrongdoing.

March

Lord Jesus,
I Want to See…

March 1

Issue: **Affirmation**

"Encourage one another and build one another up, as indeed you do."
(1 Thessalonians 5:11)

Reflection

We all like to be acknowledged and receive affirmation as praise and compliments. Such accolades tell us that we are heading in the right direction, and we are not alone. These little acts of kindness often do not cost us anything, but have great potential to create a positive impact on people around us. Unfortunately, most people would rather spread rumors and innuendos about others than give someone an affirmation or a kind compliment.

Lord Jesus, I want to see

Lord Jesus, you fully understood the power of affirmation and kind acts. For they not only make a person feel good but also point him/her in the right direction with God. That is why you usually shared with us messages in the language of the Beatitudes (Matthew 5:1-12), namely, "Blessed are you…" Help me learn to avoid spreading rumors and innuendos and try to give affirmation and compliments generously to people around me.

Resolution

Today, I will find something nice or positive to share with someone who I run into.

March 2

Issue: **Alienate**

"You who were once alienated and hostile in mind because of evil deeds; Christ has now reconciled in his fleshly body through His death to present you holy without blemish." (Colossians 1:21-22).

Reflection

There is nothing worse than feeling lonely and alienated from other human beings. That is why there is no worse form of punishment than being condemned to isolation or confinement in prison. Still, many folks, in our already lonesome, high-tech society, have chosen to be alienated from their Creator. They want their Spirit to be isolated from God and the entire spiritual world. Can anyone truly live a life of alienation and isolation?

Lord Jesus, I want to see

Lord Jesus, you came to set us free from the bondage of sin and gather us all into the family of God. No longer do we feel alienated from God and one another with the presence of Jesus. For in Christ we have become brothers and sisters and get re-connected to God the Father. Help me to stay connected to you Lord always and avoid anything that might make me feel alienated from you.

Resolution

Today, I will review my relationship with Jesus and remove anything that might alienate me from Him and a good spiritual life.

March 3

Issue: **Awake**

"I in justice shall behold your face; on awaking I shall be content in your presence." (Psalms 17:15)

Reflection

When we awake, nothing can sneak up on us, and we are ready to deal with anything that might confront us. Hence, during Advent Season, we Christians are called to stay awake to welcome the birth of our Lord and be ready for Christ's Second Coming. To stay awake means that we need to keep vigil in prayers and make amends with God and others with the help of the Reconciliation Sacrament. Certainly, none of us wants to be caught asleep and unprepared for Christ's Second Coming!

Lord Jesus, I want to see

Lord Jesus, you are the groom who will be coming at midnight to call us to your wedding banquet. The wise ones will stay awake and have their lamps ready for the chance of a lifetime to be at that special banquet. I am honored to be invited to your wedding banquet. But, it is difficult for me to get ready and stay focused on it. Help me to keep vigil in prayers for your Second Coming and continue to share your Good News with the world.

Resolution

Today, I promise to stay awake and wait for Christ's Second Coming by keeping a faithful prayer life and participating regularly in the Sacraments.

March 4

Issue: **Betray**
"While they were eating, Jesus said, 'Amen I say to you, one of you will betray me.'" (Matthew 26:21)

Reflection
If someone close to you has betrayed you, you must admit that it is an extremely painful experience. You will feel like your whole world is turned upside down, and your life is at an end. You will lose all trust in humanity and what life might be able to offer you. But, there is always tomorrow, and our faithful and loving God has a mysterious way of healing us and restoring our trust over time.

Lord Jesus, I want to see
Loving Jesus, you were a victim of betrayal committed by Judas, one of your chosen apostles. That experience hurt you so badly that you screamed out in frustration and wished that Judas had never been born. Yet, you overcame that painful experience and learned to forgive your betrayer. Help me avoid betraying others by committing myself to a life of faithfulness and teach me to be merciful to everyone around me, even forgiving people who betray me.

Resolution
Today, I will try to leave behind any painful experience of betrayal and commit myself to a life of loyalty and faithfulness.

March 5

Issue: **Condemn**

"Stop judging and you will not be judged. Stop condemning and you will not be condemned. Forgive and you will be forgiven." (Luke 6:37)

Reflection

We live in a culture that likes to condemn and blame others. We do not hesitate to pass judgment and destroy anything we do not like. When we do that, we subject everyone and everything to our current culture of death and destruction. Such a judgmental and angry attitude will also turn us into judges and demonize our neighbors if they go contrary to what we like or believe.

Lord Jesus, I want to see

Lord Jesus, you are the Judge of the living and the dead, but you never condemned us for our sins. Instead, you offered your own life on the Cross to save us. Then, like a Good Shepherd, you continued to search for us and give us another chance. You are a merciful judge, and you put salvation over condemnation. Help me adopt the attitude of saving over condemning. Make me be a person who finds ways to lift others up instead of condemning them, to restore things instead of destroying them.

Resolution

Today, I will try to stop judging and condemning others. Instead, I will look for ways to help our world be more compassionate and forgiving. I will leave the job of judging to God.

March 6

Issue: **Conquer**

"What will separate us from the love of Christ? Will anguish, or distress, or persecution, or family, or nakedness, or peril, or the sword? ... No, in all these things we conquer overwhelmingly through Him who loved us."
(Romans 8: 35-37)

Reflection

Humans love to conquer new things and be a victor or a discoverer. But, we seem to have difficulty conquering old habits or personal problems. We are either afraid to tackle problems or try to avoid them altogether. Hence, little problems, with time and potential, metastasize causing havoc for us in the future. Over time, the power of darkness will have control over our lives, all because we fail to conquer our personal problems or old habits.

Lord Jesus, I want to see

Christ Jesus, you showed us how you conquered sins, death, and darkness with your Cross and resurrection. You did it by making many personal sacrifices. Help me conquer my own demons and bad habits in my life by following a life of faith and sacrifices. Give me courage and guidance to follow through with that commitment and find a life of happiness and peace with you.

Resolution

Today, I will name some bad habits or personal problems and try to conquer them by turning to Jesus for encouragement and guidance. By doing so, I will become a better Christian.

March 7

Issue: **Cost**
"Which of you wishing to construct a tower does not first sit down and calculate the cost to see if there is enough for its completion?" (Luke 14:28)

Reflection
Nothing is free in this life. Everything in this life has a cost associated with it. Even our salvation demanded the sacrifice of God's Son Jesus on the Cross. The problem with our time is that everyone wants everything free and likes the idea of entitlement. Everyone cannot wait to enter Heaven, but many folks in our time do not want to do anything about it. The cost is a good measure of our willingness to pay for what we believe in.

Lord Jesus, I want to see
Christ Jesus, you knew better than anyone the cost of salvation and being your disciple. Our salvation cost you your life on the Cross. Being your disciple surely cost all your followers many things in this life, even their own lives. But, many of them are not willing to pay for it. Help me realize the cost of being your disciple and give me the courage to pay for it without any hesitation. For that cost will show the world where I stand regarding my relationship with you and the Kingdom of Heaven.

Resolution
Today, I will try to think, talk, act, and pray as a good Christian. This might mean I must make certain sacrifices or changes in my life.

March 8

Issue: **Cross**
"Jesus summoned the crowd with His disciples and said to them, 'Whoever wishes to come after me must deny oneself, take up one's Cross, and follow me." (Mark 8:34)

Reflection
Crosses are part of our challenges on earth. But, for us Christians, they are not something we should avoid or despise. Rather, they are part of our journey of faith with Jesus on the way to Heaven. As the Cross of Jesus led us to His tomb and the Easter joy of His resurrection, our daily crosses will eventually lead us to the Gate of Heaven and our own resurrection. For now, our crosses might look meaningless and intimidating to us. But, over time, they will make us a better Christian and help us be prepared for Heaven and the eternal life.

Lord Jesus, I want to see
Savior Jesus, you did not run away from the Cross. Instead you embraced it with open arms and carried it all the way to the top of Mount Calvary. The Cross was the road for you to move toward the empty tomb and the bridge for us to get to Heaven. Like most people, I do not like to see crosses in my life. Give me strength and courage to embrace my daily crosses as the royal road to Heaven, much like you once did for me with your Cross.

Resolution
Today, I will review all the crosses I might be facing and try to carry them forward with the hope that they will make me a better Christian and help me get ready for Heaven.

March 9

<u>Issue:</u> **Dark Night of the Soul**

"The Dark Night of the soul explains the passive purification of both the senses and the Spirit and fulfills John's promises on how to deal with the low points in one's life." (St. John of the Cross).

<u>Reflection</u>
We all have a Dark Night of the Soul at some point in our lives. Those are the moments in which we feel hopeless, desperate, overwhelmed, disappointed, hurt, pained, betrayed, totally empty, and other bad emotions. We think our whole world is caving in, and the end is imminent. We run out of options and do not know what to do next. The worst part of this awful night is that we feel all alone. But, we Christians are never alone or totally hopeless, because Jesus, our source of hope, is always with us and will bring us a fresh morning with a new day.

Lord Jesus, I want to see
Jesus, the Lord of day and night, you had to face the Dark Night of the Soul in the Garden of Gethsemane when all your disciples left you, and you felt betrayed by Judas and abandoned by God the Father. However, you did not let those negative feelings and the power of darkness consume you. Help me come to you in dark moments and let you lift me up with your grace and encouraging messages. For you are my one true source of hope and guidance.

<u>Resolution</u>
Today, I will see what troubles my soul and pulls me down. Then, I will come to the Lord in prayer and let Him lift me up and show me the way with His revealed solutions.

March 10

Issue: **Dead End**
"Sometimes a way seems right to you, but the end of it leads to death. Even in laughter the heart may be sad and the end of joy may be sorrow."
(Proverbs 14:12-13)

Reflection
When our life runs into a dead end, we might feel trapped and overwhelmed at that moment. Sometimes, we seem to run out of life options and become exhausted and hopeless. There seems to be no tomorrow for us, and we would like to give up on living. That is how Judas must have felt after he betrayed his Master. However, we Christians are eternal optimists and never stop looking forward to a new day and all the new promises that come with it.

Lord Jesus, I want to see
Loving Jesus, Source of Hope and Life, you once said, "I am the way, the truth, the life" to remind us that if we trust and follow you, you will show us the way, and we will never feel lost or think that we're running into a dead end in life. You also give us the strength and courage to deal with those despondent and difficult moments of our lives. Open my eyes to see that your way might be long and rough at times, but it will never lead me to a dead end. Give me courage and guidance, so that I will always come to you for help and encouragement in the challenging moments of my life.

Resolution
Today, I will see what makes me feel fearful and hopeless and then try to bring it to Jesus for a solution or some clarification through prayer.

March 11

<u>Issue:</u> **Demons**
"They drove out many demons and anointed with oil many who were sick and cured them. (Mark 5:13)

<u>Reflection</u>
We fool ourselves when we say that demons are not real or that we do not have bad habits. The truth is that we are surrounded by all sorts of demons and their evil tricks. Each of us carries within ourselves all sorts of bad habits and weaknesses that can develop into something big and awful, like a demon, and can cause severe harm to us and others. We need to keep these bad habits in check and try to get rid of them over time so that our souls will not become permanent homes for them.

<u>Lord Jesus, I want to see</u>
Lord Jesus, you drove out many demons and evil spirits during your ministry. You also advised your patients to live a life free of those demons and fill their live up with God's grace. Additionally, you shared with us how you confronted some powerful demons and their temptations before you could fully embrace the Passion and the Cross. Give me strength and courage to confront all the demons in my life and leave behind bad habits so that I might experience your love and blessings fully.

<u>Resolution</u>
Today, I will examine some of the bad habits in my life and try to find ways to eliminate those demons without any hesitation or regret.

March 12

Desert

"...Jesus was led by the Spirit into the desert for forty days, to be tempted by the Devil." (Luke 4:1)

Reflection

Since ancient time, the desert or wilderness has been a place where a person can confront his/her demons and wrestle with evil spirits in order to become purified. Many legendary figures, including John the Baptist and our Lord Jesus, entered the desert to fast, pray, face their demons, and strengthen their resolve to complete a serious mission. Warriors who did not go into the wilderness for a period of spiritual purification were doomed to fail on their mission or battle.

Lord Jesus, I want to see

Jesus Christ, Savior of the World, you humbly entered the desert to strengthen your Spirit and get yourself ready for the Cross and the Passion. Surely, the desert helped prepare you for that tremendous mission, much like a training gym does for an Olympic athlete. Open my mind and heart to see the importance of entering the desert to prepare myself for a serious mission and become successful. One of these missions for us Christians is making it through the Gate of Heaven.

Resolution

Today, I will enter the desert and face some demons in my life by making a retreat or committing a good part of my free time in self-examination prayer.

March 13

Issue: **Fasting**

"...Anna, a prophetess never left the temple, but worshipped night and day with fasting and prayer." (Luke 2:37)

Reflection

We live in a world that uses food as one of the sources that gives us pleasure and satisfaction, instead of simply sustaining and nourishing us. Hence, we see all sorts of ads that constantly talk about dieting and a slim figure to help us deal with our eating problem. However, we Christians have a much more effective and spiritual way to discipline our eating habits, namely, fasting. In this spiritual exercise, we only eat two big meals and one small for a day without any snacks between meals. Besides teaching us the value of discipline, fasting gives a Christian extra spiritual strength to combat all the temptations and challenges during the day.

Lord Jesus, I want to see

Gentle Jesus, you once reminded your disciples that they need to fast and pray harder to deal with certain demons and evil spirits. This is how one can acquire all the necessary strength and preparation to win any spiritual battle without fear. I pray that you will help me commit myself to the fasting discipline and gain some spiritual strength to handle temptations and daily challenges.

Resolution

Today, I will try to fast for a day or do it at other times throughout the year to boost my spiritual strength and grow closer to Jesus.

March 14

<u>Issue:</u> **Fear of the Lord**

"By kindness and piety, guilt is expiated; and by the fear of the Lord human avoids evil." (Proverbs 16:6)

<u>Reflection</u>

In our secular world, people do not seem to have any respect and concern for God, faith, or anything sacred. It is difficult for us to promote the idea of fear of the Lord as one of the gifts of the Holy Spirit. Yet, this idea is so crucial for establishing a faithful relationship with the divine and a loving rapport with other human beings. Anyone who can show fear and respect to the Lord will try to avoid all the world's wrongs and live a life of accountability to prevent future consequences. Certainly, such a person will be blessed in this life and the next.

<u>Lord Jesus, I want to see</u>

Lord Jesus, you once said, "…Do not be afraid of those who kill the body but cannot kill the soul. Rather, be afraid of the One who can destroy both soul and body in Hell." (Matthew 10:28) The irony is that our world does not seem to take that advice or its God seriously but subjects itself to human authority. Help me to show honor and reverence to your name in my thoughts and actions so that our world may come to appreciate your love for it.

<u>Resolution</u>

Today, I will promise not to use the name of the Lord in vain or do anything that is disrespectful to you, my God.

March 15

<u>Issue:</u> **Forgiving**

"If you forgive others their transgressions, your Heavenly Father will forgive you. But, if you don't, then neither will your Heavenly Father forgive you." (Matthew 6:14-15)

<u>Reflection</u>

We all have heard the saying, "It's better to give than to receive." Yet, most of us find it difficult to forgive and forget about past hurts. Perhaps those hurts were too painful and personal for us to let go easily. Only with God's grace and time can we forgive someone who has harmed us. However, every time we pray the Lord's Prayer, we Christians are called to forgive one another as God has forgiven us daily for our sins. Certainly, it is a tough task to carry out, but with regular practice, we will be able to forgive others like it is second nature to us.

Lord Jesus, I want to see

Merciful Lord, you taught your disciples to love not only their neighbors but also their enemies. With that teaching, you imply that I need to forgive first before I can love. You also showed us how you forgave Judas and everyone who condemned you to death on the Cross. I pray that, with your help, I will learn to forgive my enemies and forget all the harms done to me. For I want to live in your love and replace hurt and hatred in my world with joy and compassion.

<u>Resolution</u>

Today, I will call to mind some of the pains and hurts I have endured and, with God's help and prayers, I will try to forgive those who hurt me.

March 16

<u>Issue:</u> **Hell**

"There will be wailing and grinding of teeth when you see Abraham, Isaac, and Jacob and all the prophets in the Kingdom of God and you yourself cast out." (Luke 13:28)

<u>Reflection</u>
Some people might not believe in Heaven, but most people know where Hell is. It is where Lucifer the Devil and all the fallen angels and unsaved people reside in the next life. Interestingly, there are many Biblical references to Hell and its living conditions, namely, "...where the fire is never quenched and there is lots of wailing and grinding of teeth." Certainly, Hell is not a fun place. Yet, many folks of our time explicitly or secretively have pledged their support of Hell with their lifestyle or sinful actions. Ironically, such a wrongful focus might come true for them in the end.

<u>Lord Jesus, I want to see</u>
Lord Jesus, you came down from Heaven not to testify for Hell. Rather, you came to show us the way to Heaven and call us to focus on it always. Your Heavenly message is often about eternity, life, blessings, joy, peace, love, caring, miracles, holiness, and Good News. I cannot bear the thought of Hell, let alone wanting to end up there someday. If anything, I would like to stay far away from it! I pray that you will not only keep me from the snares of Hell but also motivate me to warn others about that awful place.

<u>Resolution</u>
Today, I will make a great effort to avoid any thought or action that might associate me with Hell and focus squarely on Heaven.

March 17

Kneel

"Let us bow down in worship; let us kneel before the Lord who made us."
(Psalms 95:6)

Reflection

Some wise person once said, "A few minutes of kneeling will bring a lifetime of blessings." This is how most Christians view kneeling. We Christians often kneel when praying and consider that gesture a sign of reverence and respect. Unfortunately, the world usually looks at kneeling as a sign of submissiveness and humiliation. Hence, most of the time the world sits or stands. In fact, the world would like to find God from one of those positions. But, history and conventional wisdom tells us that when a person is on one's hands and knees, one has a better chance of finding God—or something we have lost, for that matter!

Lord Jesus, I want to see

Lord Jesus, most of the pictures that depict you praying have you kneeling as you look up to the Heavenly Father. That image makes me realize how much respect and reverence you had for God the Father. In return, God the Father never failed to show His love and support for you. Help me spend more time kneeling before you so that I may have the right attitude toward you and everyone around me.

Resolution

Today, I will spend a few minutes kneeling in prayer without worrying if I can stand up afterward.

March 18

Issue: **Lost**

"The lost I will seek out, the strayed I will bring back, the injured I will bind up, the sick I will heal, says the Lord." (Ezekiel 34:16)

Reflection
If you have ever been lost, you realize how scary that experience was, and probably prayed to be found. Sadly, many lost folks of our time do not admit these feelings. Hence, they keep going in circles and end up feeling hopeless about their lives. We Christians certainly have the solution for this problem. It can be found in our loving and compassionate God, who never stops searching for us and wishing that we would come home. Anyone who is found or can find the way home is always elated and thankful, much like the Prodigal Son in the arms of his compassionate father.

Lord Jesus, I want to see
Merciful Lord, you are the Good Shepherd who will do anything to search out his lost sheep. Your whole ministry on earth focused on looking for the lost, the outcast, and the forsaken, and welcoming them home to the family of God. I am thankful to have you as my Lord and Savior. I feel at peace in this confusing world to have a loving and compassionate God who will not abandon me and leave me for dead. For these reasons, I want to come home to you, Jesus.

Resolution
Today, I will be open to God's messages to me and try to come home to Jesus, especially welcoming all the lost souls back to His Church.

March 19

"If you keep my commandments, you will remain in my love, just as I have kept my Father's commandments and remain in God's love...This is my commandment: Love one another as I love you." (John 15:10, 12)

Reflection

Love is one of a few topics that even an atheist believes in and shares with a believer. Indeed, everyone likes to share love with another person and be loved in return. There are an endless number of songs, poems, and plays that talk about love. But, for us Christians, love is not just a nice, romantic idea. It is also an important virtue in our Christian faith and an essential quality of our God. In fact, John's Gospel says, "God is love...and anyone who loves remains in God."

Lord Jesus, I want to see

Loving Jesus, you summarized your teachings in one word—Love— as you commanded your disciples to love God and love their neighbors. However, you did not just talk about love. Rather, you lived it and spent your whole ministry doing the work of love by healing the sick, feeding the hungry, and forgiving sinners. Help me follow your example and live a life of love toward God and my neighbors. Give me courage and strength to promote this virtue in my daily life and help my angry and violent world experience God's love.

Resolution

Today, I pledge to embrace love as one of the essential virtues of my life and try to be a loving person toward everyone around me.

March 20

"Be kind to one another, compassionate, forgiving one another as God has forgiven you in Christ." (Ephesians 4:32)

Reflection

It is not easy to extend mercy to others, especially people we do not like or worse yet people who might have harmed us. Being a merciful person demands that we forget all past hurts and would be willing to forgive all the wrongs done against us. Certainly, it is always easier said than done. For we humans tend to hold grudges and want to get back at others over every little thing. Wars and fighting over the years are good evidence of that. However, our Christian God is a merciful one who calls us to emulate Him and do the same.

Lord Jesus, I want to see

Merciful Lord, your life and ministry taught us that mercy is one of the qualities you desire and want us to pattern. You once said, "…It is mercy I desire, not sacrifice." Hence, you liked to remind the Jewish religious leaders and us that we must treat one another with compassion and focus less on religious rituals and regulations. Soften my heart and help me to be more compassionate with everyone around me.

Resolution

Today, I vow to be less judging and more merciful in dealing with people around me.

March 21

Issue: **Mountain**
"Jesus took Peter, James and John and led them up a high mountain to pray. He was transfigured before them." (Mark 9:2)

Reflection
In the Bible, mountains are often considered holy, sacred places. It is where God resides. It is also the highest point on earth that could touch Heaven. In fact, Moses met God on Mount Horeb to receive the Ten Commandments on the two stone tablets. Many other prophets and holy figures have had extraordinary revelations shown to them on a mountain as well. Surely, mountains are a special mysterious place and have a symbolic meaning for many believers, especially Christians. This is why many folks love the thrill of climbing mountains, especially the Mountain of God, despite all sorts of challenges along the way.

Lord Jesus, I want to see
Almighty Jesus, you took some of your disciples up on Mount Tabor to let them have an encounter with God the Father. They were so mesmerized by it that they wished to be there forever. Often, I find my life on the level plain too dull and difficult to encounter God. Take me up on the mountain and let me have a glimpse of God and Heaven. That is all I need to complete my faith journey on earth.

Resolution
Today, I will make a journey up to the mountain with Jesus by leaving behind some of my bad habits and being like Him in my thoughts and actions.

March 22

Issue: **Prayerful**

"Ask and it will be given to you; seek and you will find; knock and the door will be opened to you." (Matthew 7:7)

Reflection

Most of us have prayed at one point or another during our lives. Sometimes we pray because we need to ask for something or because we are in danger. Other times we pray because we want to give thanks and show gratitude to God for all the blessings in our lives. However, we are encouraged to pray early and pray often. Prayer should be about reconnecting ourselves with God and strengthening that relationship. A prayerful person will usually be at peace and full of wisdom and joy.

Lord Jesus, I want to see

Gentle Jesus, when facing with your Dark Night of the Soul and impending arrest, you called on your disciples to stay awake and keep vigil in prayer with you. You also tried to find time for prayer whenever there was a break in your work. I can see there is a great need and abundant blessings for prayer in my life. Open my heart and mind to your messages in my daily life and help me embrace a faithful and intense prayer life.

Resolution

Today, I will commit a short and regular time of my day to prayer. Then I will increase that time over a period of some months and seek out time for prayers when possible during my day.

March 23

<u>Issue:</u> **Reconcile**

"God has reconciled us to Godself through Christ and given us the ministry of reconciliation." (2Corinthians 5:18)

<u>Reflection</u>

Reconciliation is perhaps one of the toughest issues for humans to deal with. If you have ever been in a fight or disagreement with someone, you know how difficult it is for two opposing parties to reconcile. Hence, there are endless fights like the one in the Middle East that drag on from one generation to the next or bitter relationships that permanently severed relationships due to past disagreements. Yet, our God knows how important it is to live in a reconciling world and hence sent His only Son, Jesus, to reconcile with us and bring us home.

<u>Lord Jesus, I want to see</u>

Lord Jesus, many of your parables were about reconciliation and repentance. The best one of all is the Parable of the Prodigal Son, as the Father reconciles with His youngest and wild son and throws a party for him without harsh judgment. You never stop creating opportunities for people to reconcile with one another and with God. Help me to have a humble attitude and peaceful spirit to seek reconciliation with God and my neighbors wherever I go, so that my world of fighting and hatred is replaced by one of peace and love.

<u>Resolution</u>

Today, I will examine my relationship with God and with everyone around me to see if I need to reconcile. Then, I promise to live in peace and love with my neighbors.

March 24

<u>Issue:</u> **Rejection**
"Come to Him, a Living Stone, rejected by human beings but chosen and precious in the sight of God." (1Peter 2:4)

<u>Reflection</u>
None of us wants our families, friends, and people around us to reject us. Yet, in our secular world, some of us have slowly rejected God and anything to do with the spiritual world despite all the love and blessings we have received from God daily. The world has replaced God with other deities and worldly things. However, it does not stop there. People have gradually rejected faith, virtues, and moral values and embraced anything that is convenient and beneficial to their worldly interests regardless of future consequences.

Lord Jesus, I want to see
Loving Jesus, you once said, "...No one who comes to me have I ever rejected." You also practiced this during your ministry. For you are the loving and compassionate God. I am deeply grateful for that. Yet, I am living in an age that enjoys rejecting God and throwing out anything that might be inconvenient to a wild lifestyle, including moral values and faith teachings. Help me imitate all the holy figures in my Christian tradition who have rejected all worldly things and embraced you as the focus and joy of their lives.

<u>Resolution</u>
Today, I will stop rejecting and pushing God away from my life by committing myself to a life of prayer and embracing the values that lead me to God.

March 25

Repent
"There will be more joy in Heaven over one sinner who repents than over ninety nine righteous people who have no need of repentance." (Luke 15:7)

Reflection
If there is one message that all the prophets could call on the people to do from the beginning of time, it would be to repent and come home to God. Some have heeded that message and decided to change their life, while others have continued on the same old path. The call for repentance simply asks us to examine our relationship with God and see what we need to change to make it better. Our relationship with God is what really matters in the end.

Lord Jesus, I want to see
Lord Jesus, you preached the message of repentance and called on people to make changes to their lives and return to God. Sadly, that call is difficult to hear and accept amidst all the temptations and secular attitudes of our world. Help me welcome that call into my life and convert myself slowly to you. For everyone who repents usually finds peace and joy in their new life with Jesus.

Resolution
It is difficult to turn one's life completely over to Jesus, but beginning today, I'll turn away some of my bad habits and slowly hand my life over to Him.

March 26

Issue: **Sacrifice**

"...Now once and for all Christ has appeared at the end of the ages to take away sin by His sacrifice." (Hebrews 9:26)

Reflection

If there is one word we do not hear a lot these days, it is sacrifice. Instead, we usually hear about what God and the world should have done for me lately; we are simply interested in the idea of entitlement. We have lost the whole sense of contributing to a community and making personal sacrifices. We cannot seem to see the honor and personal satisfaction of putting the good of the church, nation, or Heaven before our own interests in a world that simply cares about "me."

Lord Jesus, I want to see

Kind and Generous Jesus, you willingly sacrificed yourself on the Cross so that we may have life and a chance to enter Heaven. That ultimate act of sacrifice shows us how much you love us. Give me courage to make sacrifices for a greater cause and your selfless Spirit to put the well-being of others before my own comfort. For like a grain of wheat that dies, my sacrifice will produce abundantly in the world around me.

Resolution

Today, I will put aside my selfish attitude and try to make some sacrifices for my family, neighbors, and Jesus.

March 27

Issue: **Save**
"...Christ Jesus came into the world to save sinners, of these I am the foremost." (1 Timothy 1:15)

Reflection
We love to hear the story of someone who saves the life of another human being. We call that person a hero. The Bible and our Christian tradition are full of heroes. The biggest hero of all is our God, who has continued to save us since the beginning of time. Our God is a God of life and hope. Unfortunately, we live in a culture that seeks destruction and death. Worse yet, it perpetuates that culture and allows anger and vengeance to run unchecked.

Lord Jesus, I want to see
Jesus Christ, you said more than once that you came to search out sinners and save them, not to condemn them. That is exactly what you did, from healing the sick and the possessed to feeding the hungry and the poor. My current culture tries to pull me away from your saving mission and discourage me from reaching out to save as many souls as I can. With your grace, I will avoid all occasions that might tempt me to destroy life, even with bad rumors, and look for various ways to save life and encourage others to do the same.

Resolution
Today, I will look back on my life to see all the times God has saved me and try to find ways to give thanks to God for those chances.

March 28

Issue: **Sorrowful**

"No longer shall your Sun go down, or your moon withdraw. For the Lord will be your light forever and the days of your sorrow shall be at the end."
(Isaiah 60:20)

Reflection
Sorrow is one of the most powerful and devastating emotions we humans must face when experiencing a tragic loss or terrible disappointment. Again, the Bible and our Christian tradition are full of examples about sorrow. Many people who have not relied on God's grace and have had to endure sorrow for a long time can easily fall into the valley of depression and hopelessness. These victims might not only gradually fall away from God, but also take drastic measures to hurt themselves and people around them.

Lord Jesus, I want to see
Merciful Lord, you were in such deep sorrow on the night you were betrayed and arrested that you felt like dying inside yourself. I have also had such moments when I've feel like my whole world is closing in on me. Sometimes, I feel as if I have no reason to live due to a devastating event. Yet, you have shown me that we have a God who can bring us joy, peace, and hope. This is where I need to come in those sorrowful moments and let God restore me and lift me out of that dark valley.

Resolution
Today, I will see if I have any sorrowful thing I still hold in my heart. Then, I will bring it to Jesus in prayer and ask Him to replace it with a peaceful and hopeful solution.

March 29

<u>Issue:</u> **Special**

"You are 'a chosen race, a royal priesthood, a holy nation, a people of his own'...For Christ called you out of darkness into His wonderful light."
(1Peter 2:9)

<u>Reflection</u>
Everyone likes to be called special. Yet, we have forgotten that every one of us is special in the eyes of God. Through baptism we have become God's chosen ones and been promised a place in Heaven. Like us, the Israelites were the chosen, special people of God. The Old Testament tells us that because of this status, God always watched over and took good care of them through all the winding roads of their lives.

Lord Jesus, I want to see
Christ Jesus, you called the first twelve apostles and later many more disciples, including us. I do not know how each one of us was called, but I consider myself and all the disciples of Jesus the chosen, special ones. I am also proud and happy to be a Christian. Unfortunately, some Christians might feel embarrassed or shameful to be recognized as a Christian in the public arena. They want you, Jesus, to help them in every way, but they do not want to stand up for you as Christians. Give me courage to acknowledge you before the world and help me to be thankful that I have been chosen as your disciple.

<u>Resolution</u>
Today, I will reflect on some of the blessings and benefits of being a Christian and ask myself if I feel honored and proud as a disciple of Jesus, a chosen one in this diverse world.

March 30

<u>Issue:</u> **Temptation**
"Jesus said to His disciples, 'Why are you sleeping? Get up and pray that you may not undergo any temptation.'" (Luke 22:46)

<u>Reflection</u>
Our lives are full of temptations. We are pulled away from God by our secular and materialistic culture. We are pushed far away from faith and moral values by worldly allurements and instant gratification. Like Adam and Eve, who were tempted in the Garden of Eden, we Christians are surrounded by all sorts of enticements, from money and power to pleasure and glamor. These temptations slowly make us replace our one true God with different kinds of idols. Over time, our spiritual life is harmed and diminished.

<u>Lord Jesus, I want to see</u>
Lord Jesus, you faced several temptations before embracing your Cross and Passion. You were also tempted and provoked by all kinds of influences throughout your ministry. But, you kept your eyes focused on God the Father and continued to maintain a strong relationship with Him in prayers. Help me follow your example and try to resist anything that might harm my spiritual life.

<u>Resolution</u>
Today, I will name some of the temptations I have dealt with in my life and then come up with a plan to remove them over the course of several months.

March 31

"The sting of death is sin…But, thanks be to God who gives us the victory through our Lord Jesus Christ." (1Corinthians 15:56-57)

Reflection

Everyone loves to be on the winning team and enjoy the smell of victory. No one wants to lose now or in the future. With the resurrection of Jesus, we Christians are currently on the winning team. The challenge for us is whether we really believe in that and will proudly live out that spirit amidst all the challenges of our uncertain world. With God's grace, over the centuries we Christians have reminded one another and shown to our world what the spirit of victory looks like as we have conquered hatred with love, violence with peace, judging with compassion, death with eternal life, and hopelessness with the Good News of Jesus.

Lord Jesus, I want to see

Jesus, my Lord and my God, you have given us the best victory over death and darkness with your resurrection and the empty tomb. I might not understand and appreciate the importance of your victory. But, with your help, I want to be a part of it and brag to the world more about it. I want the world to know more about you and what you did for all of us. I hope others will want to come over to the winning side in the end.

Resolution

Today, I will take a moment to acknowledge the victory of Christ at Easter and look for ways to proclaim that joy to the world.

April

Lord Jesus,
I Want to See…

April 1

<u>Issue:</u> **Afraid**

"…You have no need to be afraid since I am with you. I will bless you and multiply your descendants." (Genesis 26:24)

<u>Reflection</u>

There are many things in this life and the next that might cause us to be afraid. We are afraid to live and die alone. We are afraid we might not have enough money to take care of ourselves and our loved ones now or in our old age. We are afraid of the pain and suffering due to health issues. We are afraid of evil things or ending up in a wrong place after this life. However, as Christians, we are called to put our concerns and worries in God's hands and let God help take care of us. The only thing we should fear is being far from God's love and the Kingdom of Heaven.

Lord Jesus, I want to see

Loving and gentle Jesus, you came to bring us the blessings of Heaven and its reassurance. You want us not to be afraid of darkness, death, sadness, loneliness, pain, suffering, or lack of possessions and glamor. For you are my comfort and fulfillment. Open my eyes to see how you protect and guide me in my daily life, how you nourish and take care of me through all the trials and turns of my life.

<u>Resolution</u>

Today, I will recall some things that might cause me to be afraid and then bring them to Jesus for some guidance and solution.

April 2

<u>Issue:</u> **Banquet**

"When you hold a banquet, invite the poor, the crippled, the lame, the blind; blessed will you be because of the inability to repay you. For you'll be repaid at the resurrection of the righteous." (Luke 14:13-14)

<u>Reflection</u>

A banquet is usually a fun and joyous occasion for our families and friends to get together to break bread and share stories. We all look forward to that special time to be with our loved ones. Surely, we will never get sick of banquets and will come to them as often as we can. One of the banquets we Christians hold on a regular basis is the Eucharistic Banquet. This is a time when we gather to commemorate the Last Supper with Jesus and prepare ourselves for the Heavenly Banquet after this life. At that banquet, we will be rewarded for what we did here on earth and given a share in the divine life.

Lord Jesus, I want to see

Jesus, Son of God, you were invited to many banquets during your time on earth, including the wedding party in Cana. You realized how many people simply invited their friends and wealthy neighbors to their banquets as social etiquette. Hence, you challenged your disciples to include the poor and the outcast in those social gatherings also. Help me to keep this in mind when I organize a social event and constantly prepare myself for the Heavenly Banquet that you have set up for all your faithful ones.

<u>Resolution</u>

Today, I will consciously give thanks with my loved ones at a dinner table and think about the Heavenly Banquet that I will share with them and Jesus someday.

April 3

Issue: **Blessed**

"…I've shown you that by hard work we must help the weak, and keep in mind the words of the Lord Jesus who said, 'It is more blessed to give than to receive.'" (Acts 20:35)

Reflection

When we think of the word "blessed," we recall the Beatitudes Sermon on the Mount that Jesus gave to the distraught crowd. Like us, they had been beaten down by life's burdens. With the comforting words of the Beatitudes, Jesus lifted them up and brought blessings into their difficult lives. Without a doubt, we all need more divine blessings in our lives to bring us comfort, guidance, reassurance, and hope. With Jesus in our lives, we will definitely feel blessed despite all the challenges we might encounter each day.

Lord Jesus, I want to see

Jesus, source of all Goodness and Blessings, you spent your whole life reaching out and sharing God's blessings with others. Your generous spirit brought life and many blessings wherever you went. Help me to come to you often, so that I may always feel blessed regardless of how much trouble I might face in my daily life. Give me a generous spirit like yours, so that I may give generously of myself and learn to share God's blessings for me with others. In doing so, I will make the world around me a blessed and better place.

Resolution

Today, I will choose to say "Bless you" to everyone as often as I can.

April 4

Issue: **Call to God**
"Call to me, and I will answer you; I will tell you things great beyond reach of your knowledge." (Jeremiah 33:3)

Reflection
Most of us are often shy about asking for help. We just do not want to be a burden to anyone or be obliged to do something for that person in return. Besides, we do not want to look bad while calling out for help. But, we all need help at some point in our lives. Hence, we should call out to God for guidance, comfort, or support at those moments. Certainly, we are encouraged to call to God often so that the Lord will come to our rescue.

Lord Jesus, I want to see
Lord Jesus, our Source of Life and Hope, you told your disciples, "…Ask and it shall be given…knock and it shall be open." (Matthew 7:7) Help me to come to you freely, day and night, in prayer and bring all my worries, anxieties, and troubles to you, without the fear of bothering you or not getting the answer I want. For you are my strength and my guide. You bring me life and hope with a new day. You guide me through all the twists and turns of my life, even in the toughest and darkest moments. You are just a call and a prayer away from me. Prayer is like that "call for help" button; I just need to push it when I feel in need of help and send you a prayer.

Resolution
Today, I will push the "call for help" button and knock on God's door to bring to God my concerns and troubles without worrying how they will be answered or if I am bothering God with my prayers.

April 5

Issue: **Compromise**

"Do not deprive each other, except by mutual consent for a time, to be free for prayer. But then return to one another, so that Satan will not tempt you through your lack of self-control." (1Corinthians 7:5)

Reflection

We're living in a world that constantly bickers and fights over all sorts of issues. Members of various groups advocate for certain issues and take extreme positions without concessions or exceptions. We have seen this level of intolerance and lack of compassion for one another played out on the world stage, in our political system, in our workplaces, in our worshipping arenas, in our schools, and so on. The word "compromise" becomes an ugly word to even think about. But, can you imagine whether a household or a relationship could exist without compromise by its members? No wonder our world is broken, hurt, and full of hatred as we see it right now!

Lord Jesus, I want to see

Lord Jesus, Source of Healing and Compassion, there were so many times in the Gospels that the Pharisees and scribes tried to raise an explosive issue or stir up a tense situation with you. But, with your wisdom and caring heart, you learned to compromise and find a solution that brought the best result and peace to everyone. Open my heart to see the wisdom in your approach and learn to make compromises in my daily life so that there will always be peace and joy around me.

Resolution

Today, I will examine what issues I have found extremely difficult to accept and try to compromise with my neighbors by seeking a new and mutually beneficial solution.

April 6

Conflict

"Where do the wars and where do the conflicts among you come from? Is it not from your passions that make war within your members?" (James 4:1)

Reflection
Since the beginning of Creation, we have seen one conflict after another happen around us. The first conflict occurred between two brothers, Abel and Cain, and resulted in the murder of Abel. Since then, we humans have faced two World Wars and thousands of conflicts around the globe. Conflict arises because two sides feel passionately about something and cannot seem to find a peaceful solution. The results of conflict are a lot of hurt, pain, suffering, destruction, chaos, death, hatred, and other long-term effects. We might not be able to cause a world-wide conflict. But, we surely we can easily create many little conflicts with our neighbors that might bring about the same deadly results.

Lord Jesus, I want to see
Christ, Prince of Peace, you came to put an end to all conflicts, especially the one between us and God the Father, by your sacrifice on the Cross. Your passion and death taught me the importance of personal sacrifice and gave me the solution for a conflict. Namely, I need to put aside my own passions and selfish desires if I want to put an end to conflicts between me and my neighbors.

Resolution
Today, I will think about some conflict I had with someone and try to end it by putting aside my own passions and selfish desires.

April 7

<u>Issue:</u> **Connected**
"Through Christ the whole structure is connected together and grows into a Temple sacred in the Lord." (Ephesians 2:21)

<u>Reflection</u>
We humans cannot survive on our own. If each one of us is left alone in the wilderness or someplace away from civilization, like the Alaskan frontier, we would find our daily life to be a struggle. Hence, feeling connected to one another is so vital to our survival on earth. Similarly, spiritually speaking, we cannot survive the onslaught and temptations by the power of darkness if we're not connected to God or Jesus Christ in a spiritual community. That spiritual connection will give us a sense of belonging and all the help we need to deal with our daily challenges.

Lord Jesus, I want to see
Lord Jesus, you are the vine, and we are the branches. I cannot imagine a branch can exist on its own without being connected to the body of a plant or a tree. After a while, a disconnected brand will gradually wither and die. Likewise, a person cannot thrive or survive without being connected to God or Jesus, the source of Life and Spiritual nourishment. Open my eyes to see this important fact of life, so that I will always stay close to you, my Lord Jesus, and find ways to be connected to you. Through you I can remain strong and thrive in the face of daily challenges.

<u>Resolution</u>
Today, I will examine my spiritual life to see if I am strongly connected to God and Jesus and then make a commitment to pray daily or come to church weekly for several months.

April 8

Issue: **Corrupt**
"Do not be led astray: 'Bad company corrupts good morals.'" (1 Corinthians 15:33)

Reflection
We have all heard the term "corrupt" in politics and daily living. A corrupted system cannot work to its best ability and deliver expected results. When something is corrupted, it is like a cancer that destroys from the inside and eventually brings death. Similarly, if our souls are corrupted, we will not be able to tell right from wrong or find true meaning in our lives and have a strong relationship with God. Therefore, it is imperative that good Christians safeguard their souls from being corrupted by worldly values or bad moral teachings.

Lord Jesus, I want to see
Almighty and Everlasting Lord Jesus, you often warned your disciples to stay away from the yeast of the Pharisees and the scribes, for they were hypocrites and a bad influence for pure and good souls. By keeping myself from bad influences, my soul will not be corrupted and will be able to stay healthy to welcome the right messages of God being revealed to me daily. Certainly, that's the perfect way for me to have a healthy, good spiritual life.

Resolution
Today, I will see if some worldly values might have influenced me in a bad way and try to fill my soul with spiritual knowledge by reading the Bible.

April 9

Issue: **Easter**

"Jesus told Martha, 'I am the resurrection and the life, whoever believes in me, even if one dies, will live; and everyone who lives and believes in me will never die, Do you believe this?'" (John 11:25-26)

Reflection

We humans love to see and experience miracles. We search high and low for them throughout our lives. Miracles are a sign of God's presence and love in our lives. Amidst the early disciples' doubt and sadness over the death of their Master, God the Father blessed them with the greatest miracle of all, Easter, the Resurrection of Jesus after being in the tomb for three days. The Easter miracle not only confirms the divine nature of Jesus but also assures us of our own resurrection on the Last Day if we would follow Him faithfully to the end.

Lord Jesus, I want to see

Risen Lord, you brought joy and hope to your disciples with an empty tomb, as they were fearful and bewildered by your unjust arrest and humiliating death on the Cross. Like the early disciples, sometimes I feel lost, scared, or overwhelmed by my life's burdens. I pray that you will bring me comfort, peace, and hope with your presence and Easter miracle. Please keep showing me many miracles like the one at Easter, so I can feel your presence and love all the days of my life.

Resolution

Today, I will see what makes me fearful and anxious at this point in my life and bring it to the Risen Christ in prayer so that He can give me a solution and bless me with His peace.

April 10

Issue: **Excitement**

They went away quickly from the tomb fearful yet overjoyed, and ran to announce this [the meeting with the angels in the empty tomb] to Jesus' disciples." (Matthew 28:8)

Reflection

There are certain things in life that make people feel excited: getting a great gift, acquiring a new car or a new home, winning something special, going on a rare trip, having a first baby, being married to a sweetheart, seeing a dear friend after a long period of separation, and so on. Sometimes, it can be as simple as being able to walk after a serious accident. In other words, people are often excited about something rare, special, or extraordinary. For the early disciples, the news of an empty tomb after Jesus' death and burial excited them wildly. They had never seen anything like that before.

Lord Jesus, I want to see

Jesus, Lord of the Living and the Dead, my faith and prayer life might be dull and boring. I sometimes feel it is a big chore to say my daily prayers and a great pain to keep a close relationship with you. Help me to see the joy and excitement in all the little miracles and blessings you bring me every day. Open my eyes to recognize your presence in every kind thing I do for others, especially the lowly ones among us.

Resolution

Today, I will try to figure out what has brought me joy and excitement as a Christian and give thanks to God for it or try to remind myself of that blessing often.

April 11

Issue: **Forbear**

"...Through the forbearance of God – to prove His righteousness in the present time, that he might be righteous and justify the one who has faith in Jesus." (Romans 3:26)

Reflection

It takes a lot of humility and courage for us to endure a tough situation or a difficult person. That is what the Father of the Prodigal Son experienced when his son left home and squandered away his resources on a sinful lifestyle. Like that father, God forbears and puts up with His people with their selfish, disobedient, and wayward lifestyles. And, time and again, God's people continue to be the heavy cross for God to carry, with their defiant attitudes and dark thoughts. But, God never abandons us.

Lord Jesus, I want to see

Lord Jesus, you were sent to carry out God's plan of salvation for God's people. You had to bear our load of sins on the Cross. Seeing you suffer and hang lifeless on the cross, I cannot imagine my God would do that for me and God's people. I wonder if I am willing to suffer and sacrifice myself for a dear friend or my God. I sometimes ask myself how much I can put up with the shortcomings of my loved ones and how long I can endure their mistakes. I am sure my level of forbearance is very low compared to God's. I pray that you, Lord, will help me learn to be more patient and forgiving to my family and everyone around me.

Resolution

Today, I will review my life to see what or who seems to bother me and then figure out ways to forbear that cross in order to keep the peace and love of Jesus in my community.

April 12

Fulfilling

"...Now acknowledge with your whole heart and soul that not one of all the promises the Lord your God made to you has remained unfulfilled. Every promise has been fulfilled for you, with not one single exception." (Joshua 23:14)

Reflection

We Christians believe that God has a plan for every one of us. God has predestined us to be saved and promised us a place in His kingdom. With the birth of God's Son Jesus and his death on the Cross, God has shown us how His plan and promises for us have gradually been fulfilled. Unlike our politicians, God does not make empty promises. Rather, God has proven to His faithful ones in the course of human history how He can fulfill His promises and make our dreams come true without one single exception.

Lord Jesus, I want to see

Ever-faithful Lord, you are the fulfillment of our loving God and a sign of God's presence in our chaotic and uncertain world. I am surrounded by empty rhetoric, broken promises, unreliable relationships, and uncertain futures. It is very rare these days to see someone who can fulfill his/her promises. Give me courage and strength to always follow through with my promises and try to fulfill all the duties I have been called to do.

Resolution

Today, I will review some of the promises I have made with God and people around me and see what I can do to fulfill those promises and follow through with them.

April 13

Issue: **Gate**
Enter through the narrow gate; for the gate that is wide and the road that is broad would lead to destruction, and those who enter through it are many." (Matthew 7:13)

Reflection
We are surrounded by all sorts of gates in our daily lives. Gates have been constructed and erected to bring security and keep out bad things. Yet, we humans have used gates to create division, hatred, suffering, and other bad purposes within our human family. Instead of opening more gates and inviting our neighbors to visit us or building more bridges to help us connect with one another, we have set up new gates, shut out more people from our lives, including God. Some of us have also thrown away the keys.

Lord Jesus, I want to see
Lord Jesus, King of David, you came to open all gates, especially the Gate of Heaven, to lead us to the heart of God and connect us with one another. You also called us to use the narrow gates that demand that we make some sacrifices in this life to enter the Kingdom of Heaven. Guide me through these moments that I find those narrow gates quite frustrating and challenging, so that I may realize their benefits. Most important, wait for me at the Gate of Heaven and welcome me into your Eternal Kingdom after my time here on earth.

Resolution
Today, I will look at some of the gates that might have kept me from God and my neighbors and see what I can do to open them to reconnect myself with those relationships.

April 14

Issue: **Glory**

"Whether you eat or drink, or whatever you do, do everything for the Glory of God." (1 Corinthians 10:31)

Reflection

Everyone enjoys five minutes of fame and loves to be in the position of glory. Yet, self-glorifying can be a dangerous thing, for it can lead us to be prideful, selfish, self-indulging, self-gloating, and so on. We Christians believe that the only one to whom we should give glory always is God. Everything we do should bring glory to God and nothing else. For God is the only one who deserves glory and worship from us due to everything God has created around us and continues to do for us.

Lord Jesus, I want to see

Jesus, Son of God, your whole life was never about seeking the limelight. Your ministry was not about self-glorifying. Rather, all your good works were about serving God's people and bringing them closer to God. In fact, you often reminded your disciples and the world about the importance of giving glory to God. Help me acquire your spirit of humility and service as I try to carry on your mission of salvation. Make me realize that all my good works and successes come from you. Therefore, you deserve all the credit for a loving and compassionate world around me.

Resolution

Today, I will commit myself to do all good works, not for my own fame but for the glory of God and for being Christ's follower.

April 15

Issue: **Holiness**
"Strive for peace with everyone, and for that holiness without which no one will see the Lord." (Hebrews 12:14)

Reflection
We all want to be close to God. For God is our source of life and our key to true happiness. The best way for us to be near God is to be holy. Yet, having anything to do with holiness is the last thing anyone in our time ever wants to think about. What many people think a lot about these days is fun, pleasure, worldly possessions, and fame. No wonder our world is messed up as it is! But, anyone who stays close to holiness will be blessed with not only happiness but also wisdom and a lot of wonderful things from above.

Lord Jesus, I want to see
Jesus, my Lord and Savior, you always had a caring heart and never failed to reach out to the hungry, the sick, the lowly, the misfortunate, and the outcast during your ministry on earth. After taking care of their basic needs, you always tried to point them to holiness and the spiritual world. Help me see the blessings of that priority and strive to live a holy life. For our world needs a lot of examples of holiness to show it the blessings of Heaven. Moreover, there is no one to whom we should be close at all times other than God.

Resolution
If I have not found being holy quite appealing, today, I'll commit myself to pray a little more, read the Bible more often, and do some more good deeds this week.

April 16

Issue: **Idolatry**

"Put to death the parts of you that are earthly: immorality, impurity, passion, evil desire, and the greed that is idolatry. Because of them the wrath of God is coming." (Colossians 3:5-6)

Reflection

We chase after various things in life: pleasures, possessions, fame, to name a few. We might even put our trust and hope in some of these things and other addictions. What we do not realize is that these are forms of idolatry. We no longer have one and only God. Rather, we turn to worldly things and make them our gods. The problem is that those gods only work for us in good times and let us down in tough times. They also do not help us discern the right decisions or find meaning and hope beyond our current life.

Lord Jesus, I want to see

Jesus, my Lord and my God, you warned your followers not to go after worldly idols. You drove out people who sold things and exchanged money in the temple, because they turned your Father's house into a market place. I am surrounded by all sorts of idols and exposed to various temptations via the Internet. Give me courage and strength to resist any bad tendencies that might cause me to worship other idols and abandon my one true God.

Resolution

Today, I will review if there is anything on which I might rely more than my Lord Jesus and try to shift my focus away from those things.

April 17

Issue: **Inspired**

"...Calling to mind your work of faith and labor of love and endurance inspired by hope of our Lord Jesus Christ before our God and Father, knowing how you were chosen." (1Thessalonians 1:3-4)

Reflection

We all love to be inspired and lifted out of the doldrums of our boring life routines. Some of us might be inspired by an uplifting song and its heartfelt lyrics, whereas others might be motivated by a great book and its wonderful messages. Or, a dynamic speaker might be able to intrigue us with his/her aspiring talk. Without these sources of inspiration, we can only imagine how boring, depressed, and hopeless our lives would be.

Lord Jesus, I want to see

Jesus Teacher, you have the words of everlasting life. You brought life and excitement wherever you went. You always drew a big crowd of people with your life-giving works and messages of Good News. You reached out and motivated so many lost and dejected souls with your inspiring messages like the Beatitudes. We need more leaders and friends like you. Let my heart and soul be inspired by your words and works so that I may be a sign of hope and life-giving to others. Let me only speak words of encouragement and be a source of hope and sunshine to everyone around me.

Resolution

Today, I will see what has inspired me most about Jesus' life and try to share it with the world around me.

April 18

Intercede

"…It is Christ who died and was raised, who is also at the right hand of God, and who indeed intercedes for us." (Romans 8:34)

Reflection

Every good cause or charity group needs a corporation or a rich and powerful person to sponsor it and get the public to accept it. We also need friends in powerful positions to speak up for us and give us a hand in times of need. This is one of the effective ways we humans have used in this life to move our lowly ideas forward. Similarly, we believe that the same concept will work for us in the spiritual world as we sinners look up to holy folks in our Christian tradition like Mary and the Saints to intercede for us from their place in Heaven.

Lord Jesus, I want to see

Lord Jesus, you saw how the idea of intercession works during your ministry. At the wedding in Cana, Mary, your mother, came to you for help on behalf of the wedding couple when they ran out of wine. Or, the Centurion interceded on behalf of his sick daughter and asked you to heal her. Help me rely on you, Mary, and the Saints to intercede for my needs here on earth. Also, give me the courage and care for others so that I can bring your Good News and salvation to the broken world around me.

Resolution

Today, I will think of someone who might need a prayer or a miracle in his/her life and commit myself to pray for this person for a week.

April 19

Issue: **Judge**
"Stop judging and you will not be judged. Stop condemning and you will not be condemned. Forgive and you will be forgiven..." (Luke 6:37)

Reflection
One thing most of us have done a lot in our daily life is to judge others freely without any concern or qualifications. We condemn people who might have done something morally wrong and look down on others who might look different than we do. Therefore, we have seen our world, country, and neighborhood explode in anger, hatred, and violence. What each and everyone needs is to put on humility, compassion, and understanding.

Lord Jesus, I want to see
Lord Jesus, Judge of the Living and the Dead, you rarely passed judgment or condemned someone during your ministry. It was not because you were not qualified or because you were afraid to do it. Rather, it was because you tried to show compassion, understanding, and forgiveness to lost sheep. Help me avoid having negative thoughts about others and have a heart of understanding and compassion for others, especially people who might be different from me.

Resolution
Today, I will try not to judge or condemn someone I see on television, hear on the radio, read about in a magazine, or pass by on the road.

April 20

Issue: **Lust**

"For you have spent enough time in the past doing what pagans choose to do in living in debauchery, lust, drunkenness, orgies, carousing, and detestable idolatry." (1Peter 4:3)

Reflection

There are many difficult sins we humans must confront. Concupiscence is one of them. This sin relates to lust and sexual desire. The Bible has many examples to show us how pervasive and difficult it is to deal with this sin. Even King David, a holy man himself, succumbed to lust, committed murder against one of his generals, and fornicated with the general's wife. St. Paul referred to this sin of the flesh when he compared it to a thorn on his side. Lust is surely a huge problem that we humans must face every day, while its temptation continues to increase all around us.

Lord Jesus, I want to see

Jesus, Son of God and Son of Mary, you were tempted before undergoing your own passion. But, you conquered it. What you taught us from your personal experience against temptation is the need for divine help and a commitment to following God's plan of salvation. Yet, I find myself not relying on God for help and often struggle to commit myself to follow you, Jesus. Help me to change this and rely on you as my strength and guidance to deal with lust and other daily temptations around me.

Resolution

Today, I will empower my spiritual strength as a way to deal with lust by focusing more on prayer and spiritual work.

April 21

Issue: **Outcast**
"For the Lord your God is merciful God, who will not abandon or destroy you or forget the covenant with your forefathers, which the Lord confirmed to them by oath." (Deuteronomy 4:31)

Reflection
It is difficult for any of us to be isolated. For we all would like to be included and belong to a community. A community gives us a sense of security, family, acceptance, support, and so on. God certainly wants us to belong to the community of God's people and will bring home any of us who might be lost. On the contrary, our world likes to create division and toss aside anyone or anything it finds useless. It shows no mercy or care to someone it considers an outcast. This is sadly a tragedy.

Lord Jesus, I want to see
Jesus the Good Shepherd, you spent your whole life reaching out to the outcast and searching for all the lost souls. You asked your disciples not to shun or cast out someone because of sin, possession, appearance, or social status. Unfortunately, we all suffer from this discrimination virus and do not hesitate to turn someone into an outcast. Help me to have your caring and compassionate heart and not to cast away someone for any reason. May I learn from your example and try to reach out to the outcast and abandoned around me.

Resolution
Today, I will review my life to see if I have excluded anyone from God's family for some reason. I will make an effort to reach out and welcome those folks when I have a chance.

April 22

Issue: **Passions**

"At one time we too were foolish, disobedient, deceived, and enslaved by all kinds of passions and pleasures. We lived in malice and envy, being hated and hating one another." (Titus 3:3)

Reflection

There are certain things about which we feel passionate, which sometimes might cause us to lose our heads. Sexual desire is a passion that has gotten a lot of people into big trouble over the centuries. Unfortunately, this problem continues to destroy many good folks and their families. It causes people to become selfish, deceptive, careless, destructive, angry, addictive, and unfaithful. A victim of a passion will do anything, including harming others, to satisfy his/her desire and get what he/she wants.

Lord Jesus, I want to see

Lord Jesus, your Passion was about the Cross and salvation for humanity. It brought the promise of a new life to others instead of death and destruction. This is because your Passion focused on helping others instead of your own needs and desires. Sometimes, I let my own passions and desire overtake my dutiful and responsible nature and lead me to do selfish, harmful things. Help me to imitate you and use my passions to do good for others and bring life and hope to the world around me.

Resolution

Today, I will examine what I feel passionate about and figure out how I can carry out my passions without causing hurt and destruction to others.

April 23

Issue: **Predestined**

"In love God predestined us to be adopted as God's sons and daughters through Jesus Christ in accordance with God's pleasure and will." (Ephesians 1:5)

Reflection

We often think that things happen and come together randomly. Or, we plan and make things come about by our own will. Certainly, those situations are true. But, God the Creator does have a plan for everything under Heaven. God predestined us to be saved and have a place in His Kingdom. It is difficult for us to see God's plan or God's hand at work in our lives and in Creation. Or, we might think we are running the show on earth. But, the truth is that God is in control and God allows good or bad things happen within His big plan for the whole Creation. We just need to trust in God and let God guide us.

Lord Jesus, I want to see

Jesus Son of God, you obediently followed the plan of God the Father and came into our world to save us with your death on the Cross. At times like the moment in the Garden of Gethsemane you wondered about that plan and wanted God the Father to take away your cup of bitterness and suffering. Help me to trust in God's plan for me every day a little more. Help me conform my will to God's will, so that I will always have your peace in my heart, even in confusing times.

Resolution

Today, I will find out something that is difficult for me to let go and try to let God take care of it for me.

April 24

Issue: **Restore**
"The God of all grace, who called you to His eternal glory in Christ, after you have suffered a little while, will Himself restore you and make you strong, firm, and steadfast." (1Peter 5:10)

Reflection
One of the buttons we love the most on our computers, cell phones, or any electronic or electric devices is "reset." This button helps us dump off all the bad stuff and restored our devices to their original state, where everything is back to normal. In our spiritual life, we would like to have a similar button that could wipe out our bad history and restore us to our original state of grace, where we can have peace and happiness. For Catholics, that "reset" button is called Confession, whereas other religions call it something else. Whatever process we use to restore our souls, it usually has something to do with forgiveness and asking God to make us a new person.

Lord Jesus, I want to see
Lord Jesus, beside spiritual restoration, you restored sight to the blind, speech to the mute, hearing to the deaf, mobility to the crippled, new look to the lepers, dignity to those who are outcast, and hope to the hopeless. It must be exciting for these folks to receive that special gift from you. When I feel lost in this confusing world, please restore me to the right path. When I feel overwhelmed by life burdens, please restore my courage to keep moving forward and my hope in your love and help for me. I thank you.

Resolution
Today, I might be physically, mentally, or spiritually off-balance. I need to come to Jesus and ask Him to restore me to the healthy, whole person.

April 25

Issue: **Reverence**
"But for you who revere my name, the Sun of righteousness will rise with healing in its wings. And you will go out and leap like calves released from the stall." (Malachi 4:2)

Reflection
Our modern age brings with it many problems. One of those problems is that nothing is sacred any more. People do not have respect for authority, institutions, and offices these days. Worst of all, many folks lose a sense of reverence to God and a higher power. Thence, they lose trust in God and slowly become distant. But, that is the worst thing they must endure. More and more people have become lonely, depressed, hopeless, and lost today. That does not include many mental and social problems that have caused many pains and hurts around the world. The best way to fix these problems is to return to a good spiritual life and show God due reverence.

Lord Jesus, I want to see
Jesus, Son of God and of Mary, you always showed reverence for God the Father and God the Spirit. You also paid respect to the Holy Temples by visiting them frequently. Because of your reverence and good relationship with the divine, your life was always fulfilled and at peace. Help me to have the same sense of reverence for anything sacred so that I may have a good relationship with you and God. This way, I will never feel alone on my journey of faith or be far away from your love.

Resolution
Today, I will be more respectful in using God's name or in treating sacred symbols, objects, and worshipping places.

April 26

<u>Issue:</u> **Reward**

"But as for you, be strong and do not give up, for your work will be rewarded." (2Chronicles 15:7)

<u>Reflection</u>
We all do things for some sort of reward. That reward could be a paycheck, a good return in an investment, or some sort of recognition. For most religious folks, their reward for following religious teachings and doing good will come in the next life. Reward has been used to motivate people to do good and avoid bad things. It is also an acknowledgement for one's hard work and contributions to a cause. The best reward that we can receive is the crown of life waiting for us in Heaven.

Lord Jesus, I want to see
Loving and merciful Jesus, you rewarded Peter and your disciples a boat load of fish for following your command. You awarded anyone who believed in you with miracles and Mary Magdalene who loved you with the Good News of your resurrection. Help me put my trust and hope in you so that I may receive your abundant rewards in this life and the next. When I want to give up on my faith journey with you, let me feel your tender and loving hand to give me the encouragement to move forward. That will be the best reward I can ask for.

<u>Resolution</u>
Today, I will do a good deed for someone or say a prayer for someone in need of it and know that the Lord will reward me for it sooner or later.

April 27

Issue: **Rock**

"Everyone who hears these words of mine and puts them into practice is like a wise person who built one's house on the rock." (Matthew 7:24)

Reflection

In our daily life, a rock can be a source of troubles and danger for us. It can prevent us from moving forward or can fall on us and cause us harm. However, in the spiritual world, a rock is a firm anchor for us in tough times and a great source of protection in stormy times. It is also a life-giving source for God's people in the Old Testament as Moses struck a rock, under God's command, to bring forth a fresh spring of water for a thirsty people who went through so much in the desert. Of course, God is the eternal Rock that would bring God's people life and protection.

Lord Jesus, I want to see

Rabbi Jesus, you taught your disciples to build their house of faith on rock and put their complete trust in you. That way when challenging time comes, that house will not be destroyed. I might think my security is material possessions, fame, glamor, or pleasures. But, building the house of faith on those is like constructing the house on sand. When tough and stormy times come, such a foundation will give in and the house will collapse. By having faith in you and practicing your teachings, my life will be built on solid rock and can withstand all the onslaught of life storms.

Resolution

Today, I will see what might be preventing me from choosing God to be the rock of my life and commit myself to a good relationship with God through a steady prayer life this week.

April 28

<u>Issue:</u> **Shame**

"Nothing impure will ever enter the Temple, nor will anyone who does what is shameful or deceitful, but only those whose names are written in the Lamb's book of life." (Revelation 21:27)

<u>Reflection</u>
Shame is how we feel after we do something wrong. We regret and feel awful about what we did in the past. Out of respect for ourselves and our family name, most of us avoid anything that brings about shame and humiliation. Unfortunately, we live in a time that many folks do not know or do not care what a shameful act is any more. They keep on doing hurtful and harmful things to themselves and others around them. If they felt ashamed, they would stop before doing any of these things, because they would feel sorrow or regret. So, shame is a wonderful mechanism to keep us from going too far with something bad and make us regret the wrong we did. Unfortunately, modern time has taken away and destroyed this decency mechanism from our daily vocabulary.

Lord Jesus, I want to see
Gentle and forgiving Lord, you know how shame and taboo work in society. Hence, you went out of your way to restore honor and dignity to the outcast and repented. Give me courage to follow your example and reach out to anyone who might feel shameful and sorry for their past sins. Most important, open my mind to see what might be shameful and try to avoid it before it harms me and others.

<u>Resolution</u>
Today, I will name what brings shame to my Lord and my family and come up with ways to avoid it.

April 29

<u>Issue:</u> **Suffering**

"We rejoice in our sufferings because we know that suffering produces perseverance; perseverance character; character hope." (Romans 5:3)

<u>Reflection</u>
Suffering is one aspect of life that most of us usually do not cherish. We often wonder why we must suffer and endure all the horrible things in this life. We do not understand why someone must carry a heavy cross and why God allows bad things happen to good people. Suffering might not make any sense to a secular world, but we the believers view suffering exactly like Paul expressed in the Scripture passage above. Its value is to bring out our character, the best within us, and ultimately our sense of hope and optimism. Perhaps it is very difficult for us to see the true meaning of suffering at the time, but in the end, it makes us a better person.

Lord Jesus, I want to see
Jesus the Suffering Servant, your whole life is about suffering for the salvation of others. Your ultimate suffering was your Passion and Cross. You have certainly shown us meaning in your suffering and given us an example of courage and trust in times of darkness. Open my eyes to see the faith values and the hidden life lessons that suffering offers me. Give me courage and strength to face my daily crosses and suffering without complaint or bitterness.

<u>Resolution</u>
Today, I will name what I might be suffering from or afraid about suffering and then see how I could use this chance to teach others about suffering.

April 30

<u>Issue:</u> **Tomorrow**
"Do not worry about tomorrow, for tomorrow will worry about itself. Each day has enough trouble of its own." (Matthew 6:34)

<u>Reflection</u>
We often take tomorrow for granted and assume that the sun will rise the next morning. But, what if tomorrow never comes? Would we be regretful about something we should have done? Should we be thankful every morning for a new day? We should live each day as if it is the last day for us and not worry about tomorrow and what our future will be like. We should give thanks to God for every new day, try to live it to the fullest and cherish every moment of it. That way we will not regret if tomorrow never comes, and we will continue to be thankful and rejoicing if it does.

<u>Lord Jesus, I want to see</u>
Jesus, God of day and darkness, you once advised your followers not to worry about tomorrow, but rather focus on today and its troubles. You also told them not try to figure out when the Last Day might be. For only God the Father knows the day and the hour. I might take tomorrow for granted or let the troubles of tomorrow worry me. With your grace, help me focus simply on today and learn to cherish it. Make me realize that, by living in thanksgiving and God's love, I will be able to take care of today and tomorrow together.

<u>Resolution</u>
If there is something about tomorrow that might concern me, I need to bring it to God in prayers today and try to make peace with it.

May

Lord Jesus,
I Want to See...

May 1

<u>Issue:</u> **Action**
"In the same way, faith by itself, it if is not accompanied by action, is dead... Show me your faith without deeds, and I will show you my faith by what I do." (James 2:17-18)

<u>Reflection</u>
One of the reasons we dislike politicians is because they tend to talk big, but do nothing. Most of us appreciate and respect people who do more and talk less. There is a saying that "Actions speak louder than words." Therefore, we Christians need to avoid big talks about our devout faith and God's love, while not reaching out to help the misfortunate and take care of the poor. When we act and live out our Christian faith, we show the world that our Christian faith is real and alive.

<u>**Lord Jesus, I want to see**</u>
Jesus, Word of God made flesh, you entered our world and died for us on the Cross to show how real the love of God is for us. But, that is not the only real action you have shown us. Over ninety percent of your ministry featured concrete actions you did for God's people, while only a small part of your ministry was involved with teaching. Open my eyes to see how effective an act of your tender care is compared to a long talk of love. Make me a disciple of action and give me courage to reach out to serve the least among us. In this way, I can show the world our God is real.

<u>Resolution</u>
Today, I will do a good deed to show God's love in action to the world around me.

May 2

Issue: **Argument**
"Do not have anything to do with foolish and stupid arguments because you know they produce quarrels... And the Lord's servant must not quarrel." (2Timothy 2:23-24)

Reflection
Whenever two or three people come together, there will surely be differences and arguments. People often argue and fight over all kinds of issues; often it is about selfish things. The problem with an argument is that it destroys relationships and allows the Prince of Darkness to pull us away from God and everyone around us. An argument also takes away the peace and joy of the daily life. In human history, we have learned that an argument can cause a long, drawn-out war. Certainly, it is not good to create arguments or feed them.

Lord Jesus, I want to see
Peaceful and gentle Lord, you once told your disciples to leave the sacrifices at the Altar and go reconcile with their neighbors if they recall that there was an argument between them. Clearly, it is not good to hang on to an argument. This situation leaves us unprepared to have a relationship, especially with God. I am sure I cannot avoid all arguments with my neighbors. For I know others around me can get on my nerves and vice versa. But, I cannot call myself a disciple of Jesus if I keep hanging on to one argument after another with my neighbors. So, let me try to make peace every day.

Resolution
Today, I will try to put aside as many arguments with my neighbors as I can commit myself to a life of peace and forgiveness.

May 3

Issue: **Attitude**
"Your attitude should be the same as that of Christ Jesus." (Philippians 2:5)

Reflection

Attitude is something not only we adults have, but our little ones and pets have attitude too. It is basically our disposition and feeling toward the world around us. Some of us might have a hopeful, positive, caring, compassionate attitude, whereas others may have a pessimistic, negative, indifferent, critical one. The kind of attitude we embrace and project to the world influences the way we view and perceive it. If we have the right attitude, then all will look and feel as if it belongs to God and the Heavenly realm.

Lord Jesus, I want to see

Christ Jesus, you came into our world to save it and did many wonderful things for us during your ministry. But, one very important thing you did for the whole of humanity was to make a major attitude adjustment of it. You did it by calling humanity to love God and love its neighbors, even its enemies. I might fall back on my old attitudes and mistreat God and everyone around me because of my pride and selfishness. Help me to have your attitude by putting the Glory of God and the well-being of others before my own. For your attitude brought salvation to the world and helped move everyone closer to Heaven.

Resolution

Today, I will banish my negative, critical attitude and try to show the world a positive, hopeful one despite how bad things might look.

May 4

<u>Issue:</u> **Burning**
"You O Lord, keep my lamp burning; my God turns my darkness into light." (Psalms 18:28)

<u>Reflection</u>
When something is burning, it radiates light and produces heat. Light comes to dispel darkness and bring about life, growth, and hope. Heat is used to give us warmth and keep us from being frozen to death. Clearly, a burning thing can produce many life-giving benefits for us. Similarly, a burning faith means it is alive and quite productive for us and the Kingdom of Heaven. On the contrary, a lukewarm or cold faith does not perform its function and slowly dies.

Lord Jesus, I want to see
Son of the Living God, your heart burnt with love and our human salvation. Your days on earth were sizzling with saving works and messages of Good News. You constantly stoked your disciples and the public to have a burning love for God and the Kingdom of Heaven. I might have a lukewarm relationship with you and struggle to maintain a lively prayer life. I also might get distracted by worldly things and lose sight of what matters the most in the end. Make my heart burn with the desire to be your dear friend and secure a place for myself in Heaven. Furthermore, make me yearn to help others often and turn our world into a better place.

<u>Resolution</u>
Today, I will try to figure out how to turn my relationship with Jesus into a hot, burning love using good prayer habits or doing an increasing number of good deeds.

May 5

Common Good
"All the believers were together and had everything in common. Selling their possessions and goods, they gave to anyone as he/she has need." (Acts 2:44-45)

Reflection

The issue above is hardly mentioned in an individualistic society like ours. Some might get quite nervous upon hearing it. For our American way is mainly focused on me and my needs. The idea of the common good is far from our first thought. In fact, not many people see the value of that idea or work hard to promote it. However, it was this exact idea that helped the early Church bond together and overcome some tough times to become a vibrant source of influence in our modern society.

Lord Jesus, I want to see

Jesus, my Lord and my God, you spent your whole life for the sake of others and the Kingdom of Heaven. You called your disciples to take care of a hungry crowd and not let them fend for themselves. I wonder if I would have followed your command and looked after those poor folks. For I have been heavily influenced by our individualistic society. Help me to have a generous heart and the spirit of a missionary like yours so that I will always put the common good before my own and promote that idea every chance possible.

Resolution

Today, I will search for something that I can do for my family, Church, or country without worrying about any cost to me.

May 6

"I speak the truth in Christ – I am not lying, my conscience confirms with it in the Holy Spirit." (Romans 9:1)

Reflection
We need a compass or a map to look for direction and avoid getting lost. Similarly, in our spiritual life, we need a moral compass to tell us right from wrong and what we should do as a believer. In fact, a healthy and thriving society needs a moral compass to keep it from doing anything unethical or reprehensible. In case we forget, we humans were born with an innate moral compass called Conscience. If we really pay attention to that voice, it usually tells us what to do and what not to do.

Lord Jesus, I want to see
Beloved Jesus, you tried to build a good moral compass for God's people by warning them what they should avoid and encouraging them regarding what they should do more often. I am living in a world that throws away the moral compass and simply follows what makes a person feel good. Everyone does not look up to a moral standard to help them make decisions and teach their young. I have begun to see the consequences of this attitude with senseless violence and the constant killing of innocent people around our country and the globe. Help me hold tight to my moral compass and remain in your love.

Resolution
Today, I will find one right thing I must do and one wrong thing I must avoid to help build up my moral compass.

May 7

Issue: **Compliment**

"Do not eat the food of a stingy man…; for he is the kind of person who is always thinking about the cost… You will vomit up the little you have eaten and will have wasted your compliments." (Proverbs 23:6-8)

Reflection

One thing many of us should do more of daily and feel at ease doing is giving compliments to people around us. It does not cost us anything, but will definitely make many people feel good and build a peaceful community. Unfortunately, we tend to be critical and judgmental of others. Kind words and compliments are difficult for us to say. But, we would rather engage in bad rumors and negative criticism, which brings about hurt and destruction to others.

Lord Jesus, I want to see

Kind and loving Jesus, your preaching brought hope and encouragement to our broken world. When someone felt sad and dejected, you reached out and lifted them up with kind and comforting words like "Come, follow me, and I will make you fishers of men" (Mark 1:17) when you saw your future disciples busy catching fish for living. Open my eyes to see the wisdom in your approach to the world and all the good it did for humanity. Give me courage to say kind words and give compliments to others without any hesitation. Help me learn to lift up others more than putting them down.

Resolution

Today, I will try to compliment my family or friends to make them feel good.

May 8

Confident

"This is the confidence we have approaching God: that if we ask anything according to God's will, God hears us." (1John 5:14)

Reflection

We feel confident when we have the answers, the solutions, and the resources to deal with the world around us. A confident person is absolutely in control of a situation. But, the only one who can qualify for all the conditions above and much more is God. God is truly the confident person in the whole Creation regardless of the situation. So, provided we are connected to God, we should feel confident and have nothing to worry about.

Lord Jesus, I want to see

Jesus Son of God, you faced many difficult and uncertain situations during your ministry, including your death and resurrection, with confidence and peace, because you were fully connected to God the Father. You knew that God the Father would never abandon you. That is surely the greatest feeling one can have. I might feel scared and worried amidst my life's burdens and daily challenges. Or, I might feel lost and alone in our ever-changing world. But, by staying connected to you and remaining in your love, I will always feel confident in the face of any challenge.

Resolution

I might feel insecure about myself or something lately. But, today I will do my best and entrust the rest of my worries to God with the confidence that He will never abandon me.

May 9

<u>Issue:</u> **Consequence**
"Now that you have been set free from sin and have become slaves to God, the benefit you reap leads to holiness, and the result is eternal life."
(Romans 6:22)

<u>Reflection</u>
One of the mistakes we humans often make is to form a decision without considering its consequences. We somehow detach our decisions from their consequences. That blindness and irresponsible thinking has brought about many hurts and destruction, not only to the doer but also everyone around us. Some consequences come and go, whereas others remain for life and leave a permanent scar on their victims. Certainly, good consequences bring us all sorts of wonderful blessings, whereas bad ones leave us with tears and regrets.

Lord Jesus, I want to see
Jesus source of Wisdom and Guidance, you taught your disciples to consider the consequences of all their actions. Adam and Eve's act of disobedience brought sin and death into our world, whereas your action on the Cross gave us salvation and the promise of eternal life. Give me wisdom to think through every action I take every day and its consequences. Make me realize that a good act will bring great blessings, whereas a bad act leads to many regrettable consequences.

<u>Resolution</u>
Today, I will deliberate carefully over every decision or action of mine and its consequences before carrying it out.

May 10

Contradiction

"...Guard what has been entrusted to your care. Turn away from godless chatter and the opposing ideas of what is falsely called knowledge, which some have professed and in so doing have wandered from the faith."
(1 Timothy 6:20-21)

Reflection

Life on earth is full of contradiction and opposing ideas. Our life's mission as a believer is to find meaning for our messy life and try to line up our will with God's. Sometimes, it is confusing and difficult for us to deal with contradicting messages in our lives and make sense of them. We feel overwhelmed and frustrated when things do not add up or line up nicely. But, it is all right to live in a messy and contradictory world if we stay connected to God, our source of life and guidance.

Lord Jesus, I want to see

Jesus, Son of God and of Mary, your whole life was full of contradictions and opposites. You were divine and human. You brought Good News to God's people and challenged them to repent. Your Cross is the ultimate sign of humiliation and loss. Yet, it is also the symbol of victory and new life. Help me embrace all the contradictions that I might run into in my life without feeling panic. Make me realize that you will not abandon me in our messy and contradictory world.

Resolution

Today, I will see what contradiction in life might frustrate or confuse me and then bring it to Jesus in prayer to make sense of it and learn to accept it.

May 11

Issue: **Counsel**
"Counsel and sound judgment are mine; I [the Lord] have understanding and power." (Proverbs 8:14)

Reflection
We come to a counselor, priest, nun, deacon, spiritual director, or lawyer for advice and counsel. We consult with a close friend or someone we respect for guidance and help in times of need. But, there is someone who many people often forget to come to for counsel, namely, God. God the Father sent us God the Holy Spirit to bring us the gift of counsel and help us make the right decisions. It is wise for us to consult with God first and often in prayer if we truly want good and sound counsel.

Lord Jesus, I want to see
Jesus, Word of God, you gave good counsel to your disciples and others in need of your help. You told your disciples to cast the nets on the right side of the boat if they wanted to catch fish. You advised the servants at the wedding in Cana to fill the jars with water if they wanted wine. By following your counsel, many people had a taste of a miracle. Help me seek your counsel above everything else. Open my ears to listen to your voice in prayer when I need help.

Resolution
Today, I will think about something for which I need God's counsel and spend some time in prayer.

May 12

Issue: **Devoted**

"They devoted themselves to the apostles' teaching and to the fellowship, to the breaking of bread and to prayer." (Acts 2:42)

Reflection

A devoted person usually dedicates his/her time, efforts, and resources to a cause or a group about which he/she feels strongly. Some devote their time to serve their family members in need, whereas others spend their efforts taking care of misfortunate strangers at God's kitchen. Some dedicate their lives to serving God and do mission work, whereas others try to use their resources to help some other charity cause. Many people around the globe are motivated daily to devote their lives and resources to doing something good. We certainly need more folks like this to make our world a better place.

Lord Jesus, I want to see

Faithful Lord, you devoted your whole life to bringing Good News to the world and serving others by healing and feeding the misfortunate. Most important, the causes of your devotion did not divide God's people and pit one group against another. Nor did you do this for your own benefit. I might or might not have someone or something to which I want to devote myself to serving and promoting. But with your grace, I will dedicate myself to serve you and your Church and follow your example of service and generosity.

Resolution

Today, I will think about God, my family, or some charity cause and pick one to which I will devote my time and service.

May 13

Difference
"There is no difference between Jew and Gentile; the same Lord is Lord of all and richly blesses all who call on Him." (Romans 10:12)

Reflection
This term is used to help us quantify something and distinguish one thing from another more clearly. In the spiritual and ethical realm, knowing the difference between right and wrong or good and bad is very important for our well-being. Knowing the difference helps us stay away from something wrong or bad and hang around something right or good instead. The problem is that our modern times cannot tell the difference between right and wrong or good and bad. It thinks that everything is in the gray area and will not tell right from wrong or good from bad. That is harmful and dangerous.

Lord Jesus, I want to see
Lord Jesus, although you try to help everyone become friends and neighbors, you always know the difference between right and wrong or good and bad. You never try to blur that difference, but during your ministry, you clarified it to the public every chance possible. Maybe my moral and spiritual vision might be blurred by the fog of modern times. However, you can help me clear it up and make me realize the importance of the moral difference for the sake of my spiritual well-being. Thank you, Lord!

Resolution
Today, I will try to avoid anything wrong or bad and do as many right or good thing things as I can. This is how I will see the moral difference and stick to the right things.

May 14

<u>Issue:</u> **Discern**
"A discerning person keeps wisdom in view, but a fool's eyes wander to the ends of the earth." (Proverbs 17:24)

<u>Reflection</u>
A thoughtful and wise person will try to discern an issue thoroughly before deciding an issue. That discerning time is vital to a good and sound decision. Without that time, chances are we will make many mistakes and regrettable decisions. Sadly, a lot of people in our time downplay the importance of this time and rush their decisions. No wonder our world is full of regrets and broken hearts! But, anyone who appreciates the importance of discerning time will be rewarded with peace and contentment.

<u>Lord Jesus, I want to see</u>
Jesus, Source of wisdom and hope, you spent much time in prayer to help you discern various decisions and find the will of God the Father for you. Of course, I recall what you did on the night you were arrested and trialed. You were praying and discerning God's plan for you. I might ignore your whispering voice in my ears every day. Or, I might not take time to discern a decision. Help me follow your example and spend time in prayer for every decision I make daily.

<u>Resolution</u>
Today, I will think through in prayer everything I do and try to discern what God might want me to do.

May 15

Issue: **Dissension**

"An angry person stirs up dissension, and a hot-tempered one commits many sins." (Proverbs 29:22)

Reflection

Wherever dissension arises, there are certainly all sorts of potential troubles. For dissension often results from the seven deadly sins such as pride, anger, and selfishness. Dissension also brings about fights, arguments, bad rumors, harm, hurts, tears, sadness, and so on. The Prince of Darkness uses these things to enslave us and destroy our faith community. Any community that goes through dissension might end up being self-destructive. There will also be all kinds of other casualties. Ironically, involved parties often cannot see the negative consequences and continue to make dissension worse.

Lord Jesus, I want to see

Jesus our Savior, you entered our world to put an end to all dissension and reconcile us with God the Father. When the scribes and Pharisees attempted to create dissension and disagreements between you and God's people, you always found ways to bring unity and reconciliation to the community of God's people. When I disagree with someone, help me avoid any temptation to create dissension and division in that community. Make me one who unites, not divides, others.

Resolution

Today, I will see if there is any dissension between me and people around me. Then, I will try to put an end to it and make peace with those people.

May 16

<u>Issue:</u> **Failure**

"Examine yourselves to see whether you are in the faith; test yourselves. Do you not realize that Christ Jesus is in you – unless of course you fail the test?" (2Corinthians 13:5)

<u>Reflection</u>

If any of us has ever suffered a failure, whether it was a test, class, game, project, business, or relationship, we know how humiliating and devastating that can be. Our world seemed to crumble and come crashing down when we experienced a failure. For the victims, this might feel like the end of their life. Certainly, if we keep experiencing one failure after another, it would be like dying repeatedly. What we need after a failure is someone who can accept us and our brokenness, regardless of our future successes.

<u>Lord Jesus, I want to see</u>

Jesus, Key to our Successes, you are the one who can help me at the moment of my failure and beyond. You know how I feel about failure by your own humiliating death on the Cross among a group of criminals. Most important, you accept me as I am, despite my failures or successes. Help me not look on moments of my failure as the end of my life; instead, help me look at them as a learning experience. That way, I can be sympathetic and resilient to building up my future successes, including securing a place in your Kingdom of Heaven.

<u>Resolution</u>

Today, I will look back to see which failure in my life might be hurting me the most and then hand it over to Jesus in prayer so that He can lift me up and give me a new life.

May 17

<u>Issue:</u> **Feet**

"How beautiful on the mountains are the feet of those who bring Good News, who proclaim peace, who bring good tidings, who proclaim salvation, who say to Zion, 'Your God reigns!'" (Isaiah 52:7)

<u>Reflection</u>

Every day, we use our feet quite a bit. We walk on them, stand on them, and even climb up places with them. Like most of our body parts, we tend to take our feet for granted until something happens. Then we will miss them terribly! A missionary like St. Paul, for example, would miss his feet the most because he walked for miles every day to bring Christ's Good News to some God-forsaken place around the world. If we do not appreciate and take good care of our body and its parts, we might regret when something happens to one of them.

<u>Lord Jesus, I want to see</u>

Jesus, Master of my body and soul, you call me every day to make good use of my body—your precious gift to me at birth—and produce abundantly for your Kingdom. I might mistakenly think I own my body and do whatever I want with it. But, you constantly reminded me that I will be held accountable for all the parts entrusted to me. With your grace, I will be committed to use my body and its parts to bring you glory and serve your Kingdom.

<u>Resolution</u>

Today, I will first give thanks to God for my feet and review my actions to determine if I have used them for the glory of their Creator and serving others and not for my own selfish reasons.

May 18

Issue: **Loyal**

"O Lord, God of our fathers Abraham, Isaac, and Israel, keep this desire in the hearts of your people forever, and keep their hearts loyal to you." (1 Chronicles 29:18)

Reflection

We are thankful when we find a loyal friend. We are happy to have a loyal customer, employee, or employer. But, it gets harder every day to find such a treasure in life. Our society these days is all about material gain, self-pleasure, or my own needs. Loyalty is no longer a virtue that we foster in our children or desire in a relationship. But, our loving God continues to lure us home and call us to commit our hearts and souls to the Kingdom of Heaven despite our personal costs.

Lord Jesus, I want to see

Jesus, my Faithful Friend, you will never abandon me, even if I might betray you time and time again. You forgave Peter after he denied you and would have welcomed Judas back if he had asked you to forgive. You indeed are a loyal friend that anyone can count on always. I might not appreciate how important it is to have a loyal friend or practice that virtue in my life. But with you as my Coach and Counselor, I will learn to appreciate the virtue of loyalty and promote it in my daily life.

Resolution

I will look back to see if I have been loyal to my God, family, friends, and benefactors and then commit myself to be loyal to those relationships, regardless of the costs and challenges.

May 19

Issue: **Fruitful**

"I am the vine; you are the branches. If one remains in me and I in that person, one will bear much fruit; for apart from me you can do nothing." (John 15:5)

Reflection
We all hope that our hard work will turn out to be fruitful and successful. Surely it takes commitment, dedication, and much patience for us to see results. Unfortunately, much our work could end up to be incomplete or at a loss. That experience certainly would make us feel bad or even devastate us. But, we believers rely on God to help us deal with our failures and disappointments. We ask God to lift us up and give us strength to overcome setbacks, for apart from God we can do nothing.

Lord Jesus, I want to see
Jesus, the Great Caretaker of God's vineyard, you pruned and trimmed us with your teachings and good works so that we can produce abundantly for the Kingdom of Heaven. I thank you, Lord, for your tender loving care that helps me remain strong in my faith and stay on the way to your Kingdom. Help me to continue to do a lot more good works and share your Good News with the world to bear great fruits for you.

Resolution
Today, I will review my life to see what I have done for God's Kingdom lately and then do something good to show that Kingdom to someone else.

May 20

Influential

"...Not many of you were wise by human standards; not many were influential; not many were of noble birth. But, God chose the foolish of the world to shame the wise..." (1 Corinthians 1:26-27)

Reflection

Our world often uses wealth and power to influence people and get what it wants. That is how things become corrupt and unfair. Influential people often try to control the world and mistreat others due to their short-sightedness. God must be the most influential one who changes us for the better and for our sake. Best of all, God does not try to control or enslave us in any way. For God always wants the best for us, instead of trying to manipulate us for His own interests.

Lord Jesus, I want to see

Jesus, Advocate of the poor and the lowly, you always used your position as the Son of God to intercede for us with God the Father. You reached out to the outcast and defended the misfortunate, even offered your own life for sinners. I might not have your kind and generous attitude right now. But with your help, I will use any influence I might have in this world to share your Good News with the world and bring you glory. May I never use that privilege to benefit myself or take advantage of others around me.

Resolution

Today, I will review the blessings and influence God has given me in this life and then think how I can use it to do something nice for someone else.

May 21

Issue: **Journey**

"… I proclaimed a fast so that we might humble ourselves before our God and ask God for a safe journey for us and our children with all our possessions." (Ezra 8:21)

Reflection
Our life is surely a journey. Our faith is also another journey. A journey is often a long and uncertain period. There will be up-and-down moments and twist-and-turn occasions along the way. We need God to safeguard us and show us the way. Without a proper guide, we will be lost and harm ourselves on our life's journey.

Lord Jesus, I want to see
Jesus, my Guide and Protector, you warned us about the "yeast of the scribes and Pharisees" because of their bad example of faith. You prayed for your disciples to be safe and well to continue their journey of faith with you before your return to Heaven. I will sure have some bad days and discouraging moments on my journey and might want to give up. Or, I might feel alone, scared, and overwhelmed along the way. But, with you by my side, I will soldier on and continue the mission of salvation that you have designed for me. For you are my strength, guide, and hope.

Resolution
Today, I will prepare myself for my journey to Heaven by packing all the necessary items such as faith, hope, and love for it, including Jesus.

May 22

<u>Issue:</u> **Lift up**

"Humble yourselves before the Lord, and He will lift you up." (James 4:10)

<u>Reflection</u>

When we are lifted up, we feel a bit taller and can see things a lot better. Imagine when we feel down and someone gives us a word of encouragement. Our troubles seem to vanish and we certainly feel a lot better. What someone does to lift up another person's spirit is nothing short of a miracle. So, keep in mind that when we lift up another's spirit, we perform a miracle for that person. Naturally, everyone loves to experience a miracle.

Lord Jesus, I want to see

Jesus, the Miracle Worker, you lifted up countless number of people with your Good News and performed all sorts of miracles for the hopeless. You not only made many folks feel better but also gave them a new life. You truly are the sunshine that brightens up our whole world. I might like to put down people; but with your help, I will try to lift up others and encourage the downtrodden at every opportunity. I will also stop being critical and negative to those around me.

<u>Resolution</u>

Today, I will say as many nice things as possible to everyone around me and bring them a big smile!

May 23

<u>Issue:</u> **Mouth**
"A wise person's heart guides one's mouth, and one's lips promote instruction." (Proverbs 16:23)

<u>Reflection</u>
Often our mouth can get us into a lot of trouble, especially when we are angry about something. We can say hurtful things that might cause harm and bring tears to others. We might think that guns and knives are the deadly weapons that hurt people. In reality, our mouths and hurtful words can cause damage and hurt people a hundred times worse than conventional weapons. We can spread bad rumors or say mean things that bring tears and heartache to people around us.

<u>Lord Jesus, I want to see</u>
Jesus, Word of God, you brought wisdom and comfort with things that came from your mouth. You used your mouth not to slander or spread bad rumors, but to bring blessings and hope wherever you went. I might be tempted to use my mouth to say bad things to someone. But by your example, I will learn to speak more words of love, kindness, peace, compassion, and hope, instead of hatred, anger, accusations, vengeance, and curses.

<u>Resolution</u>
Today, I will try to control my mouth not to hurt someone, even if I am upset. Instead, I will say only kind and nice things to the people around me.

May 24

<u>Issue:</u> **Persecution**
"Among God's Churches we boast about your perseverance and faith in all the persecutions and trials you are enduring." (2 Thessalonians 1:4)

<u>Reflection</u>
We Christians have been persecuted over the years and paid a dear price for following Jesus. These persecutions might be a hurdle on our journey of faith, but they can never destroy our beliefs. Today, we Christians face a new kind of persecution, which is much more subtle and cunning, but no less painful and deadly compared to past persecution. We need to be street smart and adaptable in dealing with the modern-day persecution of Christians.

Lord Jesus, I want to see
Lord Jesus, Savior of the world, you were persecuted for your Good News and call for repentance. You warned your disciples that if the world persecuted you, it will persecute them also. I realize that the persecution of Christians happens around the world every day. Sometimes those persecutions might take the form of public policies that are anti-faith and Christian beliefs. With your protection and the guidance of the Holy Spirit, I will remain true to my faith and continue your mission of salvation.

<u>Resolution</u>
Today, I will pray for Christians being persecuted around the globe and continue to do good for the world despite its persecution.

May 25

Issue: **Purpose**
"Listen to advice and accept instruction, and in the end you will be wise. Many are the plans in a human heart, but it is the Lord's purpose that prevails." (Proverbs 19:20-21)

Reflection
Everything in life goes better if we have a purpose. In fact, a life purpose gives us a reason to wake up every day. It motivates us to work hard and brings joy to our hearts. It gives our lives a focus and helps us overcome difficult moments in our lives. It does not let us give up or give in that easily. Most important, a person with purpose makes all his/her plans come true and continues to prosper.

Lord Jesus, I want to see
Jesus, the incarnated Son of God, your purpose for entering our world was to call us back to the fold and save us from sin and death. You never let any worldly things distract you from that purpose. I might not see my purpose in life clearly, but with your help, I will try to focus on what makes me happy daily. I will also commit myself to meaningful things without being distracted by worldly things.

Resolution
Today, I will see what I am called to do and try to focus on that calling for at least a week.

May 26

Reach out

"She [a wife of noble character] opens her arms to the poor and extends he hands to the needy." (Proverbs 31:20)

Reflection

Many of us find it difficult to extend our hands and reach out to the needy and the misfortunate. This is partly because we are shy and simply minding our own business. It is also because we do not have enough time and resources to share with others. Furthermore, our modern society does not strongly encourage or publicly promote this positive idea. But, our Christian faith calls us and commends us to reach out and help our neighbors. It makes us feel good for doing so.

Lord Jesus, I want to see

Caring and compassionate Lord, you never stopped reaching out to the lowly and the outcast. When you encountered folks in trouble, you gladly extended your hands to help them. I might not always reach out to the needy and the misfortunate for one reason or another. But with your encouragement, I will practice it daily until it becomes second nature for me to help others without worrying about its costs.

Resolution

Today, I will put aside my own concerns and extend my hands to someone in need with a smile.

May 27

Issue: **Sacred**
"If anyone destroys God's Temple, God will destroy him. For God's Temple is sacred; and you are that Temple." (1Corinthians 3:17)

Reflection
The Bible and our Christian tradition are full of sacred objects and holy sites. No wonder people back then felt God's constant presence all around them. In contrast, today we lack the sense of sacredness and have a tough time finding something sacred around us. We struggle to find God's presence in our world. In fact, many people in our time feel lonely, lost, hopeless, and overwhelmed, while our world turns angry and violent. All of this can be traced back to the lack of God's presence around us.

Lord Jesus, I want to see
Jesus, Immanuel God-with-us, you were sent into our world to remind us of God's ever-presence in our lives. You had a great respect for sacred things such as the Temple and were quite upset when you discovered how people mistreated this sacred place. I might not understand or appreciate the importance of having sacred things in my life right now. But with your guidance, I will pay more respect to sacred things and surround myself more with their presence.

Resolution
Today, I will show some respect to a sacred object or site by giving it a simple bow, even if that sacred place belongs to another religion.

May 28

<u>Issue:</u> **Salt**
"You are the salt of the earth. But if the salt loses its saltiness, how can it be made salty again? It is no longer good for anything, except to be thrown out and trampled by all." (Matthew 5:13)

<u>Reflection</u>
If you have ever tasted hospital food, you can appreciate how important salt is for our foods. Without salt, our foods are bland and tasteless. As the Scripture passage above indicates, Jesus compares Christians in the world to salt in our daily life. Like salt, we Christians bring taste, joy, hope, excitement, a different outlook, and much more to the life of the world. This is not only a resounding endorsement for our role as Christians in the world but also a great challenge for us to live up to our potential every day.

Lord Jesus, I want to see
Jesus, the Taste of New Life, you came into our world not only to bring us salvation but also to give us a taste of eternal life. Your preaching and miracles always pointed people to life in Heaven. I might try to be the salt of the earth by living out my Christian way of life and showing the world how wonderful it is to be a Christian. But, I should keep in mind that our Christian hope is to make it to Heaven, not to be stuck right here on earth forever.

<u>Resolution</u>
Today, I will do a good deed or something nice for someone around me to show the world that I am the salt of the earth.

May 29

"Those who live according to the sinful nature have their minds set on what that nature desires; but those who live in accordance with the Spirit have their minds set on what the Spirit desires." (Romans 8:5)

Reflection
One of the reasons why most religions have a tough time attracting more followers is because they deal with the unseen world. Their product is the spirit, not things that people can see or touch. Moreover, people in our modern time seem to give the physical world more credit than the spiritual world. But, we all know that without our spirit, even our strong body and smart mind become useless. So, a healthy spirit is crucial to our survival here on earth, as well as our longevity in Heaven. After all, our spirit never dies.

Lord Jesus, I want to see
Jesus, my Spiritual Guide, during your ministry, you continuously emphasized how important it is for us to nurture our spirit. Many times, you healed someone's physical body and also tried to take care of their spirit by forgiving their sins. I might not have paid enough attention to my spirit all these years, because I have been busy worrying about material things, fame, pleasures, and other worldly issues. But with your guidance and encouragement, I will pray more and take actions that will empower my spirit.

Resolution
Today, I will spend time in prayer or reading the Bible to strengthen my spirit and try to keep it free from worldly corruption.

May 30

Issue: **Understand**
"A patient man has great understanding, but a quick-tempered man displays folly." (Proverbs 14:29)

Reflection
Many arguments and conflicts happen because of a misunderstanding. In fact, our world would experience more love, peace, and compassion if everyone tried to understand one another a little better. Relationships would last longer if all parties had more understanding and forgiveness for one another. To understand a person or an issue means that we must put ourselves in someone else's shoes and try to walk, live, and breathe in his/her difficult situation.

Lord Jesus, I want to see
Compassionate Jesus, you showed a lot of patience and understanding to God's people during your ministry on earth. You never judged anyone harshly or acted without compassion toward sinners and the misfortunate. Sometimes, I can be mean to and judgmental of others around me. With your grace, I will try to be a lot more compassionate and understanding in dealing with people daily.

Resolution
Today, I will try not to judge or treat others harshly. Rather, I will be gentle, kind, and understanding to people that I run into throughout the day.

May 31

<u>Issue:</u> **Witness**

"You will receive power when the Holy Spirit comes on you; and you will be my witnesses in Jerusalem, in all Judea, and Samaria, and to the ends of the earth." (Acts 1:8)

<u>Reflection</u>

At a wedding ceremony, we have two witnesses who stand next to the couple to observe their exchange of marriage vows and later sign an official document that the marriage took place. At a trial, both sides call on witnesses to testify that the truth is on their side. So, a witness stands up to testify about something he/she might have seen or experienced by telling the truth. A witness does not fear any threats or reprisals.

Lord Jesus, I want to see

Jesus Master, you call us to follow you and sent your disciples into the world to witness what they saw, heard, experienced, and believed. You also reassured their confidence and testimony by giving them the Holy Spirit as their companion. I might tend to shy away from my Christian duty as a witness of your teachings and Good News. Give me courage and zeal to stand up for you and show the world all the blessings and wonderful messages you offer for its spiritual and daily life.

<u>Resolution</u>

Today, I will witness Jesus to someone when given a chance, by being kind and compassionate to that person.

June

Lord Jesus,
I Want to See…

June 1

<u>Issue:</u> **Accusation**

"…Bold and arrogant, these people are not afraid to slander celestial beings; yet even angels, although they are stronger and more powerful, do not bring slanderous accusations against such beings in the presence of the Lord." (2Peter 2:10-11)

<u>Reflection</u>

Arguments and fights start out with exchanging accusations. Most accusations are leveled at people with malicious motives and hatred. We use our mouths as a deadly weapon to spread rumors and false accusations about those we consider our enemies. We do not care how much damage such accusations might do to our enemies and their reputations. But, anything comes out of the mouth cannot be taken back.

<u>**Lord Jesus, I want to see**</u>

Kind and Gentle Jesus, you did everything possible to avoid accusations and fights with the scribes and Pharisees even though they kept on annoying and attempting to hurt you. For you knew that slanderous accusations would lead both sides down a dangerous road. I might be tempted to engage in a war of accusations with people around me, especially when I am mad at them. But with your wisdom and guidance, I will stay away from making accusations and causing pain and heartache by stoking further arguments. I will say more kind and hopeful words instead.

<u>Resolution</u>

Today, I will double-check my daily language and see if I have been mean to someone and wrongfully accused that person of something. Then, I will try to correct my error.

June 2

<u>Issue:</u> **Adapt**

"Jesus said: 'I tell you the truth, unless you change and become like little children, you will never enter the Kingdom of Heaven.'" (Matthew 18:3)

<u>Reflection</u>

In life, unless we adapt to our circumstances, we will never be able to make it a day longer. Any business, including the Church, cannot survive over the years if it does not make necessary changes with time. Certainly, change is never easy for us. Sometimes, it makes us swallow our pride and accept a new way of thinking. But, in the long run, adaptation proves to be the right way to go. It is the law of nature.

<u>Lord Jesus, I want to see</u>

Jesus, Word made flesh, you made the first drastic change by taking on our human form and entering our world as the Son of God. But, that is not the only time you adapted. Throughout your ministry, you adapted from one situation to the next and called your disciples to do the same. I might hate to adapt because of one reason or another. However, for the sake of my survival and longevity, I must learn to adapt and make necessary changes along the way. I cannot remain rigid and refuse to change. Otherwise, I will die or face inevitable failure and bring others along as well.

<u>Resolution</u>

Today, I will try to understand what I consider difficult to change and will force myself to adapt. Then, I will do it over again until changing becomes second nature for me.

June 3

Advice

"The way of a fool seems right to him/her, but a wise person listens to advice." (Proverbs 12:15)

Reflection

When we must discern an issue or decide about something, we need good advice. In fact, good advice can help us make it through each day and our entire life with purpose and joy. People look for good advice in books, literature, customs, traditions, famous people, among other sources. The problem is that they have looked for good advice in the wrong places. The world has duped people for years and given them terrible advice about life and other daily issues. The best and most qualified person to give us good advice is God, the Source of Wisdom.

Lord Jesus, I want to see

Lord Jesus, the Wisdom of God, you shared with your disciples not only the way to get to Heaven but also the key to a life of purpose and joy here on earth. Your advice to them was clear and reassuring on their journey of faith. I certainly can use some good advice from you in my daily life. May I always come to you, and no one else, to seek guidance and advice in times of discernment and of need.

Resolution

Today, I will examine the issues in my life for which I need advice from our Lord and then spend time with the Bible to see what He might tell me.

June 4

Issue: **Anxiety**

"Do not be anxious about anything, but in everything, by prayer and petition and with thanksgiving, present your request to God. And the peace of God will guard your hearts and minds in Christ Jesus." (Philippians 4:6-7)

Reflection

Our lives are full of anxieties. We are anxious about necessities, monthly bills, our health, jobs, homes, the needs of our children or grandchildren, retirement, the future, and the list can go on. With the threat of terrorism and increasing violence around our country and the globe, we worry for our safety and loved ones' security. We are concerned about the rising costs of healthcare, housing, foods, gas, heat, college tuition, and so on. We feel overwhelmed by the burdens of our daily life and an uncertain future.

Lord Jesus, I want to see

Jesus, Source of comfort and peace, you once told Mary's sister, "Martha, Martha, you are anxious and worried about many things. One thing only you should be concerned about and Mary has chosen the better portion of it." During this time, Mary was sitting at the feet of Jesus while Martha was running around the house and worrying about every detail of hospitality. I might be like Martha at times and worry sick about every little thing in my life. But, you want me to take a seat at your feet often and let you help me with my daily concerns and uncertain future.

Resolution

Today, I will spend some time in prayer at the feet of Jesus and bring to Him some of my anxieties so that He can comfort me and help me deal with them.

June 5

Issue: **Bewildered**

"... What shall I choose? I do not know! I am torn between the two: I desire to depart and be with Christ, which is better by far; but it is more necessary for you that I remain in the body." (Philippians 1:22-24)

Reflection

Some moments we feel bewildered and do not know what to do next. Some days we are lost and overwhelmed by our daily duties and expectations. Like someone who stands at the forked road and does not know which way to turn, we could face the same situation and wonder where we should turn or what we should do. Sometimes, the road ahead is so foggy that we cannot see anything, and we are confused on our next move. It is during those times that we need to come to God for guidance.

Lord Jesus, I want to see

Jesus my Guiding Star, you once said to Thomas and your disciples, "I am the way, the truth, and the life." You want to assure your followers that they have nothing about which to worry or be confused if they follow you. When I feel overwhelmed by my life's burdens or lost on what I need to do next, I need to call on you and ask for guidance. Better yet, I should stay close to you and let you show me the way all my life.

Resolution

Today, I will check to see if there is something in my life that is bewildering and will then ask Jesus to help clarify it for me.

June 6

<u>Issue:</u> **Calm**

"A hot-tempered person stirs up dissension, but a patient person calms a quarrel." (Proverbs 15:18)

<u>Reflection</u>

When we are on the water or in the air, we want everything to be calm. When on the ground, we want a calm household and to form relationships with people who have a calm personality. A violent storm or personality not only brings us fear but also has a potential to harm us. None of us wants to be in the middle of a tumultuous situation. All we want is a peaceful and tranquil environment where everyone lives in love and harmony with one another.

<u>**Lord Jesus, I want to see**</u>

Jesus, Prince of Peace, amidst a terrible storm at sea, you quieted it down and restored calm to a boat full of your disciples. Our lives are full of terrifying and chaotic moments. There is no one else I would rather come to for help when my life and everything around me turns stormy but you, Lord. For you have the power and magic touch to keep all things calm. Help me come to you for support and remain calm regardless of how chaotic things can be around me.

<u>Resolution</u>

Today, I will examine what might be causing me to get upset or anxious. I will then call on you, Lord, for help and remain calm while you perform your magic and bring peace to my problem.

June 7

Issue: **Cheerful**
"Each person should give what one has decided in one's heart to give, not reluctantly or under compulsion, for God loves a cheerful giver."
(2Corinthians 9:7)

Reflection
Everyone wants to be around cheerful folks. They are fun and easy to deal with. They are also generous and forgiving. Nothing in life makes them bitter or easily upset. For a cheerful person has a complete trust in God and never loses hope in God. There is always joy in a cheerful person's heart despite the tough circumstances and uncertain future. For this person believes God watches over them and guides their whole life always.

Lord Jesus, I want to see
Jesus, the Love of my life, you always brought a smile to everyone you met with your Good News and life-giving miracles. Your generous spirit touched many lives and challenged them to have a generous spirit, particularly the repentant tax collector Zacchaeus. I might be tempted by our selfish and greedy world to take in more from God and others, but give out less to God and the misfortunate. However, with your generous and joyful example, I will work hard to be a cheerful and thankful giver to God and everyone around me despite my situation.

Resolution
Today, I will bring a smile to someone around me by sharing some kind words or doing a good deed without expecting anything in return.

June 8

Issue: **Community**
"All the believers were together and had everything in common... Every day they continued to meet together in the Temple courts. They broke bread in their homes and ate together with glad and sincere hearts." (Acts 2:44-46)

Reflection
The whole idea of community does not seem to appeal to a lot of people these days. Many might think that a community limits their freedom and holds them back from all sorts of possibilities. Besides, most Westerners do not like the concept of Communism. They simply do not like to have things in common such as universal health care. They prefer individual freedom and responsibilities. Yet, the Church loves to preach on the idea of community and taking care of one another, especially the needs of the poor, the lowly, and the outcast.

Lord Jesus, I want to see
Jesus, Head of the Church, you constantly called on your followers to work together and look after the poor, the lowly, the widow, the orphan, and the outcast. You started the whole idea of Church and community, so that we can care for one another. God knows that governments will not save us or look after our needs. In this modern age, I might mistakenly assume the government can replace the Church or wrongfully reject community because of the world's individualistic tendencies surrounding me. Help me to appreciate all communities.

Resolution
Today, I will volunteer to help at my Church or some local community with some of its projects.

June 9

Complain

"Do everything without complaining or arguing so that you may become blameless and pure children of God without fault in a crooked and depraved generation in which you shine like stars in the Universe."
(Philippians 2:14-15)

Reflection

We humans are very good at complaining and criticizing one another. Yet, we find it difficult to express compliments or provide a positive solution to a problem. What we do not realize is that complaining is a passive-aggressive way of attacking someone and destroying an atmosphere of unity and peace. A complainer would rather pull everything down than building it up. A complainer prefers to see a glass half empty than a glass half full. This person is truly a downer and bad influence.

Lord Jesus, I want to see

Jesus, the Hope of my Life, you rarely complained how bad or sinful God's people were. Instead, your message focused on the positive changes and wonderful possibilities of a new life in God. Crowds by the thousands could not wait to flock to you to hear that positive message. I might follow the way of the world and simply look on the negative side of things all the time. Or, I might tend to criticize and complain when things do not go my way. Help me be a positive force for change; help me to roll up my sleeves to make a difference.

Resolution

Today, I will restrain myself from saying negative things about someone or something. Instead, I will try to give compliments or do something positive for the community.

June 10

Issue: **Considerate**

"Remind the people to be subject to rulers and authorities, to be obedient, to be ready to do whatever is good, to slander no one, to be peaceable and considerate, and show true humility toward all." (Titus 3:1-2)

Reflection

It is not easy to find a thoughtful and caring person in a busy and me-centered society. Everyone seems to care simply about themselves and their interests and has very little concern for their neighbors. We often make decisions without concern for its effects on the people around us. We rarely ask others, "What can I do for you?" Instead, we usually hear this question, "What have you done for me lately?"

Lord Jesus, I want to see

Jesus, Compassionate Lord, when the disciples saw a hungry crowd, they immediately wanted to dismiss everyone and let them search for food themselves. But, your heart was moved with pity, and you wanted your disciples to take care of that need themselves. I might be bitten by the "me" bug of our modern times and care only about myself. Command and urge me to show some concern and consideration for the people around me. Give me your compassionate and caring heart.

Resolution

Today, I will see how I can give my family or neighbors a hand on some chores and ask someone this question, "What can I do for you?"

June 11

Issue: **Convenient**

"Woe to you who are rich, for you have already received your comfort. Woe to you who are well fed now, for you will go hungry. Woe to you who laugh now, for you will mourn and weep." (Luke 6:24-25)

Reflection

Everything these days is focused on being fast and convenient. If we cannot provide things quickly, we end up on the losing side. But unlike our modern world, our spiritual world is about sacrifices and patience. For the spiritual roads are full of challenges and tears. Our prayers might take a long time to be answered. The road to Heaven is paved with personal sacrifices and crosses. There is nothing too convenient about the spiritual world or the road to Heaven.

Lord Jesus, I want to see

Jesus, Spiritual Master of the Cross, you asked your disciples to go through the narrow gate if they would like to make it to the Kingdom of Heaven. Your whole life was about embracing the Cross and facing the inconvenience in our daily life. I might be influenced by the modern age bug and try to look at the spiritual world from "easy and convenient" lenses. But with your guidance, I will learn to walk the way of the Cross and choose the narrow gate and the road less traveled. For that is how I will meet you and make it to the Kingdom of Heaven.

Resolution

Today, I will pick out what is inconvenient in my spiritual life, such as daily prayer or weekly churchgoing, and commit myself to following through with no exceptions.

June 12

<u>Issue:</u> **Danger**

"Who shall separate us from the love of Christ? Shall trouble or hardship or persecution or famine or nakedness or danger or sword?" (Romans 8:35)

<u>Reflection</u>
Our body is programmed to avoid danger and run away from anything that might pose us harm. If our body takes that much precaution to avoid anything dangerous, should we not do the same for our soul or spirit? Unfortunately, many folks in our time ignore signs of spiritual danger and continue to flirt with harmful things such as sins. They seemed to prefer darkness to light, death to life, or bad habits to virtues.

<u>Lord Jesus, I want to see</u>
Lord, my Shelter and Fortress, you never stopped warning your disciples about avoiding hypocrisy and other bad influences that might endanger their souls. One of those bad influences is material possessions. As you once said, "What good is it for a person to possess the whole world and lose one's soul in the process?" I might not realize the hidden and obvious dangers that harm my spiritual life. But with your wisdom and guidance, I will learn to recognize spiritual dangers and try to avoid them at all costs.

<u>Resolution</u>
Today, I will pause to reflect on some spiritual dangers in my daily life such as substance abuse, lust, greed, envy, and so on. Then, I will make a positive effort to avoid them.

June 13

Issue: **Deceitful**

"Rid yourself of all malice, deceit, hypocrisy, envy, and slander of every kind. Like newborn babies who crave pure spiritual milk so that by it you may grow up in your salvation." (1Peter 2:1-3)

Reflection

None of us wants to be deceived. But, every day we have seen all sorts of deceit play out all around us. A wicked person preys on a gullible neighbor and deceives him/her for selfish motives. Of course, the best deceiver is the Devil. Each day it commands its cohorts to trick God's people and lure them away from the fold and God's love. It lures them with empty promises and seductive trophies, like the apple to Adam and Eve.

Lord Jesus, I want to see

Jesus, my true Friend and Savior, you are someone I can count on and trust with my life. Unfortunately, many folks in our time turn their back on you and let the world deceive and trick them with empty promises. The result is many broken hearts and a cynical world. I hope I will choose the right friends in this deceitful world. With you, Jesus, as my trusted friend, I will imitate your example and promise not to deceive anyone even just for a profit of one cent.

Resolution

Today, I will review my life to see if I am deceiving anyone, try to fix it right away, and then promise to steer clear of any deceitful act in the future.

June 14

Dedicated

"I [the Lord] have selected your fellow Levites from among the Israelites as a gift to you, dedicated to the Lord to do the work at the Tent of Meeting."
(Numbers 18:6)

Reflection

In any family or group, it is a blessing to have a dedicated person. A household, for example, is in better shape if there is a dedicated mother or father. A church can complete its mission when there are dedicated members. A business will last much longer with dedicated employees. A dedicated person not only completes his/her duties but also goes out of his/her way to do other things to put his/her group ahead. Certainly, the Kingdom of Heaven can use a few more dedicated members for the sake of its mission.

Lord Jesus, I want to see

Faithful Lord, you dedicated your whole life to save God's people and call them back to the fold. You always went an extra mile to help everyone around you and called your disciples to do the same. I might not be a dedicated Christian; but with your example, I will try to be a dedicated member at home, work, Church, and other groups in which I am involved.

Resolution

Today, I will work hard to be a dedicated person at home and Church by following through on my duties with joy and ownership.

June 15

Issue: **Despise**
"The fear of the Lord is the beginning of knowledge, but fools despise wisdom and discipline." (Proverbs 1:7)

Reflection
When we despise something or someone, chances are we do not have any love and respect for it due to some bad past experiences. That something or someone might have done something to offend us, leaving a bad taste in our mouth. The only being who can create such havoc is the Devil or the Prince of Darkness, certainly not God. Ironically, our world often despises God and religion, but loves the Devil and its empty promises.

Lord Jesus, I want to see
Jesus, my Source of Life and Hope, you are the one who I should love and respect because of everything you have done for me. You brought me into this world and continue to love and sustain me daily. Unfortunately, the world tries to convince me to despise you and turn my back on you. But, I cannot picture my life without you. For you are my strength and hope, my guide and fortress, my purpose and consolation. If anything, I should be thankful for and respect you.

Resolution
Today, I vow to love and respect what brings me life and hope, namely God. I also vow to despise and avoid what is bad and evil.

June 16

<u>Issue:</u> **Distraction**
"But Martha was distracted by all the preparations that had to be made. She came to Him [Jesus] and asked, 'Lord, don't you care that my sister Mary has left me to do the work by myself? Tell her to help me!'" (Luke 10:40)

<u>Reflection</u>
If we are driving on the road and get distracted, you bet that we might cause an accident. The same is true on the spiritual road. If we are not focused on the Kingdom of Heaven and get distracted by worldly things, we will not only lead ourselves into an accident but also keep ourselves away from Heaven. That is why we Christians have spent countless hours in prayer—to keep ourselves less distracted by the world and more focused on Heaven.

Lord Jesus, I want to see
Jesus, Lord of Heaven, you never lost focus on your mission of salvation, even at the worst moment of your life, having been betrayed by Judas and condemned on the Cross. You always had your eyes focused on Heaven. I might let worldly things distract me from my goal of getting to Heaven. But with the help of your grace, I will try to resist these worldly temptations and dream instead about Heaven.

<u>Resolution</u>
Today, I will train myself to focus more on Heaven and get less distracted by the world with the help of 10-minute time of reflection reading the Bible.

June 17

<u>Issue:</u> **Doubt**

"When Peter saw the wind, he was afraid and, beginning to sink, cried out, 'Lord, save me.' Immediately Jesus reached out His hand and caught him. 'You of little faith,' He said, 'why did you doubt?' And when they climbed into the boat, the wind died down." (Matthew 14:30-32)

<u>Reflection</u>
When we are in doubt about something or someone, we usually have questions about it or our relationship with that person. If we go ahead with those doubts in mind, we are certainly asking for trouble. Interestingly, the world continues to live in doubt with many things and relationships. No wonder our world is so messed up and full of trouble!

<u>Lord Jesus, I want to see</u>
Faithful Lord, you brought faith into our doubtful world and called us to commit to God. You asked us to put our trust in God and let God guide us in our daily life. I might have a lukewarm relationship with you and have many doubts about Christianity and Heaven. But with your grace, I promise to learn more about you and open my heart to your daily revelations. I will create opportunities for you to strengthen my faith, much like doubting Thomas did, so that I can say, "My Lord and my God!"

<u>Resolution</u>
Today, I will hand over to you, Lord, some of my worries and let you help me deal with them. That way, I can slowly put away any doubt I might have about God and Heaven.

June 18

Issue: **Endurance**

"...If you suffer for doing good and you endure it, this is commendable before God. To this you were called, because Christ suffered for you, leaving you an example so that you should follow in His steps." (1Peter 2:20-21)

Reflection

For a marathon runner, being able to endure is very important for a successful run and winning a trophy in the end. Similarly, our spiritual world and faith life take time to mature and need much endurance on our part. Any faithful Christian who wants to make it to the end and receive the crown of eternal life at the Gate of Heaven must endure all the hardships of the journey of faith and follow the way of life Christ called them to live.

Lord Jesus, I want to see

Jesus, the Victorious King, you endured the trial, mocking, spitting, beating, wrongful conviction, and crucifixion for our salvation. You also called us to pick up our daily crosses and follow you. At times, I might want to run away from those crosses and give up on my faith journey with you. But with your grace and encouragement, I will endure all the hardships and keep on carrying your Cross to the end.

Resolution

Today, for the sake of Christ, I will try to endure some of the difficulties of my day and some of the pains of being a Christian without complaining.

June 19

Issue: **Enriched**

"The apostles said to the Lord, 'Increase our faith!' Jesus replied, 'If you have faith as small as a mustard seed, you can say to this mulberry tree, 'be uprooted and planted in the sea,' it will obey you." (Luke 17:5-6)

Reflection

There is nothing better for us humans than to see our relationships with God and people around us enriched. For this means our daily communication is improved, and we have learned to appreciate God and one another much more. We should feel excited and hopeful about our spiritual life. We will know how to treat others and love God with all our being. We must find every opportunity possible to be with God, even in a busy lifestyle.

Lord Jesus, I want to see

Jesus, our Faithful and Ever-Living God, you came into our world to awaken our spiritual life. You called us to a better prayer life, a deeper relationship with God and one another, and a stronger desire to enter Heaven. I certainly want my spiritual life and my relationship with others to be enriched and deepened. That way, my spirit and relationships will survive all the challenges of a mundane, boring life and mature into the kind of life you want me to live.

Resolution

Today, I will try to enrich my spiritual life by spending five minutes of my day praying for someone and doing a good deed for someone. I will try to keep this up as long as possible.

June 20

"Each one is tempted when, by one's own evil desire, one is dragged away and enticed. Then, after desire has conceived, it gives birth to sin; and sin, when it is full-grown, gives birth to death." (James 1:14-15)

Reflection
We may not realize this, but we are surrounded by all sorts of temptations every day. Like Adam and Eve in the Garden of Eden, we are constantly enticed by worldly things, including lust, envy, and greed. The Prince of Darkness certainly knows us well and continuously probes us 24/7, seven days a week about things we enjoy. He knows what our heart desires and wants to control us with harmful desires.

Lord Jesus, I want to see
Jesus, Son of God, the Devil and all the demons know who you are and cannot wait to run far away from you. You are certainly a threat to them and never stopped warning your disciples about the snares and enticements of the power of darkness. I know I do not stand a chance in the face of the allurements and traps of the Devil. Worse yet, I continue to flirt with temptations and occasions for sins. With your help, I will steer clear of any enticement and realize its harmful potential to my soul and spiritual life.

Resolution
Today, I will confront what entices me the most and find ways to limit my exposure to such temptations. I will replace that enticement with a new devotion activity in my spiritual life.

June 21

Issue: **Excuse**
"...A certain man was preparing a great banquet and invited many guests... But, they all alike began to make excuses. The first said, 'I have just bought a field, and I must go and see it. Please excuse me.'" (Luke 14:16-18)

Reflection

When we do not like to participate in something, we make excuses. We also make excuses when we lie about something. Basically, excuses are not good. Plenty examples of excuses are in the Bible, from the excuses of Adam and Eve after they ate the forbidden fruit to the one Peter spoke when he was asked about being the disciple of Jesus. If we build our spiritual life on excuses, a complete mission will never happen. We might run into lots of troubles along the way.

Lord Jesus, I want to see

Jesus, Judge of the living and the dead, you have invited us to attend your Heavenly Banquet and be a part of the Kingdom of Heaven. Unfortunately, some people have not realized that honor and declined the invitation by making one excuse after another. Sometimes I might follow the same tendency of the world and push away your love for me. I might also put my daily schedule and worldly concerns above the Kingdom of Heaven. With your guidance, I will respond to your call daily and try to grow closer to you.

Resolution

Today, I will respond to your invitation by committing myself to do everything in my power to make it to Heaven and not make any excuses about it.

June 22

<u>Issue:</u> **Experience**
"If the ax is dull and its edge unsharpened, more strength is needed but skill will bring success." (Ecclesiastes 10:10)

<u>Reflection</u>
Some people might assume money, power, or fame are a sign of success. But, a wise person considers life experience to be an invaluable treasure. Life experience is not something one can buy or exchange. Hence, it is cannot be bribed or corrupted. Life experience is rather personal and something that remains with a person until one dies. It is certainly not something with which one was born or can learn from books and classrooms. Life experience comes from real-life lessons and mistakes a person might have made in the past.

Lord Jesus, I want to see
Jesus, Wisdom of God, you entered our world not only to bring us salvation but also give us life experiences. Your teachings were always full of wisdom and life experiences. Unfortunately, our modern time lacks the wisdom of your teaching and does not seem to desire it desperately. With your guidance, I may learn to appreciate and cherish the value of life experiences. That is what will last and matter the most in the end to help us distinguish the champions.

<u>Resolution</u>
Today, I will recall a life experience that has made me a better person and helped me see things differently. I will then thank God for this abundance.

June 23

Fairness

"...For attaining Wisdom and discipline; for understanding words of insight; for acquiring a disciplined and prudent life, doing what is right and just and fair." (Proverbs 1:2-3)

Reflection

We all want to be paid a just wage and be treated fairly. Anything short of that causes a huge outcry, perhaps even an angry outburst. Fairness is one of the foundational principles for a peaceful and well-functioning society. Anyone who supports this principle and practices it consistently demonstrates this great quality in him- or herself. Amidst the rampant greed and selfishness of our modern time, promoting fairness strongly will be a great breath of fresh fair.

Lord Jesus, I want to see

Jesus, Merciful and Just God, you urge our world continuously to be fair to everyone and not take advantage of the poor and the lowly. You often stood up for the outcast and defended the widow, because society never treated them fairly and respectfully. When I attempt to mistreat someone for one reason or another, help me realize your expectations of me. Make me see the importance of treating others fairly.

Resolution

Today, I commit myself to live according to the principle of fairness, by watching how I deal with others daily. Next, I will try to correct myself when I treat someone unfairly.

June 24

<u>Issue:</u> **Friendship**
"Do not forsake your friend and the friend of your parents, and do not go to your siblings' house when disaster strikes you – better a neighbor nearby than a sibling faraway." (Proverbs 27:10)

<u>Reflection</u>
We all need friends to share stories, bounce around ideas, ask questions, find companionship, give comfort, and exchange laughs. Our lives would certainly not be the same without friends. But, finding a right and good friend is not easy. Often people make mistakes and pick the wrong friends when they begin to hang around the wrong crowd and take on bad influences. Having only a few but good friends makes a big difference in our lives, because those folks will influence us positively and make us better people.

<u>Lord Jesus, I want to see</u>
Jesus, my Dear and Faithful Friend, you called your first disciples friends and gave them great examples of a special, good pal yourself. As you offered yourself on the Cross for their sins and mine, you said, "There is no greater love than to lay down one's life for one's friend." I want to be able to share that same love for my friends and family. I want you to be my friend and teach me to pick the right friends and be a good influence on them.

<u>Resolution</u>
Today, I will review my list of friends to see which ones have been a positive influence and which ones have not. Then, I will decide to wean out bad friends and keep the good ones.

June 25

<u>Issue:</u> **Fun**
"They will be paid back with harm for the harm they have done. Their idea of pleasure is to carouse in broad day light. They are blots and blemishes, reveling in their pleasures while they feast with you." (2Peter 2:13)

<u>Reflection</u>
"Fun" is one of the words in our modern day vocabulary that everyone loves to hear. People want to have fun in everything: vacations, parties, weddings, work, school, charitable work, even church. Anything without fun will not draw a crowd to it. But, our faith journey to Heaven is not about fun. Doing the right things or good things for others is not always fun. Keeping a consistent prayer life and a good relationship with God is not fun all the time. We should not use fun as a set of lenses to judge something.

<u>Lord Jesus, I want to see</u>
Jesus, my Faithful and Dependable God, you always follow through with your mission, even if it was a long and painful one like the mission of the Cross. You did not reach out to help the misfortunate and the outcast because it was fun. Rather, it was because your heart was moved with pity for them. May I have your caring and compassionate heart to do good things for others. May I also commit myself to carrying my daily crosses and following you.

<u>Resolution</u>
Today, I will try to help around the house or do something good for someone, not because it was fun. Rather, I will help because it is the right thing for me to do.

June 26

<u>Issue:</u> **Gentle**
"Your beauty should not come from outward adornment, such as braided hair and the wearing of gold jewelry and fine clothes. Instead, it should be that of your inner self, the unfading beauty of a gentle and quiet spirit, which is of great worth in God's sight." (1Peter 3:3-4)

<u>Reflection</u>
We live in a world that glorifies power and promotes strength and toughness. It judges people and values them based on those criteria. Anything related to gentleness is considered weak and useless. No wonder we have seen all kinds of violent outbursts and powerful attacks all over the world! We must realize gentleness is a great gift of the Holy Spirit and a wonderful quality that we should promote in schools and workplaces. We should coach our young to be gentle.

<u>Lord Jesus, I want to see</u>
Jesus, Gentle Soul and Kind Spirit, you used your whole ministry to teach us how to act in a kind and gentle manner with one another. You were always gentle and compassionate to the broken and sinners. I must follow your example and learn to be gentle, kind, and merciful in dealing with others, regardless of how the world might treat me. I must also try not to be harsh and condemning in my words and thoughts.

<u>Resolution</u>
Today, I will talk and act in a gentle manner with everyone around me, even when things go haywire or people are rough and mean to me.

June 27

<u>Issue:</u> **Gladness**

"... They gathered the Church together and delivered the letter. The people read it and were glad for its encouraging message." (Acts 15:30-31)

<u>Reflection</u>

Our days are full of moments of sadness and regret. It is very rare for us to find a few moments of gladness. We got to cherish those rare moments and make them last, because we are often glad when things go our way and please us. This is a special and uplifting feeling we have about something. We certainly would like to have that feeling remain with us and encourage things to run smoothly for us in our lives.

<u>Lord Jesus, I want to see</u>

Jesus, the Source of my Joy and Hope, you did many wonderful things for God's people. But, the most important thing you did was to bring glad tidings to them. After all, these people were surrounded by much bad and tragic news. I might be too pessimistic and down in the dumps at times. But, with your inspiration, I will try to be a person of joy and a bearer of glad tidings to the world around me. I will be less condemning and more uplifting in my words and actions to others so that there will be no more tears and sadness in my world.

<u>Resolution</u>

Today, I will see if I can cheer someone up by bringing some glad tidings to that person. This experience will make me glad that I can do a good thing.

June 28

<u>Issue:</u> **Hand**

"After the Lord Jesus had spoken to them, He was taken up into Heaven and He sat at the right hand of God." (Mark 16:19)

<u>Reflection</u>
Unlike the heart, the hand is considered less important as far as the whole body's functioning is concerned. Yet, our lives would not be the same if one of our hands is harmed or removed. In Holy Scriptures, the hand reference is heard in phrases such as, "…Sitting at the right hand of God" or "…Do not let the left hand know what the right hand is doing." Generally, the hand symbol conveys the message of power and connection. But, we also shake hands with someone when we greet and welcome them.

Lord Jesus, I want to see
Jesus, the Hand of God in the world, you showed us the face of God in flesh and blood. Through your healing and compassionate hands, God touched many broken lives and changed them for the better. Your hands are certainly better than the hands of a successful surgeon. I would surely love to have a pair of hands like yours to bring healing and good things to the world. I do not want to use my hands to do bad things or hurt others. With your help, I believe my dreams about my hands will come true.

<u>Resolution</u>
Today, I will use my hands to help lift up an elderly person, wash dishes at home, or write a thoughtful card to a broken soul.

June 29

Issue: **Sincere**

"Now that you have purified yourselves by obeying the truth so that you have sincere love for your brothers and sisters, love one another deeply from the heart." (1Peter 1:22)

Reflection

In any relationship—personal or business—we hope all parties will be sincere with one another. There is nothing worse than learning our friends or business partners lied to us or betrayed us. A sincere person not only shows his/her true intentions, but also makes a serious commitment to a relationship or a task. Surely sincerity is one of the most desirable qualities in a friend or a business partner.

Lord Jesus, I want to see

Christ Jesus, whose heart is full of sincere love and mercy, you were devastated to learn that Judas, one of your disciples, would betray you. You also warned your disciples to avoid the hypocrisy of the scribes and Pharisees because of their lack of sincerity. It truly takes courage and humility to be a sincere person. Our modern age might tell me to be crafty and deceitful if I want to succeed. However, by your great example, I pledge to be sincere in all my relationships.

Resolution

Today, I will share with people around me my true thoughts and feelings on the issues at hand, without fear of being judged. Then, I will practice this honesty daily.

June 30

Issue: **Vineyard**
"What more could I have been done for my vineyard than I have done for it? When I looked for good grapes, why did it yield only bad?" (Isaiah 5:4)

Reflection
It gets tougher for us to find a vineyard these days due to all kinds of construction and suburban sprawl. But, after we have found a vineyard, we want to linger around it as long as we can to enjoy what it has to offer us. If we have been in a garden, we know how peaceful and relaxing it can be. We can forget all the stress and worries when we enter a garden. A vineyard has that same magical touch of a garden and many more hidden blessings.

Lord Jesus, I want to see
Jesus, the Manager of God's Vineyard, you were sent to invite people to enter it and take part in caring for it. You promised its workers a just wage and many wonderful blessings. Sadly, some make up excuses to turn down that invitation, whereas others mistreat you and your helpers. I certainly want to be a part of your vineyard and help it produce abundantly. Its fruits are love, joy, peace, patience, kindness, goodness, generosity, and many other blessings. I would love to stay in this vineyard forever.

Resolution
Today, I will spend time in my own garden or a quiet place in a park and take in all the wonderful feelings it offers me. I will then come back and visit it many more times.

July

Lord Jesus,
I Want to See...

July 1

Issue: **Adversity**
*"Although the Lord gives you the bread of adversity & the water of afflic-
tion, your teachers will be hidden no more; with your own eyes you will see
them." (Isaiah 30:20)*

Reflection
Our life is full adversities. Some might be small and less painful,
whereas others are big and unbearable. We often wonder why we must
face difficulties and endure adversities. Most of us pray that adversities
will soon be gone and that we will be left with peace and hope. But,
adversities often make us stronger and, in some cases, more compassionate and understanding. St. Paul confirmed it when he wrote,
"...We even boast of our afflictions, knowing that affliction produces
endurance, and endurance proven character, and proven character
hope, and hope does not disappoint." (Romans 5: 3-5)

Lord Jesus, I want to see

Jesus, my guiding Light, your short life on earth was never a walk in
the park. Yet, you always faced your adversities head on and called us
to pick up our daily crosses and follow you. I hope to have a life free
of adversities and may want to run away from my daily crosses. But,
with your inspiring example, I will embrace my adversities as opportunities to grow closer to you and be a stronger and better person.

Resolution
Today, I will face my life's adversities without fear or bitterness. For I
know Jesus is always there to give me a hand and guide me through it.

July 2

<u>Issue:</u> **Anger**
"A fool gives full vent to one's anger, but a wise person keeps oneself under control." (Proverbs 29:11)

<u>Reflection</u>
Certainly, we have been angry about one thing or another in our lives. It is not a good feeling to have. Yet, our world is constantly in anger, which has caused all sorts of violence and senseless killing around us. We Christians realize that anger is one of the seven deadly sins and want to eliminate it or at least keep it under control. Otherwise, it could destroy us and cause great damage to the world around us. Indeed, it has immense power. If we could harness that great power from anger to do good, like we do with nuclear power, we would surely accomplish many fabulous things.

<u>Lord Jesus, I want to see</u>
Jesus, Prince of Peace, several times you felt frustrated and upset because of the crazy things God's people did to the Temple or the spiritual laws and tradition. Yet, you never once attempted to kill or hurt your neighbors. In fact, when Peter chopped off the ear of a servant in anger, you touched the servant's ear and healed it. I live in a violent and angry world where people blow each other away over small disagreements. Give me your gentle spirit and courage to be an advocate of peace wherever I go so that my broken world may experience your healing peace.

<u>Resolution</u>
Today, I will try to be calm and peaceful, even when I find myself in an upsetting situation. I will try to practice peace.

July 3

Issue: **Fight**
"What causes fights and quarrels among you? Don't they come from your desires that battle within you? You want something but don't get it. You kill and covet, but you cannot have what you want. So, you quarrel and fight. You do not have, because you do not ask God." (James 4:1-2)

Reflection
Humans fight sometimes over silly things; other times, they fight about something big and valuable. However, the cause of a fight always comes from selfishness, lack of caring, and an inability to compromise and make peace with one another. If only we would learn to be generous and sacrifice a little more of ourselves, there would be less fighting among us. If only we would teach our children and grandchildren to share their blessings and resources with one another, then that would help prevent future fights around the world.

Lord Jesus, I want to see
Loving Jesus, Source of Life and Hope, you often reminded your disciples to focus on Heaven and try to win the crown of eternal life by following a life of love and peace on earth. We can do so by detaching ourselves from all worldly possessions, which are the source of fights and quarrels. St. Paul agreed with your advice as he wrote this reflection during his last moments on earth, "…I have fought the good fight; I have finished the race; I have kept the faith. Now there is in store for me the crown of righteousness, which the Lord, the righteous Judge, will award to me on that day…" (2Timothy 4:7-8). That is the reward I would like to receive in the end.

Resolution
Today, I will review what fights might arise from envying my neighbors and try to diffuse that anger by focusing on my dream on Heaven and eternal life.

July 4

"Get rid of all bitterness, rage and anger, brawling and slander, along with every form of malice. Be kind and compassionate to one another, forgiving each other, just as in Christ God forgave you." (Ephesians 4:31-32)

Reflection

People become bitter after they have been beaten down by life's burdens again and again. Their speeches are sour and their outlook on life is cynical. They lose trust in people and slowly turn their back on life. They have no desire to live and sometimes do not hesitate to hurt other people around them. That is what we see a lot around the world these days: many bitter and angry people. Is there a cure for it? Can bitter people ever be healed?

Lord Jesus, I want to see

Jesus, Kind and Compassionate Lord, you never displayed any sign of bitterness, even after you had been mistreated by the religious leaders repeatedly. Rather, you became more caring and compassionate to everyone around you. You also called on your disciples to give thanks for all their daily blessings. I might not realize how important that daily exercise is to prevent me from becoming bitter with my life. But, with your grace, I will try to live in thanksgiving, kindness, and compassion always.

Resolution

Today, I will give thanks for something in my life and try to perform an act of kindness for someone. I will do this for several days.

July 5

Conformed

"Do not conform any longer to the pattern of this world, but be transformed by the renewing of your mind. Then you will be able to test and approve what God's will is – His goodness, pleasing, and perfect will."
(Romans 12:2)

Reflection
Most people find it difficult to conform themselves to human laws and regulations, let alone God's Laws. We usually assume that conforming means giving up our freedom and losing our normal ways of life. But, conforming our will to God's will helps us choose the right things in this life and end up in the right place in the end. Following God's will also guarantees us a life of joy and peace here and the eternal life after this one.

Lord Jesus, I want to see
Jesus, the Incarnated Word of God, you never tried to avoid conforming yourself to God's will. Even in the Lord's Prayer, which you taught your disciples, you hope that God the Father's will would be done first. And, at the darkest moment of your life, you still prayed, "Abba, Father, all things are possible to you. Take this cup away from me, but not what I will, but what you will." (Mark 14:36) I sometimes find it difficult to seek out your will for me and follow it at times. With your grace, I will see what you call me to do each day and for the rest of my life.

Resolution
Today, I will avoid doing what the world wants me to do, namely, searching for pleasures. Instead, I will see what I can do to help someone.

July 6

Issue: **Content**

"Keep your lives free from the love of money and be content with what you have because God has said, 'Never will I leave you; never will I forsake you.'" (Hebrews 13:5)

Reflection

Whenever we hear the word "content," we are reminded of the words of John the Baptist during Advent. This great prophet called us to prepare for the coming of the Savior of the world by changing our current way of life, being content with what we have, and trying not to extort others to make up for our wicked desires. A content person is always happy and thankful for who he/she is and what he/she has. Nothing in this world could tempt or make this person desire more.

Lord Jesus, I want to see

Jesus, Lord of Heaven and earth, every Lent you let us reflect on your preparation for the upcoming Passion and the Cross by having us face various temptations. What the Devil does not know is that you have the entire Heaven and earth; hence, you could desire nothing else. You are absolutely content with yourself and your mission. So, if I have you, I will have everything and be content with myself. With you, nothing in this world can tempt me and make me desire for more. I will live a happy and thankful life.

Resolution

Today, I will see how content I am with my life by reviewing how often I am thankful or how much I still desire from the world. Then, I can begin to list things for which I am thankful.

July 7

<u>Issue:</u> **Controversy**
"...Those who have trusted in God may be careful to devote themselves to doing what is good. These things are excellent and profitable for everyone. But, avoid foolish controversies and genealogies and arguments and quarrels about the Law, because these are unprofitable and useless." (Titus 3:8-9)

<u>Reflection</u>
Our modern world craves controversies, for that is how it sells news and keeps the public entertained. We just need to look at the number of talk shows and around-the-clock news networks to see how important controversies are today. In fact, many attention-seeking folks make up fake disputes or try to copycat some bad altercation to get on the news. But, we the believers are advised to avoid controversies and scandals, because they set a bad example to people around us.

Lord Jesus, I want to see
Jesus, Prince of Peace, you warned your disciples not to create scandals and controversies to the little ones. Otherwise, they would deserve severe punishment in the end. I might like to cause fights and love to argue to bring attention to myself. Or, I might enjoy coming up with controversies for my benefit or some other reason. But, you cannot see anything good come from a controversy. With your gentle spirit and good example, I will try to avoid foolish controversies and commit myself to doing good deeds and bringing peace to the world around me.

<u>Resolution</u>
Today, I will avoid anything that might cause arguments and controversies with others and choose to be a peacemaker.

July 8

Issue: **Gracious**

"May God be gracious to us and bless us and make God's face shine upon us, that God's way may be known on earth, God's salvation among all nations." (Psalms 67:1-2)

Reflection

We often hear the term "gracious" being used in various contexts. We are often given a "grace" period to pay a bill. Or, someone has been a "gracious" host to us and let us take a seat at a busy event or use something without charging us. A gracious person is always thoughtful, kind, caring, giving, generous, thankful, and cheerful. This person puts the needs of others before his/her own. This person sees God in other people.

Lord Jesus, I want to see

Jesus, Loving and Gracious God, you were always concerned about the well-being of others and their needs. Your heart was often moved with pity for the downtrodden and misfortunate. I live in a dog-eat-dog world where people lack courtesy and often act rudely to one another. Help me have a gracious heart and learn to be kind and generous with others. Give me strength to act graciously toward people, even when I have a bad day.

Resolution

Today, I will try to be gracious toward people I meet and extend my hands to greet and welcome them, just as I do to Jesus.

July 9

Issue: **Destroy**

"Now we know that if the earthly tent we live in it is destroyed, we have a building from God, an eternal house in Heaven, not built by human hands." (2Corinthians 5:1)

Reflection

We humans have built many things since Creation, but we have also destroyed much more along the way. In fact, we have done extreme damage to God's Creation, especially the human soul and spiritual life. With wrongful life principles and crooked spiritual goals, we humans have set out to destroy everything around us at an alarming rate. We destroy anything to do with God and spiritual life, the family structure, sacred relationships, tradition, human life, the environment, and so on. Worse yet, we annihilate anything we hate or deem it useless in our short-sighted viewpoint.

Lord Jesus, I want to see

Jesus, Author of Life and Builder of the Church, you came not to destroy sinners, but to save them. Your whole life and mission was to lift people from their life burdens and build up the Church. I might be influenced by our current culture, and we like to destroy things. Perhaps I do not carry out acts of destruction constantly, but I might do equivalent damage with words through rumors or by slandering my neighbors. But, with your help and example, I will stop destroying things and try to build more good things around me each day, including my strong relationship with you.

Resolution

Today, I will avoid anything that might bring destruction, such as bad rumors about someone. Instead, I will rally around anything that is constructive, such as giving thanks to God and others often.

July 10

Disappointment

"Hope does not disappoint us because God has poured out God's love into our hearts by the Holy Spirit, whom God has given us." (Romans 5:5)

Reflection
Our lives are full of disappointments, big and small ones alike. Successes often come few and far between. It is up to us to figure out how to handle these disappointments. Some bury them in tears and regrets, while others try to deal with them head on. These people want to see what they must do to turn disappointments into successes. Unfortunately, many people do not know how to do this, and they end up hurting themselves in various ways. They might even take their own life or bury themselves in depression.

Lord Jesus, I want to see
Jesus, my Hope and Salvation, you faced many disappointments in your disciples and religious leaders. For they not only paid no attention to your messages but also created all sorts of scandals for God's people. But, you never gave up on them or turned away from them. I have surely disappointed you and others countless times. However, with your forgiveness and encouragement, I will never give in to my disappointments and other misfortunate things in my life. Rather, I will learn to hope again.

Resolution
Today, I will look back on things that have disappointed me. Then, I will bring them to God in prayer to ask for help to move forward and hope again with a new focus.

July 11

Issue: **Duty**

"Paul looked straight at the Sanhedrin and said, 'My brothers and sisters, I have fulfilled my duty to God in all good conscience to this day.'" (Acts 23:1)

Reflection

Every day we have many duties to complete. In fact, our whole life is a series of duties for us to get done. Our duties might look daunting at times. But, a responsible person always makes sure his/her duties are finished. Sadly, our modern society does not encourage or reinforce the importance of fulfilling our duties. This includes our duties to God, country, family, friends, work, and so on. Many people in our time neglect or fail to complete their duties. The consequence is lack of ownership and honor and, ultimately, a complete mess.

Lord Jesus, I want to see

Jesus, Faithful Servant of God, you always knew what your duty was, namely, to save God's people. You completed this duty even when you were tempted to abandon it. You took your duty call seriously and considered it a great honor to carry it out and serve God the Father. Maybe I have not realized what my duty is in the course of a day. Or, perhaps I might try to run away from my duty and avoid it. With your example and encouragement, I will fulfill my daily duties as a parent, child, worker, student, church member, and so on with honor and pride.

Resolution

Today, I will look at my role in my family or work and then fulfill it without complaining. I will try to keep this attitude until it becomes second nature.

July 12

Issue: **Promise**

"For no matter how many promises God has made, they are 'Yes' in Christ. And so through Him the 'Amen' is spoken by us to the glory of God." (2Corinthians 1:20)

Reflection

People make many promises to each other these days, especially our politicians. Unfortunately, most of these promises are empty rhetoric or meaningless. Some of us are gullible enough to buy into these empty promises and expect something great from them. For us Christians, the only promise that matters is the eternal life in God's Kingdom. The reason we can trust this promise is because it has been paid in full by our faithful God with the Cross of Jesus, God's only Son. This hope will help us make it to the end.

Lord Jesus, I want to see

Jesus, my Hope and Salvation, you were the fulfillment of God's promise to God's people. You brought hope and promise of a new life with your Good News and kind acts. The difference between you and other promise carriers is that you do not benefit from your promise. I have made promises to family and friends, but sometimes I do not follow through with them. Or, I sometimes, I do not bring hope to people around me or uplift them with my work and life routines. But, with your guidance and example, I will commit to bringing true hope and lasting joy to people around me.

Resolution

Today, I will do something nice and simple for my family, or neighbors instead of making a spectacular promise. I will also focus more on real actions rather than giving false hope.

July 13

Freedom

"My dear brothers and sisters, you were called to be free. But, do not use your freedom to indulge the sinful nature; rather serve one another in love." (Galatians 5: 13)

Reflection

One of the most important gifts we have enjoyed as Americans is freedom. Unless we have lived in an oppressive society, we have no idea how special the gift of freedom is. But, we can also misuse this gift. Some of us use it to do whatever we want at the expense of others around us or indulge in destructive activities. However, freedom has its limits, and we all have the responsibility to carry out checks and balances on it. Otherwise, freedom will become licentiousness and bring harm to society.

Lord Jesus, I want to see

Jesus, my Lord and Savior, you came to set us free from the slavery of sin and death. For years, we have suffered under that horrible yoke. But, thanks to you, we have been given the gift of freedom and new life. I might not realize the potential for good and the danger of harm that freedom brings us. But, with your guidance, I will learn to make good use of this gift and reduce its harmful dangers. I will subject it to your Laws and not have it the other way around, as is seen in the world these days.

Resolution

Today, I will stop doing whatever I feel like doing, but will consult with my Lord in prayer regarding my daily decisions to conform my freewill to God's will.

July 14

<u>Issue:</u> **God's will**

"Be joyful always; pray continually; give thanks in all circumstances, for this is God's will for you in Christ Jesus." (1 Thessalonians 5:16-18)

<u>Reflection</u>

Some people think of God's will as Karma or a bad omen. They cannot seem to explain it, but they feel its effects in their daily life. For believers, God's will is what we discern daily in our prayers. We want to know what God wants us to do or which choice is the best for us as we look at different issues each day. Surely, God's will for us is to become like our God, namely, to do the right things, as God does, and perform good deeds for others regardless of the personal cost.

<u>Lord Jesus, I want to see</u>

Jesus, Son of God, you always did everything according to the will of God the Father even if it meant you had to suffer and died on the Cross. For you knew well that it is through God's will that we humans must be saved. I might not realize how important it is to discern God's will for my daily decisions as well as my life. But, now that I know about God's will and follow it, I will certainly be at peace with everything I do and can live my life in true happiness.

<u>Resolution</u>

Today, I will look at several issues that have arisen recently and discern what God wants me to do—not what I want to do—as I review all the pros and cons.

July 15

Issue: **Hero**
"When they saw the courage of Peter and John and realized that they were unschooled ordinary men, they were astonished and they took note that these men had been with Jesus." (Acts 4:13)

Reflection
Our world would not be the same without heroes. They were ordinary folks like us; and yet they do extraordinary, maybe even impossible, things for humanity. They risk their lives and sacrifice what they have to save the misfortunate and do good for others. We need a lot more heroes in our world. For us believers, heroes are called saints because they have not only lived a remarkable way of life but have also shown us a wonderful role model for our journey of faith.

Lord Jesus, I want to see
Jesus, my Faithful and Loving Savior, you did all kinds of selfless acts for God's people and ultimately sacrificed your life on the Cross for us. I am honored and happy to have you as my hero. You have touched my life and influenced me in a positive way. I do not know how to thank you enough. May I always look up to you as a great role model for my life and share your example with others. May I also learn to be a hero and a good example of Christian living to people around me.

Resolution
Today, I will show Jesus to someone through an act of kindness and let Him work on the person through my kindness.

July 16

Issue: **Honorable**

"Pray for us. We are sure that we have a clear conscience and desire to live honorably in every way." (Hebrews 13:18)

Reflection

We do not hear the term "honor" a lot these days. We only hear about it at a school awards event or when we address a judge. An honorable person is someone who lives by a code of respect and care for other human beings. This person does not do anything that might bring disgrace and shame to his/her family and friends. Such folks avoid anything that might be scandalous or corruptible to their souls. Surely, our society should expect its citizens to live honorably and compassionately with one another. Imagine how our world might look like if everyone followed the code of honor.

Lord Jesus, I want to see

Jesus, most honorable King of the Universe, even though you have equal power with the other two persons of the Holy Trinity, you always showed respect and consideration to them. You called on your followers to honor their fathers and mothers with your Commandments and teachings. I live in a world that focuses simply on "me" and has no concern for family reputation or anything else. Help me always live in an honorable manner and be considerate to people around me.

Resolution

Today, I will show some honor and respect to my family, friends, and people around me by the way I address them and take care of them.

July 17

Issue: **Jealous**

"Place me like a seal on your heart, like a seal on your arm; for love is as strong as death, its jealousy unyielding as the grave. It burns like blazing fire, like a mighty flame." (Song of Songs 8:6)

Reflection

Jealousy is one of the seven deadly sins and the cause of many fights and bloodshed in the Bible, as well as our world today. People become jealous over others' material possessions, reputations, appearance, achievements, affections, and so on. A jealous person is selfish, petty, controlling, ungrateful, unhappy, dissatisfied, and uncaring. This person is like a blazing fire that will burn down anything that might be threatening without worrying about the consequences.

Lord Jesus, I want to see

Jesus, Loving and Generous God, you are always concerned about the needs of others and willing to give them everything you have, even your own life. During your ministry on earth, when the religious leaders became jealous of you and your reputation, you did not fight with them. Rather, you kept giving your whole self to others and preaching the message of reconciliation. I might be tempted to become jealous of my family members, friends, neighbors, or co-workers over something. But, with your guidance and encouragement, I will be happy for their blessings and thankful for my own.

Resolution

Today, I will review what might be making me jealous of someone. Then, I'll congratulate that person and say a prayer of thanksgiving for all the blessings in my life.

July 18

"This is what the Lord Almighty says: 'Administer true justice; show mercy and compassion to one another. Do not oppress the widow or the father-less, the alien or the poor. In your hearts, do not think evil of each other.'"
(Zechariah 7:9-10)

Reflection
One quality we humans want to see on earth is justice. For we all want to be treated justly in the court room, grocery store, work place, school, or wherever we go. Unfortunately, since the beginning of time, the poor and the lowly have felt mistreated and realized that justice was not on their side. So, they must rely on God to deliver justice. God also helps hold everyone accountable for their actions. The wicked and the powerful will not get away with anything, whereas the just and the lowly will have their justice served.

Lord Jesus, I want to see
Jesus, Judge of the living and the dead, you called on everyone to change their life and stop mistreating one another. You often tried to defend the poor and the lowly, while holding the rich and the power-ful accountable for their actions. The Beatitudes is a good example of how seriously you take justice for the poor and the lowly. If I have treated anyone unjustly, help me change and repay that person accordingly.

Resolution
Today, I will commit myself to live by God's justice and fix any injus-tices I might have committed recently.

July 19

Issue: **Laugh**
"When the Lord brought back the captives to Zion, we were like men who dreamed. Our mouths were filled with laughter, our tongues with songs of joy. Then it was said among the nations, 'The Lord has done great things for them.'" (Psalms 126:1-2)

Reflection
Everyone loves to laugh or at least smile as often as possible. It is a sign that all is well, and there is nothing about which they should worry or be concerned. People only stop laughing when something serious or fearful is about to happen. God's people stopped laughing and began wailing when they were driven into slavery and away from home. They started laughing again when they were allowed to return home or when they were blessed with a successful harvest.

Lord Jesus, I want to see
Jesus, God's smiling face in our world, you certainly came to earth to put a smile on our face. You are always concerned about the well-being of God's people and want them to cry less and laugh more by reaching out to help at every chance possible. I might not laugh a lot lately due to my life's burdens or other daily concerns. But with you by my side to help and cheer for me, I know I can laugh again and more often.

Resolution
Today, I will choose to laugh the whole day, even though there are all kinds of pressures or concerns in the back of my mind.

July 20

<u>Issue:</u> **Licentious**
"For certain people whose condemnation was written about long ago have secretly slipped in among you. They are godless people, who change the grace of our God into a license for immorality and deny Jesus Christ our only Sovereign and Lord." (Jude 4)

<u>Reflection</u>
The "licentious" idea is very harmful and dangerous to a spiritual life, but a true diagnosis of the current problems with our world. A licentious person is someone who lacks moral discipline and disregards all accepted rules or standards. This person thinks and does whatever he/she wants to do without any accountability. This not only creates absolute chaos in society but also gives a person a false sense of moral certitude. Unfortunately, this is exactly the situation we see in our society and around the world these days. There are no moral standards and no accountability.

<u>Lord Jesus, I want to see</u>
Jesus, Source of my moral and spiritual life, you did not come to abolish the Laws, as some might think, but you came to fulfill them. You reiterated this message by announcing the new Commandments, but this time the Laws related to love. It is surely easier for me to follow the licentious way in my spiritual life and do whatever I want. But, with you as my moral standard, I will follow all your Laws and Commandments so that I can be counted among your children and the chosen ones in your Kingdom on the Last Day.

<u>Resolution</u>
Today, I will try to live up to one of your Commandments or the Ten Commandments by practicing concrete acts.

July 21

<u>Issue:</u> **Lonely**

"God sets the lonely in families, God leads forth the prisoners with singing; but the rebellious live in a sun-scorched land." (Psalms 68:6)

<u>Reflection</u>
We all feel a bit lonely at one time or another, even if we are involved in all sorts of relationships with people around us. There are moments we feel empty inside, scared, abandoned, or sad. Adam, after being in the Garden of Eden by himself, felt lonely and asked God to create Eve as his companion. However, even with a spousal companion and all kinds of friends, we humans continue to feel lonely at an exponential rate. This is because we will not feel complete until we find God. St. Augustine summarized it neatly this way, "My Soul will not rest until it rests in you, my God."

Lord Jesus, I want to see
Jesus, my Dear Friend and Companion, you had moments of loneliness, even with all the disciples around you. In the Garden of Gethsemane, you felt so alone and saddened that you called on God the Father to come and comfort you. I have surely had lonely moments along the way. But, I hope I will soon realize that I can call on you to come and walk with me any time. For only in you will my soul find rest and true companionship. Thank you for your friendship!

<u>Resolution</u>
Today, I will call on you, Jesus, if I feel a bit lonely and will choose you to be my friend for the rest of my life.

July 22

<u>Issue</u>: **Malice**

"Now you must rid yourselves of all such things as these: anger, rage, malice, slander, and filthy language from your lips." (Colossians 3:8)

<u>Reflection</u>
No one likes to be around mean people at work or school. Yet, a malicious spirit is quite prevalent in our society today. It takes the form of hatred, vengeance, retribution, punishment, threats, slander, bad rumors, and so on. Everyone seems to have more negative and malicious things to say about one another than positive and kind things. How will anything survive in this kind of toxic environment? It will simply breed more negative and malicious acts. We must break out of this vicious circle.

<u>Lord Jesus, I want to see</u>
Jesus, Gentle and Kind Spirit, you broke out of the vicious circle by performing good deeds and are calling us to do the same. When the scribes and Pharisees acted maliciously toward you, you simply turned the other cheek and did not return the same mean act. Help me to conquer malice with kindness, not return malice for malice. By doing this, I can help change our world slowly for the better.

<u>Resolution</u>
Today, when someone says or does something malicious to me, I will try not to lash out. Instead, I will keep calm and pray for peace. If possible, I will say or do something nice in return.

July 23

Issue: **Loud**

"When Jesus came near the place where the road goes to the Mount of Olives, the whole crowd of disciples began joyfully to praise God in loud voices for all the miracles they have seen... Some of the Pharisees in the crowd said to Jesus, 'Teacher, rebuke your disciples!' 'I tell you,' Jesus replied, 'if they keep quiet, the stones will cry out.'" (Luke 19:37-40)

Reflection

Our world believes that the louder a person becomes, the faster and better the results will be. Hence, people keep yelling and screaming at each other instead of listening and paying close attention to each other. In fact, some even use loudness to intimidate their opponents and neighbors. But, this is not how God acts toward us, despite God's immense power. The Prophet Isaiah discovered through his personal experience that God was not in a strong and heavy wind, an earthquake, or a fire. Rather, God was in a tiny, whispering sound.

Lord Jesus, I want to see

Jesus, soft and gentle Voice of God, you never tried to be loud in your speech or actions, even when you dealt with screaming and violent spirits. For you knew that is not how a person would likely meet God. Instead, people will have a divine encounter in a gentle, tender moment. I sometimes like to be loud when I am upset or frustrated. Help me control my volume at all times and not to consider being soft and gentle as a sign of weakness. Doing so is how I might meet God.

Resolution

Today, I will try not to raise my voice or yell at people around me, even if I become upset or tense.

July 24

Prejudice

"I charge you, in the sight of God and Christ Jesus and the elect angels, to keep these instructions without partiality, and to do nothing out of favoritism." (1 Timothy 5:21)

Reflection
We have each been raised in certain ways and taught to believe in certain things. Over the years, we formed certain beliefs and viewpoints that slowly hardened into prejudices. These are the lenses through which we look at the world and judge it. Sometimes, those lenses do not create any problems for us, and those prejudices are not a threat to society at large. Other times, those lenses show us things in a negative, harmful way and prejudices become problematic. These negative lenses need to be identified and fixed.

Lord Jesus, I want to see
Jesus, true and clear Vision of my life, you tried to have an open mind and block any preconceived notions when dealing with the world. You strengthened prejudice-free thinking by not having a judgmental attitude. I would certainly like to imitate your example and avoid any prejudices I might have about a certain group of people. I want to see you in everyone around me and treat them as I would treat you.

Resolution
Today, I will discover something nice and positive I can say or think about someone or a certain group of people that I might have viewed negatively.

July 25

Issue: **Protection**

"The Lord holds victory in store for the upright, He is a shield to those whose walk is blameless, for He guards the course of the just and protects the way of His faithful ones." (Proverbs 2:7-8)

Reflection

We count on our government for many things, one of which is protection. We want our government to protect us and bring us security. For what good is our success in business, the harvest, or inventing if we get attacked and harmed? Unfortunately, our government often fails us and leaves hurt everywhere. Many of us have wised up and come to God instead to ask for protection and security. After all, God is the Creator and Owner of the Universe and cannot be swayed by worldly power like the government can.

Lord Jesus, I want to see

Jesus, my Shield and Fortress, during your ministry on earth, you always felt the need to defend the poor, the weak, the lowly, and the misfortunate. You want to make God's people feel safe and well protected always. Hence, you left the Holy Spirit upon your return to Heaven. I have relied on other worldly things for protection. But, it is time for me to seek protection from you and nowhere else. For it is in you, God alone, that I trust.

Resolution

Today, I will call upon you, Lord, when I feel scared or threatened by something or feel my life's burdens are heavy.

July 26

<u>Issue:</u> **Resentful**

"The Lord's servant must not quarrel; instead, one must be kind to everyone, able to teach, not resentful. Those who oppose him/her, he/she must gently instruct..." (2Timothy 2:24-25)

<u>Reflection</u>
The Bible is full of stories about resentful folks. This includes Cain, who resented Abel because God seemed to favor him and the ten disciples, who discovered that James and John asked Jesus to sit at His right and left in God's Kingdom. Apparently, resentment arises when someone becomes jealous or envious of someone else. This creates anger and bitterness about the whole experience to the point that it hurts others.

<u>Lord Jesus, I want to see</u>
Jesus, Kind and Generous Lord, you experienced resentment firsthand as the religious leaders felt that they had been sidelined by your preaching. Hence, they tried to hurt you at every chance possible. But, you counteracted that resentment by being merciful and grateful. I have certainly become resentful of someone over something. The best way for me to fix this feeling is to adopt your attitude of mercy and gratitude.

<u>Resolution</u>
Today, I will examine what might be making me resentful recently and then give thanks for the many things in my life.

July 27

Rude

"Love is patient, love is kind. It does not envy, it does not boast, it is not proud. It is not rude, it is not self-seeking, it is not easily angered, it keeps no record of wrongs. Love does not delight in evil but rejoices with the truth." (1 Corinthians 13:4-6)

Reflection

None of us likes it when someone treats us rudely or behaves meanly toward us. We all want to be treated with respect. When people are rude to us, they might be having a bad day or lack any care and consideration. Rude people are often selfish, inconsiderate, uncaring, disrespectful, and childish. None of us wants to be a rude person. Unfortunately, our world is full of people suffering from this affliction.

Lord Jesus, I want to see

Jesus, Kind and Thoughtful Lord, you never stop worrying about God's people. Like a Good Shepherd, you keep helping and caring for them every chance possible. Having lived in our world for some time, I have been influenced by the "rudeness" virus and can display some rude behaviors, especially when I am upset. But, with your example and good influence, I will try to show respect and consideration for others, even when things do not go my way.

Resolution

Today, I will say "thank you" or "please" to everyone I encounter throughout the day and show them respect, even if I am having a bad day.

July 28

Issue: **Self-control**
"Like a city whose walls are broken down, it is a person who lacks self-control." (Proverbs 25:28)

Reflection
Everything in life is better in moderation. If we know our limitations and watch for what we take in and give out, everything should be all right. Unfortunately, sometimes we do not know how to control our desires, which causes us to do something illegal or stupid. Anyone with a lack of self-control usually acts on impulse and does much damage to people around him/her. Sadly, our current world does not teach people how to have self-control and restrain themselves. Instead, it allows people do whatever they want and then blames our problems on mental health when they are caught doing something bad.

Lord Jesus, I want to see
Jesus, my Guide and Moral Standard, although you show mercy to God's people, you also advise them to control their desires and impulses. For these emotions can easily cause people to do dumb things and hurt others. Sometimes I might let my guard down and forget to practice self-control in my speech and actions. But, with your help and encouragement, I will try to follow your Laws better and not to do anything harmful to others.

Resolution
Today, I will watch everything I do carefully and have good reasons for each of my actions. Otherwise, I will stop my bad behavior.

July 29

Soul

"Come to me, all you who are weary and burdened and I will give you rest. Take my yoke upon you and learn from me, for I am gentle and humble in heart and you will find rest for your Souls. For my yoke is easy and my burden is light." (Matthew 11:28-30)

Reflection

We humans have many valuable possessions: houses, cars, gold, diamonds, boats, and the list can go on. But, the possession that is worth more than all these worldly things combined—and one that many of us often overlook—is our soul. Unlike all worldly things, our soul lives beyond this life and forever. Everyone who has such a precious possession should spend nights and days polishing it up and taking great care of it. Sadly, most folks in our modern world do not seem to know the value of their soul or care enough to give it proper attention.

Lord Jesus, I want to see

Jesus, Spirit of the Living and Strength of the Soul, you slowly revealed to God's people through your miracles during your ministry that a spiritual world exists beyond our physical one. In that world, our soul or spirit lives, and it is up to us to nurture and strengthen it. I may not appreciate the spiritual world as much as I should. But, if I do not take care of my soul or spirit, it will weaken and become badly damaged like a sick person.

Resolution

Today, I will feed my soul or spirit by reading the Bible, spending time in prayer, or doing some acts of charity.

July 30

Issue: **Tolerance**

"Your eyes are too pure to look on evil; you cannot tolerate wrong. When then do you tolerate the treacherous? Why are you silent while the wicked swallow up those more righteous than themselves?" (Habakkuk 1:13)

Reflection

"Tolerance" is the most hated term in our highly charged and sharply divided political environment right now. No one wants to give up a little bit and compromise with others for the sake of peace and love. Those who do try to tolerate and make some compromises are considered sellouts or betrayers. The result of this stance is constant fighting and lack of love. This is exactly what the Devil wants, and he enjoys every bit of it. Meanwhile, the community of God's people is divided and hurting.

Lord Jesus, I want to see

Jesus, my Peacemaker and Reconciler with God, you have definitely tolerated my sins and tolerated the pesky attitude of the scribes and Pharisees during your ministry on earth. Yet, you never once called on your disciples to hate and fight your opponents as I see happening all around me now. I must follow your example and learn to tolerate others, even my enemies. I must be the servant of all and have that humble attitude, as your teaching tells me, if I want to be the greatest in your eyes.

Resolution

Today, I will try not to talk back or react angrily to an upsetting or annoying situation at home, at work, or on the road. Instead, I will say a quick prayer asking for tolerance.

July 31

Unity

"May the God who gives endurance and encouragement give you a spirit of unity among yourselves as you follow Christ Jesus so that, with one heart and mind, you may glorify the God and Father of our Lord Jesus Christ." (Romans 15:5-6)

Reflection

Unless we have lived in a divorced family, a divided situation, or a civil war, we have no idea how important and precious the gift of unity is. It hurts everywhere when a division or separation exists. People do not talk or care about each other in such a situation. In fact, the only result is fighting and destruction for both sides. The Church went through many schisms, and it knows the pain of disunity. Heaven was divided between Light and Darkness, and it has paid a dear price for that ever since.

Lord Jesus, I want to see

Jesus, the Second Person of the Most Holy Trinity, you came to earth to reconcile us with God the Father and bring us back into the fold. Your whole life's mission on earth was to restore unity to the whole person, to relationships, and to war-torn factions. Sometimes, I might want to fight and go my own way. I might not appreciate the value and importance of maintaining unity. Help me learn to put aside my own agendas and selfish desires so that I spread peace and unity wherever I go.

Resolution

Today, I will participate in an activity with my family or a project at my church or at work to help bring unity and promote it in my little community.

August

Lord Jesus,
I Want to See...

August 1

<u>Issue:</u> **Conversation**

"Let your conversation be always full of grace, seasoned with salt, so that you may know how to answer everyone." (Colossians 4:6)

<u>Reflection</u>

Every day we have conversations with people around us. Sometimes, the conversation is for us to vent, share our feelings about something, or seek comfort and reassurance. Other times, we explore something new, show our appreciation to each other, or explain certain subjects. For us believers, we have conversations with God daily in the form of prayer. Our prayer conversations are often used to ask God for help or other needs.

<u>Lord Jesus, I want to see</u>

Jesus, the Voice of God among us, you entered our world to make our conversations with God more intimate. You were often found having a conversation with God the Father in a quiet place, especially the one in the Garden of Gethsemane before your Passion and Cross. I might not have regular conversations with you due to my busy schedule or fear of being close to you. But, I cannot imagine keeping myself away from you or having no contact with you. Help me build a strong relationship with you and have many conversations with you throughout my days. For that is how you can be my best friend, and I will not feel alone on my faith journey.

<u>Resolution</u>

Today, I will try to have a few conversations with you, Lord, throughout my day regardless of how busy it becomes.

August 2

Issue: **Cooperation**
"It was for the sake of God that they went out, receiving no help from the pagans. We ought therefore to show hospitality to such people so that we may work together for the truth." (3John 7-8)

Reflection
It is rare to see people cooperate with each other for the common good these days. It is difficult for people to hold hands and work together for the good of the whole due to pride or selfishness. Hence, all kinds of arguing and fighting are swirling around us all the time. Perhaps, cooperation might not work well in our human world. But, in the God-Head, the three persons of the Holy Trinity always cooperate and help each other achieve the common good. Gods' way has had great results and worked better than our human tendencies.

Lord Jesus, I want to see
Jesus, Peacemaker and Reconciler, you were mistaken to be a rabble-rouser. But, you constantly called on your disciples to cooperate with one another, even with the authorities, to bring about love and wonderful blessings to the community. I might not want to cooperate with you or my neighbors to bring about common good. But, with your example and encouragement, I will always put the good of the community before my own and work together with others to make peacefulness reality.

Resolution
Today, I will put aside my own plans and try to cooperate with others at home or work to bring about something good for the whole community.

August 3

<u>Issue:</u> **Cursing**

"But I [Jesus] tell you who hear me: Love your enemies, do good to those who hate you, bless those who curse you, pray for those who mistreat you. If someone strikes you on one cheek, turn to him/her the other also. If someone takes your cloak, do not stop him/her from taking your tunic." (Luke 6:27-29)

<u>Reflection</u>
We curse when we are mad about something. We also put a curse on our enemies or people we hate. Cursing is a sign of frustration and disapproval of something or someone after we have felt mistreated or wronged somehow. In the Bible, we learn that God put a curse on the snake, as well as Adam and Eve after they violated God's Command and ate the forbidden fruit. Clearly, cursing is not a pleasant experience and can become a bad habit for us over time.

<u>Lord Jesus, I want to see</u>
Jesus, God's Blessing to us humans, you once put a curse on a mulberry tree for not bearing any fruit, and it immediately withered. You certainly had power over your curse. But, you never used it in a derogatory way to put someone down. I might not be shy about cursing someone out of hatred or frustration. Yet, cursing can hurt people and become a bad habit. But, with your grace, I will try not to curse, even when I am frustrated or mad about someone or something.

<u>Resolution</u>
Today, I will watch my words carefully and control my emotions, so that I will not curse even when things do not go my way.

August 4

<u>Issue</u>: **Delight**

"But, the Lord said to me, 'My grace is sufficient for you, for my power is made perfect in weakness.' Therefore, I will boast all the more gladly about my weakness, so that Christ's power may rest on me. That is why, for Christ's sake, I delight in weaknesses, insults, hardships, persecutions, and difficulties. For when I am weak, then I am strong." (2Corinthians 12:9-10)

<u>Reflection</u>

We usually feel delighted and content when things run smoothly in our lives or go our way. God the Father must be delighted after He completed His wonderful Creation. Mary, Joseph, and all the Heavenly hosts must have been delighted upon the birth of Jesus. Mary Magdalene, Peter, and John must have been delighted when they saw the empty tomb. We all welcome these delightful moments any time and will do anything to make them last.

Lord Jesus, I want to see

Jesus, my Delight and Salvation, you certainly had some moments when you restored someone to full health. You also loved to bring a delightful moment to as many folks as possible. I sure could use a moment like that once a day. But, I also realize that my faith journey on earth is full of crosses. Having you by my side is all the delight I need to make it through each day.

<u>Resolution</u>

Today, I will try to bring a moment of delight to someone by sharing light humor or doing a kind deed for someone who might be in need.

August 5

<u>Issue:</u> **Deny**

"Jesus said to His disciples: 'If anyone would come after, one must deny oneself and take up one's cross and follow me. For whoever wants to save one's life will lose it, but whoever loses ones' life for me will find it.'"
(Matthew 16:24-25)

<u>Reflection</u>

Humans learn to deny the moment we learn how to talk. We might do something wrong, get caught, and then try to deny it. The Bible is full of examples of this. Both Adam and Eve denied that they ate the forbidden fruit. Cain denied that he killed his brother Abel. Peter denied that he was Jesus' disciple. When an alleged perpetrator is confronted about a wrongful act, he/she usually tries to deny it. But, this behavior often leads the person into more troubles.

<u>Lord Jesus, I want to see</u>

Jesus, Source of Truth, you once said, "Yes means yes; No means no." You also advised your disciples not to lie or do anything that might damage their soul. Rather, we should deny ourselves, take up our daily crosses, and follow you. I might take up the bad habit of denial when I am caught doing something bad. I need to get rid of that habit. The only denial I need is to deny myself, take up my daily crosses, and follow in your footsteps, for that is the way to Heaven.

<u>Resolution</u>

Today, I will work hard to not deny my wrongdoing if I am confronted. Instead, I will try to sacrifice myself and carry my daily crosses without any complaints.

August 6

Issue: **Disaster**

"Do not be a terror to me; you are my refuge in the day of disaster. Let my persecutors be put to shame, but keep me from shame; let them be terrified, but keep me from terror. Bring on them the day of disaster; destroy them with double destruction." (Jeremiah 17:17-18)

Reflection

When disasters strikes, things often turn chaotic. Some of us might wonder where God is and why God would allow something terrible to happen. Most disasters are natural, whereas some are man-made. A disaster often gives us a sense of helplessness and shows us the mighty power of God. Unfortunately, some folks blame the disaster on God and get angry at God when facing such circumstances. But, usually a disaster rallies a whole community and gets everyone to pitch in and help the least fortunate. After all, something good can still come out of a disaster.

Lord Jesus, I want to see

Jesus, Lord of the storm and God of thunder, you came to the rescue of the disciples when their boat was caught in a fierce storm and you calmed the sea. Your heart was always moved with pity at the sight of a disaster. I might feel numb or indifferent upon seeing something disastrous and do nothing to help its victims. However, with your grace and encouragement, I will try to reach out to the misfortunate at every chance possible.

Resolution

Today, I will see if any disasters surround me for which I can offer help or make a difference. I will see how I can ease some of the pain and hardship for its victims.

August 7

<u>Issue:</u> **Exploit**
"You gladly put up with fools since you are so wise! In fact, you even put up with anyone who enslaves you or exploits you or takes advantage of you or pushes himself forward or slaps you in the face. To my shame I admit that we were too weak for that..." (2Corinthians 11:19-21)

<u>Reflection</u>
Humans exploit other human beings or a situation if we are given an opportunity. This tendency arises often because we are proud, selfish, envious, jealous, and greedy people. We will do anything to make ourselves number one at the expense of other people, even intimidate and cheat on others. We learn in the Bible how God's people were the victims of this problem for centuries. Sadly, the problem of exploitation continues to occur in our time and even thrives in certain parts of the world.

Lord Jesus, I want to see
Jesus, kind and generous Giver of all blessings, you are the most generous person who will give anyone even the shirt off your back. You showed us that generous spirit by offering your life on the Cross for our sake. I might want to exploit the lowly, the misfortunate, or even the system for my selfish benefits. With your example and inspiration, I will learn to give more of myself and share your blessings for me with others. For it is better for me to give than receive and hence I can help create a generous and caring society.

<u>Resolution</u>
Today, I will try to avoid exploiting or using someone for my own benefit. Instead, I will do at least one good deed for someone without expecting anything in return.

August 8

Issue: **Favor**

"Blessed is the one who listens to me [Wisdom of God], watching daily at my doors, waiting at my doorway. For whoever finds me finds life and receives favor from the Lord. But whoever fails to find me harms oneself; all who hate me love death." (Proverbs 8:34-36)

Reflection
Favor is something nice or kind we do for someone without expecting anything in return. Since the beginning of Creation, you, Lord, have done one favor after another for us. Yet, it is difficult for us to realize and acknowledge this important fact. And, it is not just God who can perform favors. Some human beings have imitated the divine example and learned to do favors for their neighbors without much trouble. A world with many folks like that will bring us close to the world of Heaven.

Lord Jesus, I want to see

Jesus, kind and merciful God, favor was not anything new to you. For you performed it every day and wished that the whole world would do the same. It is very rare for someone to do a favor for another without expecting something in return. I sometimes share that same thinking when doing something nice and kind for someone. With your help and example, I will continue to do favors for people around me as often as possible.

Resolution
Today, I will do something nice and kind for someone without expecting anything in return.

August 9

<u>Issue:</u> **Feed**

"Just as the living Father sent me and I live because of the Father, so the one who feeds on me will live because of me. This is the bread that came down from Heaven. Your forefathers ate manna and died, but anyone who feeds on this bread will live forever." (John 6: 57-58)

<u>Reflection</u>
For anything to live and survive in our world, it needs some sort of nourishment. We must feed it something. Otherwise, it will lack energy and die. Similarly, our soul and spiritual life need to be fed if we want it to live and thrive. The best way to nourish it is by following a consistent prayer routine and having a strong desire to do good for others. With that source of nourishment and other spiritual foods, our soul and spiritual life will survive through any tough conditions in this life.

Lord Jesus, I want to see
Jesus, source of Life and Hope, every time you performed a miracle and fed a hungry crowd with bread and fish during your ministry on earth, you always pointed people to the importance of caring for their souls. Without proper care and nourishment, our souls will become famished and die of hunger. I might not have given much care and attention to my soul and spiritual life up to this point. But, you have opened my eyes to see how crucial it is to feed it daily and take good care of it. I thank you, Lord, for that great insight.

<u>Resolution</u>
Today, I will commit to feeding my soul and spiritual life by setting up a short time each day to pray and find other ways to nourish it regularly.

August 10

Issue: **Flexibility**

"Anyone who remains stiff-necked after many rebukes will suddenly be destroyed without remedy." (Proverbs 29:1)

Reflection
We all like routines, structure, and stability. Rules and regulations are necessary for us to achieve such goals. Without guidance, the world will turn chaotic. But, for every rule or regulation, there is an exception to it. For every yin, there is a yang. Even a wise and just King like Solomon had to be flexible and merciful in his approach to every case coming before him. In fact, throughout our human history, our God has not been too rigid in dealing with His people. Rather, our God been flexible and merciful in every case.

Lord Jesus, I want to see
Jesus, Judge of the living and the dead, you have given us a set of Commandments that help guide your teachings and daily work. But, you never let rules and regulations restrict you on how to deal with a case before you. I might have been rigid and stubborn in my approach to a problem or an issue in life. But, after reviewing your years of ministry, I have realized that I cannot succeed or survive in this world without being flexible in dealing with issues in life.

Resolution
Today, I will review some routines in my life, such as hanging around a certain group at a social gathering. I will challenge myself to be flexible and mingle with other people outside my circle of friends.

August 11

<u>Issue:</u> **Soil**

"...But the one who received the seed that fell on the good soil is the one who hears the Word and understands it. One produces a crop, yielding a hundred, sixty, or thirty times what was sown." (Matthew 13:23)

<u>Reflection</u>
Soil is an image we find many times in the Bible as well as around us. It might look simple and mundane in our view, but it carries powerful spiritual messages. Good soil brings us spectacular harvests, whereas bad soil gives us nothing. If our spiritual life is good soil, it will produce thirty, sixty, or a hundredfold. On the other hand, if it is bad soil, God's words cannot take root in it and very little or nothing will be produced at harvest time. We must cultivate good soil by having the right spiritual nutrition and proper care.

Lord Jesus, I want to see
Jesus, Word of God, you were sown into our world to bring us the Good News of Heaven and spiritual help. You certainly want us to have good soil and produce abundantly for the Kingdom of Heaven. I might not realize how important it is for me to become good soil and produce great results for you. It must disappoint you a great deal if I become bad soil and bring you nothing. But, with your great support, I promise to tend my spiritual life carefully to become good soil.

<u>Resolution</u>
Today, I will prepare my spiritual life to become good soil by searching for ways to make me more interested in the spiritual world, such as learning more about God and Heaven.

August 12

<u>Issue:</u> **Gracious**
"The Lord said to Moses: ... This is how you are to bless them... 'The Lord bless you and keep you; the Lord make His face shine upon you and be gracious to you; the Lord turn His face toward you and give you peace.'"
(Numbers 6: 22-26)

<u>Reflection</u>
Gracious is one of those terms we rarely hear these days. Indeed, our modern society is all about "me" and "what I can get for myself at the expense of others around me." Our secular and materialistic world is a dog-eat-dog environment where everyone tries to win everything at all costs. A gracious person will do one's best to be kind, patient, generous, understanding, friendly, tender, gentle, and merciful. This person will show others how to act in a tough situation by imitating our kind and merciful God.

<u>Lord Jesus, I want to see</u>
Jesus, my Loving and Merciful God, you are always gracious and kind to everyone, even your opponents and sinners. I remember when one of the robbers hung on the cross by your side asked you to forgive and remember him in your Kingdom. You graciously said, "Today, will be with me in Paradise." You did not judge and condemn him for his past sins. I need to have your gracious spirit and learn to act more kindly and mercifully toward people around me, regardless of how they treat me.

<u>Resolution</u>
Today, I will learn to be gracious by acting kindly and mercifully toward everyone I meet during the day.

August 13

<u>Issue</u>: **Guidance**
"For lack of guidance a nation falls, but many advisors take victory sure."
(Proverbs 11:14)

<u>Reflection</u>
If we want to get to Heaven, but follow the wrong guide or the blind guy, we will never make it. That is why God's people were lost and wandered in the desert for forty years as they looked for the Promised Land. Worse yet, without proper guidance, we might hurt ourselves and everyone around us. This seems to be the problem with our current society—it continues to seek guidance in all the wrong places. It will end up hurting itself and will never make it to Heaven.

<u>Lord Jesus, I want to see</u>
Jesus, my Guide and my Hope, you came into my world not only to save me but also show me the way to Heaven. You opened the eyes of many blind folks to help them see the way. You also tried to show God's people how to have a happy life on earth and later make it to the Gate of Heaven. I might feel lost at times due to our confusing world and life's pressures. But, with your guidance, I know what to do in this life to achieve true happiness and end up in Heaven someday.

<u>Resolution</u>
Today, I will pick one of the issues with which I am currently struggling and bring it in prayer to God. I will ask Him for guidance on how to deal with it.

August 14

Issue: **Harm**

"…Whatever other commandments there may be are summed up in this one rule: 'Love your neighbor as yourself.' Love does no harm to its neighbor. Therefore, love is the fulfillment of the Law." (Romans 13:9-10)

Reflection

All sorts of things can harm us physically. Some of these harmful sources can be seen with our naked eye, whereas others can only be observed under a microscope. If we do not take these harmful sources seriously, we will get hurt badly and inflict grave damage on others around us. Similarly, our world is full of spiritually-harmful things. If we are not careful in dealing with them, we might end up hurting our souls and damaging our spiritual life.

Lord Jesus, I want to see

Jesus, my Protector and Healer, you know how harmful the power of darkness and its bad influences in our world might be to my soul. That is why you tried to drive out demons and warn God's people about the potential harm to their spiritual life during your ministry on earth. I might not take spiritual harm seriously and keep hanging around bad influences. It is time for me to wake up and stay away from these influences or anything that might harm my soul.

Resolution

Today, I will think of some bad influences or harmful things that might affect my spiritual life and try to stay away from them.

August 15

<u>Issue:</u> **Harmony**

"Finally, all of you, live in harmony with one another; be sympathetic, love as brothers and sisters, be compassionate and humble. Do not repay evil with evil or insult with insult, but with blessing, because to this you were called so that you may inherit a blessing." (1Peter 3:8-9)

<u>Reflection</u>
We can tell if whether a community is harmonious by the way its members treat one another. A harmonious community will have love, kindness, caring, understanding, compassion, and humility as its important characteristics. It also knows how to put the common good above individual possessions and learns how to get along with one another. Clearly, Heaven and the Holy Trinity are great examples of what a harmonious community might look like.

<u>Lord Jesus, I want to see</u>
Jesus, Prince of Peace, whenever the disciples argued or the religious leaders tried to agitate the crowd, you tried to bring peace and harmony to the community. For you knew how important it is to be in harmony and get along with one another. Sometimes, my life or family might not have any harmony and instead be in turmoil. Help me seek you at those moments, so that you can restore peace and harmony to my heart and home.

<u>Resolution</u>
Today, I will endeavor to avoid arguments and fights. Instead, I will look for ways to promote peace and harmony in my home and community around me.

August 16

Issue: **Hate**
"Love must be sincere. Hate what is evil; cling to what is good. Be devoted to one another in brotherly and sisterly love. Honor one another above yourselves." (Romans 12:9-10)

Reflection
If there is one thing we have a lot around us these days, it is hate and anger. So many people are filled with these vicious emotions that we constantly see violence and killing all around us. The best way to put an end to this circle of evil is to replace hate and anger with love and tolerance. The cause of hate and anger can be resentment, envy, vengeance, ignorance, selfishness, and so on. But, the real root of all that evil is lack of love. Ironically, there is a lot of talk about love, not real acts of love surrounding us.

Lord Jesus, I want to see
Jesus, the Love of God in our midst, your life was full of love and rooted in God's love. You did everything out of love and never let any hateful and evil thoughts around you sway or influence you and your actions. Being human, I am not completely free of hate and evil thoughts. Yet, our current world does not bring me much peace and love either. With your help and example, I will try to think and act out love as often as possible and not let hate rule my heart.

Resolution
Today, I will examine my heart to see if I might have any hateful feelings toward someone or some group and try to let go of it. I will then replace that hatred with the love of Jesus.

August 17

<u>Issue:</u> **Heart**
"Do not store up for yourselves treasures on earth, where moth and rust destroy, and where thieves break in and steal. But, store up for yourselves treasures in Heaven, where moth and rust do not destroy, and where thieves do not break in and steal. For where your treasure is, there your heart will be also." (Matthew 6:19-21)

<u>Reflection</u>
The heart is always a sweet and romantic symbol of love. Over the centuries, people have used the heart symbol to communicate love for someone or something. But, the heart, which is the opposite of the mind, is where we hide all our feelings. It is difficult for anyone to know our true feelings about something, because no one can have access to our heart except God. This is why the heart can be a hiding place for many deep, dark, and evil feelings.

Lord Jesus, I want to see
Jesus, the Living Heart of God in our world, you always showed the world how you truly felt about various issues. In fact, the Gospels often said that your heart was moved with pity when you saw a hungry, desperate crowd. I might try to hide my feelings and not honestly tell others how I truly feel about everything around me. That certainly might cause me to form bad habits and lie about my true feelings. But, with your role model, I will always speak the truth.

<u>Resolution</u>
Today, I will see what I might be trying to hide in my heart and then find ways to express how I truly feel. I hope this sharing will be my new habit from now on.

August 18

<u>Issue:</u> **Hand**

"If I go up to the Heavens, you are there; if I make my bed in the depths, you are there. If I rise on the wings of the dawn, if I settle on the far side of the sea, even there your hand will guide me, your right hand will hold me fast." (Psalms 139:8-10)

<u>Reflection</u>

To our surprise, the hand is a symbol we read a lot about in the Bible. The right hand or being "on the right hand" are usually good things. If there are two lines waiting for Heaven, we will better off be on the right-hand side. For folks on the right-hand side often refer to people who are good, kind, caring, loving, compassionate, and faithful to God's Commandments and teachings all the way to the end. Because of their lifestyle, these folks will receive great rewards in the end.

<u>Lord Jesus, I want to see</u>

Jesus, the Right Hand of God the Father, you were once asked by the mother of James and John if her two sons would be able to sit on your right hand and on your left. You quickly enlightened her that it is not be up to you to decide but it is God the Father's choice. I might be a right-handed person or a left-handed one. But, one thing you have taught me well is to be a great helping hand to everyone around me. I certainly do not want to become an exploiting hand of the poor, the lowly, and the misfortunate.

<u>Resolution</u>

Today, I will extend my hand to help someone with some kind act and thank God for my ability to help others.

August 19

<u>Issue:</u> **Humor**
"Abraham and Sarah were already old and well advanced in years, and Sarah was past the age of childbearing. So, Sarah laughed to herself as she thought, 'After I am worn out and my master is old, will I now have this pleasure?'" (Genesis 18:11-12)

<u>Reflection</u>
We believers often focus on serious faith matters and totally forget about the importance of humor. Yet, laughter and humor play an important part in our spiritual life. In fact, there is a saying, "A good laugh is wonderful medicine for the soul." A laugh brings joy to the soul and lifts up the spirit. Also, a person with a good sense of humor generally has peace and joy in his/her heart and is able to make light a situation or diffuse it before it gets ugly.

<u>Lord Jesus, I want to see</u>
Jesus, the Joy of my life, the Gospels might not share with us the laughs you might have had during your ministry on earth. But, I am sure you must have had light-hearted moments that you shared with your disciples. For example, your disciples were scared when they saw you walk on water one night toward them and thought you were a ghost. Then, you came aboard and assured them that it was you. That must have brought a roar of laughs for them all. I might be taking my life too seriously, but you can help me laugh and enjoy it a little more.

<u>Resolution</u>
Today, I will try to laugh as often as possible and not take things too seriously.

August 20

Issue: **Hurt**
"Lord, who may dwell in your sanctuary? Who may live on your holy hill? Anyone whose walk is blameless and who does what is righteous, who speaks the truth from one's heart and has no slander on one's tongue, who does one's neighbor no wrong and casts no slur on one's fellowman, who despises a vile person but honors those who fear the Lord, who keep one's oath even when it hurts..." (Psalms 15:1-4)

Reflection
It is not fun when we are hurt. We are often in much pain, anguish, and distress. Some wounds are visible, whereas others are not. The Bible shares with us many examples on these wounds: physical, emotional, mental, and spiritual. Some of them take years to heal. But, with God's healing grace, a person can be restored to full health in no time. Hopefully, we will do the same and try to bring more healing to the world around us instead of causing more hurt.

Lord Jesus, I want to see
Jesus, Source of Healing and Comfort, during your ministry on earth, you saw first-hand some of the hurts people endured, especially those who felt hopeless or were under the influence of demons. You tried to relieve them from their troubles as fast as possible, even doing so on the Sabbath. I surely see how much pain and suffering our world endures each day. With your help, I will try to hurt others less and bring more healing to people around me every day.

Resolution
Today, I will pray for people who I might have hurt or anyone who might feel hurt right now and ask for God's healing grace for them.

August 21

<u>Issue:</u> **Lack**

"The Lord your God has blessed you in all the work of your hands. He has watched over your journey through this vast desert. These forty years the Lord your God has been with you, and you have not lacked anything." (Deuteronomy 2:7)

<u>Reflection</u>

We humans lack many things in this life: from material things to spiritual and mental strength. Even the rich and the powerful in our world still feel that they lack more worldly stuff and need to desire more. Ironically, what the world lacks the most now and should desire at all times is spiritual richness. But, we believers know that the only one who can fulfill and satisfy what is lacking in us is God. As the Creator and owner of the Universe, God can take care of our needs.

<u>Lord Jesus, I want to see</u>

Jesus, my Security and Hope, everyone comes to you for help and guidance. For you not only can fulfill whatever they might be lacking but also have the words of everlasting life. In the miracles of multiplying the loaves and fishes, the crowds left completely satisfied and still some was left over. I lack many things in my life, but most significantly I lack faith. I pray that you will increase my faith a little more each day and help me learn to trust you more.

<u>Resolution</u>

Today, I will see what I might lack in spiritual richness and come to God to fulfill it for me.

August 22

<u>Issue:</u> **Neighbor**
"Love does no harm to its neighbor. Therefore, love is the fulfillment of the Law." (Romans 13:10)

<u>Reflection</u>
In Jesus' time, the concept of neighbor was defined along the lines of ethnicity, religion, culture, and tradition. Hence, there were parables such as the Good Samaritan to help expand the concept of neighbor and help us to see the image of a neighbor in every human being. For only neighbors were obliged to help one another according to tradition back then. So, it came as a big shock for everyone to learn that a Samaritan would reach out to help a Jew and treat him as his neighbor. People who lived in Jesus' time on earth were challenged to change their old concept of neighbor.

<u>Lord Jesus, I want to see</u>
Jesus, my Faithful and Kind Neighbor, you not only called us to love our neighbors but also challenged us to change our old points of view about who is our neighbor. You ask us to love our neighbors as ourselves. I might not pay enough attention to my neighbors or care enough to help the people around me. But, your Commandment to love my neighbors continues to echo louder in my ears. Help me live up to that Commandment, even when my neighbors do not act like one toward me.

<u>Resolution</u>
Today, I will try to do a good deed for a neighbor or someone else, even if I might not get the same treatment back.

August 23

<u>Issue:</u> **Pleasure**
"At one time we too were foolish, disobedient, deceived, and enslaved by all kinds of passions and pleasures. We lived in malice and envy, being hated and hating one another. But, when the kindness and love of God our Savior appeared, He saved us, not because of righteous things we had done, but because of His mercy..." (Titus 3:3-5)

<u>Reflection</u>
If there is a word that people of our time love to hear, it is definitely the word "pleasure." For most people these days like to have fun and will do anything to get it. Some squander their entire life, even their souls, simply to have some fun or pleasure. They certainly do not realize the consequences of their actions. For their little bit of fun might ruin everything and destroy the lives of others around them as well.

<u>Lord Jesus, I want to see</u>
Jesus, the Joy of my life, you certainly do not object us to having some fun and enjoying our lives. After all, you attended the wedding in Cana and had some fun there. But, you caution us that pleasure should not be allowed go so far as corrupting our souls. I like to have some fun in my life, but it should not amount to the point of destroying my soul. For the true joy in my life should be you and only you.

<u>Resolution</u>
Today, I will review my life to see where I look for pleasure that hurts my soul and try to replace it slowly with better habits.

August 24

Issue: **Refresh**

"I, Paul, am writing this with your own hand. I will pay it back — not to mention that you owe me your very self. I do wish, brothers and sisters, that I may have some benefit from you in the Lord; refresh my heart in Christ." (Philemon 19-20)

Reflection
There is a button on our Windows software program called "refresh." When we push that button, it shuts down the program and immediately brings up a new, updated version. We go through each day with the same routines and get stuck on the same attitudes week after week. Our lives can become boring and monotonous after a while. We need to come to God in prayer and ask God to push our "refresh" button to give us new energy, perspectives, and great excitement to deal with daily issues and challenges in our lives.

Lord Jesus, I want to see
Jesus, Fresh Spring of New Life, you came to bring us new Commandments and fresh perspectives for our spiritual life and relationship with God. This might create some anxieties and concerns on my part. For, like most people, I do not like change. But, with your help and guidance, I will push the "refresh" button and call on you to give me new strength and excitement to take care of my daily duties and challenges.

Resolution
Today, I will depart from my daily routines by going out to dinner with a friend or visiting a church to give me a fresh start in my routine life.

August 25

<u>Issue:</u> **Relief**

"God is just: God will pay back trouble to those who trouble you and give relief to you who are troubled, and to us as well. This will happen when the Lord Jesus is revealed from Heaven in blazing fire with His powerful angels." (2Thessanolians 1:6-7)

<u>Reflection</u>
When we are in trouble or crisis, we pray and are thankful for some relief. God sends us help to deal with the problem at hand. Often that help comes from our families, friends, churches, and charity groups. Sometimes, it comes from unlikely sources. God's people have experienced this first-hand when facing turmoil, hardship, and slavery for years. They called for rain in times of drought, protection in times of plagues and danger, healing in times of sickness and hurt, and freedom in times of slavery. God also brought them some relief through interesting alliances and foreign kings.

Lord Jesus, I want to see
Jesus, my Help and Salvation, amidst my broken world you came to bring me some relief and show me what to do. When God's people faced hunger and sickness, you were there to lend them a helping hand and give them moral support. I might feel scared and alone in this tough and ever-changing world. But, with you by my side, I will always find some relief and have nothing to worry about, even in difficult times.

<u>Resolution</u>
Today, I will ask the Lord for some relief and guidance on a problem that has worried me lately. Then, I will let Him surprise me by revealing His way.

August 26

<u>Issue:</u> **Sign**
"Then Isaiah said: 'Hear now, you house of David. Is it not enough to try the patience of people? Will you try the patience of my God also? Therefore, the Lord Himself will give you a sign: The virgin will be with child and will give birth to a son, and will call Him Immanuel." (Isaiah 7:13-14)

<u>Reflection</u>
Signs are an important part of God's Creation, whereby God and God's creatures communicate to each other in subtle ways. Our society is full of signs and symbols. They help us convey long messages in a shorter form. In fact, many mysterious, lengthy, spiritual messages have been conveyed to us as signs and recorded in the Bible. The story of Joseph and his ten brothers in the Book of Genesis tells us how Joseph became a sign-and-dream interpreter. If we can interpret spiritual signs around us, we can certainly have a fruitful life.

<u>Lord Jesus, I want to see</u>
Jesus, Sign of God's Love for us, quite a few times you have called on the crowd to read the spiritual signs around them and turn their lives back to God. Your whole ministry was focused on pointing out spiritual signs and interpreting them for God's people. I might have closed my eyes to the signs that God has sent me daily to point me on the right path. With your help, I will learn to pay close attention to them and interpret them in the correct way.

<u>Resolution</u>
Today, I will look for a spiritual sign and try to see what God is trying to tell through that sign.

August 27

<u>Issue:</u> **Slander**

"In your hearts, set apart Christ as Lord. Always be prepared to give an answer to everyone who asks you to give the reason for the hope that you have. But, do this with gentleness and respect, keeping a clear conscience, so that those who speak maliciously against your good behavior in Christ may be ashamed of their slander. It is better to suffer for doing good than for doing evil." (1Peter 3:15-17)

<u>Reflection</u>

We live in a time in which people slander freely and accuse one another wrongfully without being held accountable. Usually, they do this out of anger and retribution. What they do not realize is that malicious words can be as deadly as a bullet, an arrow, or a knife. Once words came out of our mouth, we cannot take them back, because the damage has been done. We have destroyed another's reputation and cannot easily restore it. We need more words of kindness and compassion than slander in our world.

Lord Jesus, I want to see

Jesus, the Word of Truth, although you spoke the truth, you tried not to slander or spread bad rumors about people you met. You also called on your disciples not to fight among themselves and to have more love and mercy for one another. Sometimes, I might imitate the world and engage in rumors about someone. Help me avoid this bad habit and speak only gracious and compassionate words about others.

<u>Resolution</u>

Today, I will catch myself from slandering someone. Instead, I will say more words of love and compassion toward people around me.

August 28

Strive

"...Rather, train yourself to be godly. For physical training is of some value. But, godliness has value for all things, holding promise for both the present life and the life to come. This is a trustworthy saying that deserves full acceptance (and for this we labor and strive), that we have put our hope in the living God, who is the savior of all, and especially of those who believe." (1 Timothy 4:7-10)

Reflection

When we want something badly enough, we strive for it. For someone who wants to get to Heaven, this person strives hard for that goal and does everything possible to make it come true. For God's people, the Promised Land was their hope. So, they strived with all their hearts and minds to get there, even though it took them more than forty years. Likewise, if our goal is to grow closer to God and be a good Christian, we will strive our best to achieve this closeness regardless of the costs.

Lord Jesus, I want to see

Jesus, my Lord and Savior, your goal on earth was to save God's people and point them to the Kingdom of Heaven. You strived hard for that goal despite your painful suffering and ultimate sacrifice on the Cross. I might be tempted to set my goals in our secular world and strive for them. But, such goals will soon disappear along with our fragile world. I need to set my goals in the spiritual world, where everything will last forever and bring me true happiness.

Resolution

Today, I will think about something noble and honorable that I can do for people around me and strive to make it come true.

August 29

<u>Issue:</u> **Temperance**

"Teach the older men to be temperate, worth of respect, self-controlled, and sound in faith, love, and endurance. Likewise, teach the older women to be reserved in the way they live, not to be slanderers or addicted to much wine but to teach what is good. Then, they can train the younger women to love their husbands and children, to be self-controlled and pure, to be kind... Similarly, encourage the young men to be self-controlled." (Titus 2:2-6)

<u>Reflection</u>

Temperance is one of the virtues that any good Christian must have. For it teaches us to have self-control and not let our passion or any worldly influences drive us into doing things that we might regret later. The Bible is full of examples of people who lacked temperance and created a series of mistakes that affected them and their future generations negatively. These folks included Adam and Eve, King David, Peter, Paul, and many others. Ironically, our current world seriously lacks self-control and yet it does not teach its young this important virtue or try to promote it at all.

<u>Lord Jesus, I want to see</u>

Jesus, Source of Peace and Guidance, you performed many miracles and shared wonderful teachings with your disciples. But, when they felt you were not warmly welcomed by a Samaritan town and wanted to call down fire from Heaven to destroy it, or when Peter drew his sword to chop off the ear of one of his opponents in the Garden of Gethsemane, you asked them all to take control of themselves and not to engage in physical violence. Help me always be a person of good temperance and peace.

<u>Resolution</u>

Today, I will renounce any act of violence and try to maintain calm and self-control even when I am upset.

August 30

<u>Issue:</u> **Treasure**
"The Kingdom of Heaven is like treasure hidden in a field. When a person found it, one hid it again, and then in one's joy went and sold all one had and bought that field." (Matthew 13:44)

<u>Reflection</u>
We all love to find a treasure in our lifetime and celebrate the wonderful result of that discovery. We certainly jump for joy and do everything possible to protect that treasure. In fact, our life is all about searching for treasures in relationships, jobs, housing, shopping, and so on. We think that the more treasures we find, the happier we will be. But, there is one treasure that everyone would die to have, namely, eternal spring of life. That is what the Samaritan woman at the well and many people in this life have been looking for. That eternal spring will keep them refreshed and young forever.

<u>Lord Jesus, I want to see</u>
Jesus, Eternal Source of Wisdom and Life, without you I would never know how important it is to search for the right treasure. But, you showed me that the eternal life is the key to a fulfilled and happy life here on earth. Perhaps I might have tried to search for treasures in the wrong places like pleasures, material possessions, fame, and so on. Yet, the right place for treasure can only be found in God and the spiritual world. Only there can we find the true eternal spring of life.

<u>Resolution</u>
Today, I will think of something valuable and meaningful in the spiritual world that I can count on as an anchor for my life.

August 31

Issue: **Willingness**

"Command those who are rich in this present world not to be arrogant nor to put their hope in wealth, which is so uncertain, but to put their hope in God, who richly provides us with everything for our enjoyment. Command them to do good, to be rich in good deeds, and to be generous and willing to share. In this way, they will lay up treasure for themselves as a firm foundation for the coming age..." (1 Timothy 6:17-19)

Reflection

We are only willing to do or participate in something when we are pleased with it or at least see some benefit for us in it. In the Bible, we learn that whenever God's people were willing to follow God's way or cooperate with God, they ended up with great results. On the contrary, whenever God's people refused to walk with God, they always landed on their face. But, even with that devastating end, God never forced them to follow His will.

Lord Jesus, I want to see

Jesus, Son of God, you were willing to follow God the Father's plan and offer yourself on the Cross to save us. Even though you did not gain any benefit from that, you were still willing to go through with the whole ordeal of the Passion and the Cross. If the world and I would follow your example and be willing to cooperate with God, as you were, our world would have a lot of wonderful things happen daily and would become a better place. Like Jesus, may I be willing to reach out and help other people in need around me.

Resolution

Today, I will be willing to give someone a hand and follow God's way, even if I might not like it.

September

Lord Jesus,
I Want to See…

September 1

<u>Issue:</u> **Build**

"For God did not appoint us to suffer wrath but to receive salvation through our Lord Jesus Christ. He died for us so that whether we are awake or asleep, we may live together with Him. Therefore, encourage one another and build each other up, just as in fact you are doing." (1 Thessalonians 5:9-11)

<u>Reflection</u>

Since the beginning of Creation, God has continued to build our world. Contrary to public opinion, God does not go on a rampage and destroy Creation one part after another because of the world's sins. No, our God does not do that. Instead, our God sent God's only Son to save us and re-build out broken relationship. In fact, every day our God searches out the lost and the broken so that they can be restored and returned to the fold.

Lord Jesus, I want to see

Jesus, the Builder of the Church, you gathered your Church members who were scattered by sins and darkness and single-handedly built the Christian faith community. In that process, you have tried to build up each member by healing, feeding, and giving hope to each broken person. I have grown up in a society that likes to destroy and throw things away. With your help and example, I promise to build up things wherever I go and never break down anything.

<u>Resolution</u>

Today, I will try to build up a good habit or a broken relationship by doing something kind and humbly letting God's love and mercy guide me.

September 2

<u>Issue:</u> **Commitment**

"If you suffer as a Christian, do not be ashamed, but praise God that you bear that name... And if it is hard for the righteous to be saved, what will become of the ungodly and the sinner? So then, those who suffer according to God's will should commit themselves to their faithful Creator and continue to do good." (1Peter 4:16-19)

<u>Reflection</u>

Commitment is one of the words that we humans have struggled to honor and appreciate throughout our human history, especially in our modern times. People today find it very difficult to commit themselves to a relationship, a calling, a duty, or service to a charity group. Everyone is fearful of commitment and do not see it as a badge of honor and a challenge. Although God's people struggle to commit themselves to God, God has never failed to be faithful to them and give help and guidance.

<u>Lord Jesus, I want to see</u>

Jesus, my Faithful Lord, you were sent for the mission of my salvation and are always committed to that calling even when things got difficult and you had to face death and the Cross. I might be influenced by the thinking of my culture and scared of a commitment. But, with your example and encouragement, I will try to live a life of commitment and not be afraid to see things through until the end.

<u>Resolution</u>

Today, I will sign up for some charity work and commit myself to see it through for a long time.

September 3

<u>Issue:</u> **Create**

"For it is by grace you have been saved, through faith – and this not from yourselves, it is the gift of God – not by works, so that no one can boast. For we are God's workmanship, created in Christ Jesus to do good works, which God prepared in advance for us to do." (Ephesians 2:8-10)

<u>Reflection</u>
If we have ever been involved in creating something new, we see what an exciting and amazing process it is. When we create something, we start from nothing and bring into existence something new that was never there before. A creator puts his/her whole heart and soul into amazing work and slowly sees its miraculous transformation. We can see the honor and joy on the face of God on the sixth day or of the parents of a newly-born child when they all gaze on their new creation.

<u>Lord Jesus, I want to see</u>
Jesus, the Master of God's New Creation, you restored the old order and brought us a new Creation with your blood and Cross. You continue to create something new every day through your healing grace and miracle. When I am afraid to create new ideas and think differently with the help of love, kindness, or compassion, help me overcome the fear of criticism or being different and just do it. Thank you for creating me in your own image, yet still making me unique.

<u>Resolution</u>
Today, I will create something new in my home, work, or church such as a positive and hopeful attitude by being kind and nice to others and criticizing less.

September 4

Issue: **Criticize**

"We want to avoid any criticism of the way we administer this liberal gift. For we are taking pains to do what is right; it is not only in the eyes of the Lord but also in the eyes of people." (2Corinthians 8:20-21)

Reflection

If there is one thing we humans are very good at, it is criticizing. People often do not hesitate to voice criticism about anyone over anything. Yet, they give very little praise or compliments to others. Indeed, God's people constantly criticized and complained to God even after everything God had given them, including manna and quails. Surely, God's people need to change their critical and negative attitude and be more uplifting and positive. For a critical person always brings about resentment, bitterness, quarrels, and division.

Lord Jesus, I want to see

Jesus, the Gentle and Loving Voice of God, you were criticized relentlessly by the religious leaders and your own people over all sorts of things. Yet, you were still able to maintain a dignified manner and pray for your opponents, "Father, forgive them, they know not what they do." (Luke 23:34) Most of us would be tempted to engage in a war of words with our criticizers and fight with them. I could do exactly that and become very critical of everything around me. But, with your help and example, I will always take the high road and try to be positive and solution-oriented instead.

Resolution

Today, I will stop being critical of everyone and everything and try to be uplifting and see something good in others.

September 5

<u>Issue:</u> **Determined**

"From one man God made every nation of human race so that they should inhabit the whole earth; and God determined the times set for them and the exact places where they should live. God did this so that all would seek God and perhaps reach out for God and find God, though God is not far from each one of us." (Acts 17:26-27)

<u>Reflection</u>

When we are determined to do something, we set our minds and hearts on it and get it done. That is what champions do. They commit themselves to their goal or mission and follow through. God's people certainly had one important goal in mind, namely, to make it to the Promised Land. Although they had to face all sorts of difficulties, including forty years wandering in the desert, they were determined to get there one way or another.

Lord Jesus, I want to see

Jesus, my Cheerleader and Supporter, you were given the tough mission of human salvation and calling God's people back to the fold. That mission is quite daunting and scary at first look. Yet, you were determined to see it through. Surrounded by many hardships and temptations, I surely have had moments of hopelessness and wanted to give up on you and Heaven. But with your support and encouragement, I am determined to stay close to you and make it to Heaven at the end of my life on earth.

<u>Resolution</u>

Today, I will review my relationship with Jesus and be determined to make it stronger by committing myself to a good, consistent prayer life.

September 6

Issue: **Diligence**
"God is not unjust; God will not forget your work and the love you have shown to the Lord as you have helped God's people and continue to help them. We want each of you to show this same diligence to the very end, in order to make your hope sure. We do not want you to become lazy, but to imitate those who through faith and patience inherit what has been promised." (Hebrews 6:10-12)

Reflection
Every time we hear the term "diligent," we are immediately reminded of King Herod's advice to the Magi, "Go and search diligently for the newborn King. When you have found him, bring me word, that I too may go and pay Him tribute." (Matthew 2:8) The Magi did look diligently for Baby Jesus and found Him. A diligent student or employee is someone who works hard and meticulously on an assigned project. With remarkable work, a diligent worker will be rewarded handsomely in the end. This work ethic is something we should imitate.

Lord Jesus, I want to see
Jesus, Faithful Son of God, you always conducted your ministry in a diligent manner. You never performed a miracle or a teaching halfway through and then abandoned it. I might feel lukewarm toward faith and God's work. I might be distracted by other worldly allurements. But with your guidance and help, I will commit myself to your mission and work diligently. I promise not to live out my faith only half-heartedly and abandon it in tough times.

Resolution
Today, I will be diligent in my work for God and Heaven by exploring various ways to show God to the world.

September 7

<u>Issue:</u> **Enterprising**
"The master commended the dishonest manager because he was enterprising. For the people of this world are more shrewd in dealing with their own kind than children of the light. I tell you, use worldly wealth to gain friends for yourselves, so that when it is gone, you will be welcomed into eternal dwellings." (Luke 16:8-9)

<u>Reflection</u>
Enterprising might sound like something out of a Star Trek movie. But, it has actually been used in the Gospels to describe a manager who was let go from his job and decided to call in all his boss' debtors and write down a lesser amount. He did that to win favor from the public as he prepared for being released from his current job. That way, he might get hired for a new job. Even though his actions conjure up cheating and stealing and deserve severe punishment, Jesus praised him for his enterprising actions and initiative.

<u>Lord Jesus, I want to see</u>
Jesus, Merciful Master, you were not only open to the story of the enterprising manager but also encouraging us to model his thinking and take the same initiative in preparing ourselves for what is coming after this life. I might be thinking only about now and not concerned about tomorrow and eternal life. But, with the help of the word "enterprising," you call us to be shrewd and prepared for Heaven and eternal life by making the best use of what was given to us here on earth.

<u>Resolution</u>
Today, I will figure out a way to win favor for myself when standing before God on the Last Day.

September 8

<u>Issue:</u> **Focused**
"They devoted themselves to the apostles' teaching and to the fellowship, to the breaking of bread and to prayer... All the believers were together and had everything in common... Every day they continued to meet together in the Temple courts. They broke bread in their homes and ate together with glad and sincere hearts praising God and enjoying the favor of all the people..." (Acts 2:42-47)

<u>Reflection</u>
We can recall times that we focused on something or someone because that thing or person mattered to us. When we care about something or someone, we usually concentrate our whole mind and soul on that thing or person. The result is a stronger bond with that subject; nothing can distract us from it. This is exactly what we need to do with our spiritual life and our relationship with God. We must focus on our soul and do everything possible to grow closer to God. This should matter to us and concern us beyond mundane things.

<u>Lord Jesus, I want to see</u>
Jesus, the Center of my life, you were always concerned about Heaven and the spiritual life. Despite all the good deeds you did for God's people, you never failed to point them to the importance of taking care of their souls and spiritual life. Seeing how focused you were on that subject, it must matter a lot to you, and I should take note of that. Perhaps I get distracted by many worldly things daily. It is time for me to focus on things that matter beyond my present life.

<u>Resolution</u>
Today, I will focus on things that bring me true peace and happiness, such as volunteering for some charity group.

September 9

Friendly

"My command is this: Love each other as I have loved you. Greater love has no one than this; that one lay down one's life for one's friends. You are my friends if you do what I [Jesus] command." (John 15:12-14)

Reflection
In our dog-eat-dog world, it is sometimes considered unwise for someone to be friendly with his/her neighbors. Some people think everyone should be well-guarded and mean to one another if they want to survive another day in this jungle of life. We wonder why our world can be so mean and vicious. The Bible, on the other hand, certainly wants us to be different from our world and calls us to be friendly to each other. For that is how we can show God's love to the world and be rewarded for our work in this life and the next.

Lord Jesus, I want to see
Jesus, the Living Proof of God's love, you were friendly with everyone around you, especially tax collectors and sinners. Most people avoid those folks and yet you hung around and ate with them. You wanted to show them God's love and bring them back to the fold. I sometimes adopt the attitude of the world and act mean toward my neighbors. But, with your example and encouragement, I will try to be friendly to others even on bad days or when I am being mistreated by the world.

Resolution
Today, I will try to greet everyone I might encounter throughout the day with a smile and show God's love to them.

September 10

Issue: **Hospitality**

"The end of all things is near. Therefore, be clear minded and self-controlled so that you can pray. Above all, love each other deeply, because love covers over a multitude of sins. Offer hospitality to one another without grumbling." (1Peter 4:7-9)

Reflection

The Bible is full of examples of hospitality. Because of that virtue, God's people had many encounters with God and received many blessings as well. A good example of good hospitality can be found in Abraham when he saw three strangers on a hot day who needed some water and food. He decided to welcome them into his home. The result of that was their blessing on Sarah to conceive on her old age, and that she did!

Lord Jesus, I want to see

Jesus, Kind and Loving God, you extended hospitality not only to your disciples at first encounter but also strangers throughout your ministry on earth. You went out of your way to offer food and drink to hungry and weary crowds when your disciples wanted to dismiss them. Sometimes I want to take the easy way out and simply care about myself. But, your example compels me to be hospitable to strangers and others around me, regardless of what I might receive in return. By doing that, I help show the world your presence and love.

Resolution

Today, I will reach out to welcome someone warmly to my home, work, or church and be kind to that person without any bias.

September 11

Issue: **Instrument of God**

"But, the Lord said to Ananias, 'Go! This man is my chosen instrument to carry my name before the Gentiles and their kings before the people of Israel. I will show him how much he must suffer for my name.'" (Acts 9:15-16)

Reflection

One of the big mistakes our world makes is to assume that it owns everything. Hence, people think they can do anything they want with their lives. Certainly, it gets worse in modern times as our world turns secular and its members often say, "It is my life. I can do whatever I like with it." Many choose to keep God's blessings all to themselves and not share anything with other misfortunates around them. What our world forgets is that God owns everything, and without God all things would cease to exist.

Lord Jesus, I want to see

Jesus, Humble Servant of God, you told many parables of stewardship. You called on God's people to share God's blessings with others and make good use of them. You were always willing to reach out to the poor and the misfortunate to give them a hand. Help me realize that I am an Instrument of God and should try to share God's blessings for me with others. By doing that, I will learn to be a good steward and allow God to touch and heal our broken world.

Resolution

Today, I will try to be an Instrument of God by reaching out to someone in need and help that person with a kind deed.

September 12

Issue: **Kindness**

"The Lord's servant must not quarrel; instead, one must be kind to every-one, able to teach, not resentful. Those who oppose you, you must gently instruct, in the hope that God will grant them repentance leading them to the knowledge of the truth..." (2Timothy 2:24-25)

Reflection

Kindness adds a wonderful aroma to our world. We cannot imagine what our world would be like if there was no more kindness in it. Everyone would be mean to each other and act selfishly toward his/her neighbors. We can say that kindness is what distinguishes us and sep-arates us from the animal world. The Bible gives us numerous exam-ples of kindness, and the Saints are certainly masters of this virtue.

Lord Jesus, I want to see

Jesus, Kind and Loving God, you have shown us one example after another of kindness in the Gospels. Yet, you never tired of it. For you knew that kindness can conquer sins and darkness and help bring a lost sheep back to the fold. There is a saying, "It is easier to win over people with kindness than with vinegar." Like the world, I might think that the best way to earn respect is to overpower and intimidate a person. But, you have shown us that kindness and love are how I can earn respect from people around me.

Resolution

Today, I will be kind to someone to show God's love and witness God's presence to that person and the world.

September 13

Issue: **Knowledge**
"Therefore dear friend, since you already know this, be on your guard so that you may not be carried away by the error of lawless people and fall from your secure position. But, grow in the grace and knowledge of our Lord and Savior Jesus Christ. To Him be glory both now and forever! Amen." (2Peter 3:17-18)

Reflection
A wise person once said, "Knowledge is the key to success." Over the years, that saying has proven to be true. Hence, every industry on earth, especially science and technology, has spent significant time, effort, and resources to research and advance its knowledge. Unfortunately, in the spiritual area, we have not done a good job studying and increasing our knowledge. We have spent very little time, effort, and resources on research and development in spirituality and the faith life. It is no wonder there is a lack of knowledge and interest in the soul and spirit in our modern times.

Lord Jesus, I want to see
Jesus, the Incarnated Word of God, you came not only to save us but also to increase our knowledge and love of God. You spent much time teaching us about God and opening our hearts and minds to learn more about the spiritual world. I might not be interested in the spiritual world yet. But with your help and guidance, I will learn more about your mysterious ways and increase my knowledge of you and the spiritual world over time.

Resolution
Today, I will think of some spiritual matter of which I might lack some knowledge and then spend some time studying it.

September 14

Issue: **Learn**
"But as for you, continue in what you have learned and have become convinced of, because you know those from whom you learned it, and how from infancy you have known the Holy Scriptures, which are able to make you wise from salvation through faith in Christ Jesus." (2 Timothy 3: 14-15)

Reflection
Our whole life is about learning and getting to know ourselves and the whole world better. The moment we stop learning, we become arrogant and ignorant about everything. Even one of the smartest people in the world—Albert Einstein—never stopped learning and trying to solve the mysteries of the universe. In that process, Einstein realized that there must be a very intelligent person who created our wonderful universe and made everything got it work together remarkably well through the complex and mysterious laws of physics. He also admitted that there are many more mysteries of the universe yet for us to discover.

Lord Jesus, I want to see
Jesus, the Wise Rabbi of all times, you are the Albert Einstein of the spiritual world. You gave us wonderful teachings and insights about that mysterious world. You also called us to keep studying and discovering more about God and the Spirit. Living in a busy world, I often have no time to learn more about you and the spiritual world. Help me make time to dig deeper into the mystery of God and be curious about the spiritual life.

Resolution
Today, I will try to learn one thing about God or the spiritual world.

September 15

<u>Issue:</u> **Materialism**

"Do not store up for yourselves treasures on earth, where moth and rust destroy, and where thieves break in and steal. But, store up for yourselves treasures in Heaven, where moth and rust do not destroy, and where thieves do not break in and steal." (Matthew 6:19-20)

<u>Reflection</u>

People who have many possessions tend to worry more than people who have less. For they must figure out how to protect those treasures from thieves and robbers. They also want to grow their piles of wealth. This can lead to all sorts of other problems such as greed, envy, self-ishness, cheating, stealing, killing, and so on. Meanwhile, they neglect other aspects of life such as their souls and spiritual life. Without proper care and attention, their souls or spirit will wither and die.

<u>Lord Jesus, I want to see</u>

Jesus, my Spiritual Master, you warned us about the danger and the corrupting nature of material possessions. They can overtake our whole life and make us completely attached to this present world. What you want us to do is to make good use of God's blessings for us in this life and try to secure for ourselves a place in the spiritual world and the eternal life. Like the rich young man in the Gospel, I might want to have the eternal life and still try to hang on to my material things. I must detach myself from this world if I would like to have a foot in the next one.

<u>Resolution</u>

Today, I will simplify my life and donate some material things I pos-sess to a charity and not replace them with something else.

September 16

<u>Issue:</u> **Meaning**
"They read from the Book of the Law of God, making it clear and giving the meaning so that the people could understand what was being read."
(Nehemiah 8:8)

<u>Reflection</u>
If we read a book or watch a movie and there is no point to it, we get bored and want to stop. Likewise, our life must have a meaning or purpose if we want it to continue on and become fruitful. Unfortunately, many folks of our time, especially youth, cannot find meaning for their lives and end up taking their own lives. They forget that the best way to have a meaningful life is with the help of faith and religion. Everything else in this world will eventually lose its attraction and fade away.

<u>Lord Jesus, I want to see</u>
Jesus, my Reason and Guide in this life, you helped refocus and bring meaning to the life of many people. Even the rich and the powerful sought you to help re-evaluate their lives and find new meaning for them. I sometimes get stuck with my busy lifestyle and do not seem to have a real purpose for my life. But, with your help and encouragement, I will commit myself to a higher calling such as caring for the sick or feeding the hungry and make my life more meaningful.

<u>Resolution</u>
Today, I will sign up and volunteer for a church or charity group to give meaning and reason to my life.

September 17

Issue: **Motivate**

"My Conscience is clear, but that does not make me innocent. It is the Lord who judges me. Therefore, judge nothing before the appointed time; wait till the Lord comes. He will bring to light what is hidden in darkness and will expose the motives of human hearts. At that time, each will receive one's praise from God." (1 Corinthians 4:4-5)

Reflection

The reason we need a coach, teacher, minister, priest, nun, monk, or deacon in our lives is because we want those people to motivate us and get us to do the right things. Without their voice of challenge and encouragement, we would never have the reason or take the initiative to do something good. During the times of the Old Testament, we had great figures like Abraham and Moses to help motivate God's people along their journey to the Promised Land. I cannot imagine where God's people might have ended up without these motivators.

Lord Jesus, I want to see

Jesus, my Coach and Teacher, you relentlessly called on your disciples to increase their prayer life and motivated them to do good things for others through your own example. Your motivation has changed many lives and created a whole generation of motivators that we call Saints in the life of the Church. With your help and the encouragement of the Saints, I will commit myself to a good faith life and follow you all the way to the end despite my life challenges.

Resolution

Today, I will try to motivate someone at home, work, church, or the store by sharing a word of praise or a compliment.

September 18

<u>Issue:</u> **Persevere**

"...We rejoice in the hope of the glory of God. Not only so, but we also rejoice in our sufferings, because we know that suffering produces perseverance; perseverance, character; and character, hope. And hope does not disappoint us." (Romans 5:2-5)

<u>Reflection</u>

Over the years, we humans have conquered the power of darkness and created champions through perseverance. In fact, what distinguishes humans from the animal world is the ability to persevere. There are many examples in the Bible that show us the amazing power of this virtue. The great example relates to how God's people persevered and endured all sorts of hardships before they made it to the Promised Land.

Lord Jesus, I want to see

Jesus, Faithful and Devoted Lord, you certainly faced many challenges during your ministry. Yet, you persevered and completed your mission. You also shared the story of the widow who kept coming to a judge and asked him to hear her case to illustrate to God's people that they must persevere in their prayers. I might want to give up on my prayers or faith life when things do not go my way. But, with you by my side, I will persevere in my faith life and keep on praying until I make it to your Kingdom.

<u>Resolution</u>

Today, I will review what I might have given up lately for God's sake and, with God's help, I vow to persevere and try to complete it.

September 19

<u>Issue:</u> **Problem**

"We sent Timothy, who is our brother and God's fellow worker in spreading the Gospel of Christ, to strengthen and encourage you in your faith, so that no one would be unsettled by these trials. You know quite well that we were destined for them. In fact, when we were with you, we kept telling you that we would be persecuted. And it turned out that way..." (1 Thessalonians 3:2-4)

<u>Reflection</u>

We all face with numerous problems daily and throughout our lives. It is part of our imperfect life here on earth. Over the years, we have seen many Saints and heroes created because of the ways they faced their daily problems. These folks do not run away from their problems or become bitter and angry about them. Rather, they embraced them with courage and trust. They have always trusted that their God would come to help them and not abandon them. Mother Teresa was one of these trusting folks who gave us this advice, "Do not pray that your life is problem-free. Rather, pray that you would be given enough strength to deal with your problems."

Lord Jesus, I want to see

Jesus, my Help and Guide, you were not born with a problem-free life, even though you were the Son of God. You always taught us to follow God's will and not let our life's problems define us. I might complain or question my faith when facing problems in my life. Help me learn to trust you more and use those trial moments to make me a stronger and more compassionate person.

<u>Resolution</u>

Today, I will face the problems of the day head on without any fear or worry. I will let God guide me through and solve my problems.

September 20

Issue: **Reasonable**

"...Always be prepared to give an answer to everyone who asks you to give the reason for the hope that you have. But, do this with gentleness and respect, keeping a clear conscience, so that those who speak maliciously against your good behavior in Christ may be ashamed of their slander."
(1Peter 3:15-16)

Reflection

We humans love to see miracles and expect something out of nothing. Sometimes our prayers can become unreasonable and we demand that God do things our way. If things do not turn out the way we want, we question God's power and assume that we know best. The problem with that logic is that we think we are in control. But the truth is that we are not. Ironically, this is the logic we have heard a lot these days from the world. We must help others to be realistic and reasonable with their thinking and expectations.

Lord Jesus, I want to see

Jesus, my Guide and Compass, you definitely have taught us many things and performed numerous miracles during your ministry. But, most of your miracles were done with existing things such as a boy with five loaves and two fishes. By giving us that fact, the Gospel writers want us to be reasonable and realistic with expectations. Sometimes I might be unreasonable in my thinking about you and others. Help me learn to meet others halfway and most importantly follow your way and not mine.

Resolution

Today, I will try not to demand too much from God and others. Rather, I will accept whatever blessings God might send my way this day.

September 21

Meditate

"I will remember the deeds of the Lord; yes I will remember your miracles of long ago. I will meditate on all your works and consider all your mighty deeds." (Psalms 77:11-12)

Reflection
Our secular and materialistic world finally realizes the importance of meditation and spiritual reflection as it sees yoga classes and mind-centered workshops pop up all over the place. Meditation is not something we do for fun or some voodoo we perform for show. Rather, it is an essential part of spiritual exercises and a healthy spiritual life. If we go to the YMCA or fitness places to exercise our bodies and get in good shape, should we not do the same for our spirit? Meditation can do the same for our spirit that aerobics does for our heart.

Lord Jesus, I want to see
Jesus, my Spiritual Master and Coach, you continuously reminded God's people to take good care of their spiritual life, even when you fed them or healed their physical ailments. Indeed, we do not feel good if our spirit is under the weather or in bad shape. I might not see my spirit, but I know how I feel when my spirit is down. It is time for me to take good care of my spirit and get it in great shape beginning with serious and daily meditation. I could also spend more time praying and reflecting.

Resolution
Today, I will spend about ten minutes in prayer and meditation with the Bible and let God take away all my worries and anything that is bothering me.

September 22

Issue: **Responsible**
"When the Jews opposed Paul and became abusive, he shook out his clothes in protest and said to them, 'Your blood be on your own heads! I am clear of my responsibility. From now on, I will go to the Gentiles.'" (Acts 18:6)

Reflection

It is difficult for us to see someone take responsibility for something, whether it is good or bad, especially in our day and age. At the beginning of Creation, we humans, represented by Adam and Eve, did not take responsibility for the bad act of disobedience and started blaming our behavior on someone and something else. That bad habit has continued down to our present time, as everyone still resists being a responsible person at home or work. But, being responsible means that one takes pride and ownership in one's duty or whatever one is doing.

Lord Jesus, I want to see

Jesus, Trustworthy Son of God, you took your responsibility for your mission seriously and never disappointed God the Father. As a Good Shepherd, you take great care of your sheep and are responsible for every one of us. You never blame the lost sheep on someone else, but go out to look for it yourself. I might try to avoid responsibilities or being a responsible person. But, with your example and encouragement, I will take pride in being a responsible person at home, work, church, and whatever duty for which I might volunteer.

Resolution

Today, I will try to be a responsible person on a certain duty and not be afraid of its consequences, but see it through to the end.

September 23

"Brothers and sisters, as an example of patience in the face of suffering, take the prophets who spoke in the name of the Lord. As you know, we consider blessed those who have persevered. You have heard of Job's perseverance and have seen what the Lord finally brought about..." (James 5:10-11)

Reflection

If there is one thing our world lacks these days, it would be good spiritual examples or role models. These are living individuals to whom our children and grandchildren can relate and look up to. They should possess great Christian values, inspire our young to love God and their neighbors, and carry the Church banner into the next century. Without inspiring role models, the Church will lose the competition with the world of sports heroes and pop stars and gradually become a thing of the past.

Lord Jesus, I want to see

Jesus, my Shining Star and Inspiring Example, you attracted a group of faithful followers and drew a big crowd wherever you went. You provide such a wonderful role model that many of John the Baptist's disciples left him and followed you. I might not realize the importance and impact of being a good example of you to my family, my friends, and other people around me. But, if I do not try to be a great role model in the matter of my faith, my family and the world will look for one elsewhere and end up with a wrong role model.

Resolution

Today, I will learn to be a good example of faith for my family and the world by being a kind Christian and loving God with all my heart and soul.

September 24

Security
"Anyone who fears the Lord has a secure fortress, and for one's children it will be a great refuge." (Proverbs 14:26)

Reflection
Most people would love to have a financially secure lifestyle. But, with all the violence and terrorism happening around the world these days, many of us pray for safe protection and good security. For God's people, the only one who has consistently been their protector and defender is the Lord God. Throughout the people's history of slavery and wrongful alliances, God was always by their side to defend them and was the last one who brought them security. For most of us, God is also the one who gives us physical and financial security in the end.

Lord Jesus, I want to see
Jesus, my Shield and Fortress, you are often concerned about the welfare and security of God's people. During your ministry on earth, you reached out to feed the hungry and drove out demons and evil spirits from their lives. Like God's people, I certainly can count on you to provide me with security in this life and the next. With you by my side, I will feel secure from all evil doers and the power of darkness, even ISIS.

Resolution
Today, I will come to you, Lord, in prayer if I feel insecure in my life or anxious about something.

September 25

<u>Issue:</u> **Serenity**

"They cried out to the Lord in their trouble, and the Lord brought them out of their distress. The Lord stilled the storm to a whisper; the waves of the sea were hushed. They were glad when it grew calm and the Lord guided them to their desired haven." (Psalms 107:28)

<u>Reflection</u>

Our life can seem like a whirlwind at times. But, everything could quickly turn into a violent storm when we must face tragedies and turmoil. Amidst all that chaos and uncertainty, we hope for a serene moment and peace. For our souls and spirits cannot survive in a constantly noisy and tumultuous world. Hence, it does not make sense for us to engage with people who want to create violence and cause tragedies in the lives of others. Only evil people want such things.

<u>Lord Jesus, I want to see</u>

Jesus, Source of Peace and comfort, you quieted the wind and calmed the water when the boat of your disciples ran into a violent storm. You also brought serenity to many folks who were possessed by the demons and evil spirits. I might feel anxious and overwhelmed by life's pressures and other burdens. By staying close to you, I will feel much more serene and safer, because you will help take away all of my worries and anxieties.

<u>Resolution</u>

Today, I will come to you, Lord, in prayer to find a serene moment and be taken away from any stress or pressure for a while.

September 26

Solidarity

"As a prisoner for the Lord, I [Paul] urge you to live a life worthy of the calling you have received. Be completely humble and gentle; be patient, bearing with one another in love. Make every effort to keep the unity of the Spirit through the bond of peace." (Ephesians 4:1-3)

Reflection

Living in an individualistic society like ours, it is difficult for people to see the importance of coming together and uniting in a community like the Church. The only example of a good union we can see is the Holy Trinity. The spirit of solidarity between the three persons of the Holy Trinity is remarkable. Other than that, people only come together when their safety is threatened or after there is a horrendous tragedy. In either case, the spirit of solidarity only comes about when people can see benefits to it.

Lord Jesus, I want to see

Jesus, Second Person of the Holy Trinity, you certainly have a strong bond with the other two persons of the Godhead. But, you also have solidarity with the poor and the misfortunate, as you went out of your way to take good care of them during your time on earth. I might feel far removed from those folks or the whole concept of solidarity. But, with your example and teaching, I will follow your way and form the same solidarity as you did.

Resolution

Today, I will form a solidarity with my family or best friends, such that nothing in this life can break it.

September 27

<u>Issue:</u> **Steadfast**

"And the God of all grace, who called you to God's eternal glory in Christ, after you have suffered a little while, will restore you and make you strong, firm, and steadfast. To God be the power for ever and ever. Amen." (1Peter 5:10-11)

<u>Reflection</u>
If one thing saved God's people throughout their tumultuous history, it was their steadfast faith in God. Despite their pains of slavery and daily difficulties, they put their total trust and hope in the Lord to remain close to Him. Eventually, their prayers were answered, and they were freed from bondage and able to rebuild their country.

<u>Lord Jesus, I want to see</u>
Jesus, my Lord and my God, throughout your ministry you healed many afflicted souls and performed many miracles for God's people on one condition. That is, you always requested that they have some faith. You also called on your disciples to remain steadfast in prayer upon your departure for Heaven in order to conquer the power of darkness. Sometimes my faith might be shaken due to tragedies, and my prayer life might slack off due to my busy schedule. But with your grace, I will keep a strong and steadfast faith in you.

<u>Resolution</u>
Today, I will spend an extra five minutes with my daily prayer to assure a steadfast relationship with my Lord Jesus.

September 28

<u>Issue:</u> **Strength**

"I am not saying this because I am in need, for I have learned to be content whatever the circumstances. I know what it is to be in need, and I know what it is to be in need, and I know what it is to have plenty. I have learned the secret of being content in any and every situation, whether well fed or hungry, whether living in plenty or in want. I can do everything through Him who gives me strength." (Philippians 4:11-13)

<u>Reflection</u>

We all have our own strengths and weaknesses. It is the goal of God's people to reduce their weaknesses and increase their strength with the help of God's grace. For that is how they will defeat the power of darkness and become more like our God. Furthermore, by being close to God, we will have the strength to endure our journey of faith and deal with other challenges along the way.

Lord Jesus, I want to see

Jesus, my Strength and Help, you did many good deeds and miracles for God's people and shared the Good News with them as well. But ultimately, what you did was restore their strength and hope in God. I often feel weak and depleted with my daily burdens and life's pressures. I am also surrounded by all sorts of worldly temptations. Without your help and strength, I cannot move on and will collapse soon. Help my weak faith and strengthen my fragile spirit, Lord.

<u>Resolution</u>

Today, I will gain some strength from the Lord by spending some time with Him in prayer and let Him restore me.

September 29

"Surely, God will save you from the fowler's snare and from the deadly pestilence. God will cover you with God's feathers, and under God's wings you will find refuge; God's faithfulness will be your shield and rampart. You will not fear the terror of night, nor the arrow that flies by day, nor the pestilence that stalks in the darkness, nor the plague that destroys at midday." (Psalms 91:3-6)

Reflection

Terror is certainly on the mind of a lot of people these days. Everywhere we look, there are all kinds of violent acts and killing of innocent victims. We feel scared, vulnerable, and insecure. Even our government and the best security teams cannot protect us from these acts of terror or reduce them somehow. Yet, terrorism comes about because of hatred and anger and continues to thrive in a world that embraces death over life, violence over peace. We believers count on God for true protection from terrorism and putting an end to it through a life of love and peace.

Lord Jesus, I want to see

Jesus, Prince of Peace, you always called on your disciples to live a life of love, mercy, forgiveness, and peace. Hence, you commanded Peter to put away his sword when he tried to carry out terror and violence against your enemies. I do not like acts of terrorism carried out against my neighbors. Cure me from any thoughts and acts of violence and evil. Help me embrace your attitude of love and peace and try to share it with the world.

Resolution

Today, I will examine my thoughts, acts, and words for any hints of violence and terror and try to avoid them.

September 30

<u>Issue:</u> **Thoughtful**
"The faithless will be fully repaid for their ways, and the good person rewarded for his/her. A simple person believes anything, but a prudent person gives thought to one's steps. A wise person fears the Lord and shuns evil, but a fool is hot headed and reckless." (Proverbs 14:14-16)

<u>Reflection</u>
We appreciate thoughtful acts and love thoughtful folks. For they make us feel good and reflect a Christ-like attitude. When the Magi saw a strange star indicating the birth of a new king, they brought gifts and paid tribute to Baby Jesus in Bethlehem. What they did was truly a thoughtful act. Similarly, when Mary heard that her cousin Elizabeth was blessed with the conception of John the Baptist in her old age, she set out on a long, dangerous journey to rejoice with her and take care of her. What Mary did was indeed a thoughtful act. These acts are praiseworthy and have the potential power to change our world and humanity for the better.

Lord Jesus, I want to see
Jesus, Kind and Caring God, you did so many thoughtful acts for God's people during your ministry and conveyed God's love to the world effectively that way. Through those profound acts of kindness, you called on our world to live by the law of love. Sometimes, I can be inconsiderate and take you and my loved ones for granted. But with your example and challenge, I will try to be a thoughtful person in words and deeds to everyone around me.

<u>Resolution</u>
Today, I will try to give people around me a helping hand or perform an act of kindness for someone without being asked.

October

Lord Jesus,
I Want to See…

October 1

<u>Issue:</u> **Abandoned**

"…I saw the Lord always before me. Because He is at my right hand, I will not be shaken. Therefore, my heart is glad and my tongue rejoices; my body also will live in hope, because you will not abandon me to the grave, nor will you let your Holy One see decay. You have made known to me the paths of life; you will fill me with joy in your presence." (Acts 2:25-28)

<u>Reflection</u>

When Jesus was left hanging high on the Cross for death, He cried out, "Father, why have you forsaken me?" Clearly, Jesus felt abandoned and distraught. That feeling is something none of us would ever want to have. We do not want to be alone and rejected or feel that everyone is against us. Yet, our world has continuously treated certain groups of people in society that way. In fact, we often abandon our elderly and veterans because they are a bit too inconvenient and overwhelming for us to deal with.

<u>**Lord Jesus, I want to see**</u>

Jesus, my Lord and Savior, you personally experienced first-hand how it felt to be abandoned. You felt unloved, rejected, scared, and alone. It is certainly not a good feeling. I do not want my God or my loved ones to abandon me. Sadly, I sometimes have done that exact thing to you and others without a second thought. With your grace, I will try not to abandon you when I am busy or when everything is going well. Nor will I abandon my loved ones and the misfortunate.

<u>Resolution</u>

Today, I will call or write to someone in my circle of family and friends with whom I have not had contact for some time.

October 2

<u>Issue:</u> **Accountable**

"Nor we know that whatever the Law says, it says to those who are under the Law, so that every mouth may be silenced and the whole world held accountable to God. Therefore, no one will be declared righteous in one's sight by observing the Law; rather through the Law we become conscious of sin." (Romans 3:19-20)

<u>Reflection</u>
One of the themes we hear a lot in the Bible is accountability. Apparently, our world has not been able to hold everyone accountable for their actions with its human system of justice. The rich and the powerful seem to get way with evil acts and keep on oppressing the poor and the lowly. Surely, there is no accountability or justice in our world. But, God's wheel of justice slowly turns things around and firmly holds everyone accountable for their actions without any partiality.

Lord Jesus, I want to see

Jesus, Judge of the Living and the Dead, although you are merciful, you constantly call on God's people to turn their lives around and be accountable for their actions. Like Adam and Eve or Cain after doing something bad, I might think I can get away with something I did that was wrong. But with your counsel, I will follow an honest lifestyle and hold myself accountable for all my actions.

<u>Resolution</u>
Today, I will say I'm sorry for something wrong I have done to someone and repay what I took from someone.

October 3

<u>Issue:</u> **Blame**

"Do everything without complaining or arguing so that you may become blameless and pure children of God without fault in a crooked and depraved generation, in which you shine like stars in the universe as you hold out the word of life – in order that I may boast on the day of Christ that I did not run or labor for nothing." (Philippians 2:14-16)

<u>Reflection</u>
It's almost funny to see many folks in our world—from an alleged perpetrator to our Congress and politicians—blame everyone else except themselves for their wrongful acts. What they cannot see is that the whole world is watching them and our children slowly imitate their actions. They do not know how to apologize and quickly blame someone or something else. But, this whole "blame game" had its origin in a classic Bible story as Adam and Eve blamed their misdeed on each other and the snake. Sadly, this "blame virus" continues to be passed down to our present time.

<u>Lord Jesus, I want to see</u>
Jesus, Source of Truth and Life, you once advised your disciples how to live a life of integrity, "Yes means Yes; and No means No." They should not try to parse a word and blame their wrongdoings on someone else. Clearly, you do not want me or anyone else to play the blame game. Instead, you call me to be an honest and accountable person and set a good example to our youngsters. It takes humility and courage to accept our wrongdoings.

<u>Resolution</u>
Today, I will humbly accept my mistakes and apologize. I will refuse to blame my errors on someone or something else.

October 4

Issue: **Caring**

"Give proper recognition to those widows who are really in need. But if a widow has children or grandchildren, these should learn first of all to put their religion into practice by caring for their own family and so repaying their parents and grandparents, for this is pleasing to God." (1 Timothy 5:3-4)

Reflection

The Bible is full of examples about caring for others. For example, Pharaoh's daughter saw a helpless Hebrew baby, Moses, on a river-bank and showed her care by rescuing him. Or, Jesus continuously let us see His caring heart when He reached out to help a hungry crowd and many misfortunate folks. A caring heart is a true miracle and can bring about many little miracles. For it is a sign of God's love and presence in a world of indifference and selfishness.

Lord Jesus, I want to see

Jesus, the Caring Heart of God, you taught the world how to love not only by your preaching words but also by your caring actions. Your personal, caring examples have touched the world and moved many people to imitate you. Today, thousands of missionaries have dedicated their lives around the world to share your caring heart with the broken and the abandoned. Help me to do the same wherever I go by having a caring heart.

Resolution

Today, I will show a caring heart by helping a widow, an elderly person, or a panhandler with whatever they might need.

October 5

Issue: **Comfort**

"Praise be to the God and Father of our Lord Jesus Christ, the Father of compassion and the God of all comfort, who comforts us in all of our troubles so that we can comfort those in any trouble with the comfort we ourselves have received from God." (2Corinthians 1:3-4)

Reflection

Someone once said, "The road to Heaven is paved with tears and sweat." This means that it takes many efforts and pains to make it to Heaven. For our life on earth is full of tears, sadness, and difficult moments. We constantly need to be comforted and have someone dry our tears. God is one of those who does that job for us. Again, the Bible is full of stories on how God comforted God's people. Like a best friend, God has always been there for us throughout our human history.

Lord Jesus, I want to see

Jesus, my Joy and Comfort, you certainly did many good things for God's people, including comforting them. When you ran into a widow who just lost her son to death, you stopped to bring him back to life and brought her comfort. You did the same thing for your friends Martha and Mary by bringing their brother Lazarus back from the dead. Sometimes, I feel shy about comforting someone. But, our world needs more people who can do that for others. Help me learn to wipe the tears of the people around me and ease their pains.

Resolution

Today, I will try to bring comfort to someone who might be in pain or anguish by being a listening ear and giving that person a helping hand.

October 6

Decent

"Let us behave decently, as in the day time, not in orgies and drunkenness, not in sexual immorality and debauchery, not in dissension and jealousy. Rather, clothe yourselves with the Lord Jesus Christ, and do not think about how to gratify the desires of the sinful nature." (Romans 13:13-14)

Reflection

One of the things we do not hear a lot about in our world these days is that something is decent, appropriate, or fitting. For everything nowadays must be outrageous, shocking, or different. All the spectacular entertainment acts are now measured by how shocking they might appear to the public. With a public that desires glamor and notoriety, it is no wonder we end up with the world we see now; namely, careless, indifferent, thoughtless, selfish, narcissistic, and destructive. It is time for our public to promote the virtue of decency if it wants a different world than the current one.

Lord Jesus, I want to see

Jesus, the most Respectful Prophet of all time, during your ministry, you kept reminding God's people that you were not a religious rebel or someone who was trying to abolish all the laws and traditions. You were upset when God's people turned the Holy Temple into a secular market place. I might fall under the same spell with the public and want everything we do to be different and outrageous. But, it is time for me to set an example for the public and only carry out decent acts in my daily life.

Resolution

Today, I will not appear drunk or sexually immoral to the public. Rather, I will show some decency in public.

October 7

<u>Issue:</u> **Distress**

"From inside the fish Jonah prayed to the Lord His God. He said: 'In my distress I called to the Lord, and He answered me. From the depths of the grave I called for help, and you listened to my cry.'" (Jonah 2:1-2)

<u>Reflection</u>
We all have been in distress at one point or another in our lives, and we surely did not like this feeling. Our hearts were filled with worries, anxieties, sorrow, and pressure. We certainly want to be freed from that stress. Moses could relate to us, because God's people complained about everything and made his life truly miserable. He could not do anything right for them and asked God to bring him relief from that misery. Clearly, no one likes to be in distress.

Lord Jesus, I want to see
Jesus, my Joy and Hope, you were in much distress and sorrow toward the end of your ministry as you tried to prepare for your Passion and death. You exclaimed, "My Soul is sorrowful even to death." I have surely had those moments of distress as I have faced my life's burdens, pressures, and challenges. Knowing that you went through the same thing makes me feel a little better. But, I certainly want you to help deliver me from such moments and take away my distress.

<u>Resolution</u>
Today, I will call on you, Lord, to take away anything that might cause me distress, including my health, relationships, or employment problems and show me a solution.

October 8

Encourage

"See to it, brothers and sisters, that more of you have a sinful, unbelieving heart that turns away from the living God. But, encourage one another daily, as long as it is called Today, so that none of you may be hardened by sin's deceitfulness." (Hebrews 3:12-13)

Reflection

There is one thing we humans can do more for one another each day, namely, provide encouragement. We should encourage one another a little more and criticize a little less. Sadly, we tend to do the opposite. When we encourage someone, we basically lift up the person and make the person feel good about him/herself. One person in the Bible who practiced this good habit often, almost to perfection, is St. Paul. He encouraged God's people regularly and yet did not hesitate to correct either.

Lord Jesus, I want to see

Jesus, Source of Comfort and Encouragement, you constantly encouraged your disciples when sending them on mission trips and corrected them when they did something wrong. I might tend to criticize and put down others, much as the world often does. But with your example and help, I will try to see the good in others and speak words of encouragement often to people around me, especially the hopeless and the condemned.

Resolution

Today, I will try to give compliments and speak words of encouragement to my family, friends, and co-workers and help make their day joyous.

October 9

Issue: **Enlighten**

"I keep asking that the God of our Lord Jesus Christ, the glorious Father, may give you the Spirit of Wisdom and revelation, so that you may know Him better. I pray also that the eyes of your heart may be enlightened in order that you may know the hope to which He has called you, the riches of His glorious inheritance in the saints, and his incomparably great power for us who believe..." (Ephesians 1:17-19)

Reflection

We have heard about the Enlightenment period, a European philosophical movement that relied on reason and experience rather than dogma and tradition to advance humanitarian goals and social progress. This movement happened around the 18th Century and forced us humans to open our minds to reasoning and logic to see how the universe works. However, God continues to enlighten us daily and gets us to see things differently through various encounters and experiences. A good example of this is seen through the Magi and how God enlightened them via their meeting with Baby Jesus to take a different road home.

Lord Jesus, I want to see

Jesus, my Source of Wisdom and Guidance, you opened the hearts of God's people to God's love with your good deeds and enlightened their minds with your Good News. Sometimes I am afraid to open my soul and let you come in, because I do not want to change. But with your grace, I want like you to enlighten me each day and help me make necessary changes in my life.

Resolution

Today, I will try to have an open mind about certain issues and let God enlighten me about how to deal with them and produce a good result.

October 10

"I eagerly expect and hope that I will in no way be ashamed, but will have sufficient courage so that now as always Christ will be exalted in my body, whether by life or by death. For to me, to live is Christ and to die is gain."
(Philippians 1:20-21)

Reflection
For years, God's people expected a Savior who could restore Israel to the good old days of King David and put an end to their painful days of slavery. It took them many generations, but their prayers were finally answered in Jesus. We can only imagine how fulfilling and satisfied God's people must have felt. We all have expected and dreamed of wonderful things for ourselves. It will be a miracle when those dreams finally come true for us. So, let us keep on dreaming and expecting more from our Lord.

Lord Jesus, I want to see
Jesus, my Dream and Hope, you brought joy and new life for many people with your ministry. You also made Heaven visible and reachable by your presence. Like the rest of the world, I have many dreams and expectations. But, most of them might be too far-fetched. It is time for me to be realistic and have concrete plans to make my expectations a reality. With your help, I will try to focus more on my spiritual expectations and each day find ways to bring me closer to you and Heaven.

Resolution
Today, I will expect myself to improve my relationship with Jesus by spending more time with Him in prayer.

October 11

Feel

"Just then a woman who had been subject to bleeding for twelve years came up behind Jesus and touched the edge of his cloak. She said to herself, 'If I only touched his cloak, I will be healed.' Jesus turned and saw her. 'Take heart, daughter,' He said, 'Your faith has healed you.' And the woman was healed from that moment." (Matthew 9:20-22)

Reflection

For humans, feeling and our senses are essential parts of our daily life. We cannot imagine what our lives would be like if we lost our ability to feel and lost our senses. What defines us as human is our ability to feel, love, think, reason, and hope. The moment we lose these abilities, we will soon be dead. But, among these abilities, feeling is the medium that keeps us closer to a lively faith and strong spiritual life. For feeling opens our hearts and connects us to God's love and tender care for us.

Lord Jesus, I want to see

Jesus, the Incarnated Word of God, you have become the face of God in our world and have allowed us humans to touch you with our hearts and senses. Your heart was moved with pity like the rest of us when you stood before a sad situation. Conventional wisdom tells me to be stoic and detach myself from any feeling. But, my faith and you call me to be in touch with all my feelings and show my honest emotions before a situation. Let me reach out and touch you daily so that I might have life.

Resolution

Today, I will try to touch you, Lord, by being kind and nice to people I might run into throughout this day.

October 12

Issue: **Habits** (good)
"They get into the habit of being idle and going about from house to house. And not only do they become idlers, but also gossips and busy bodies, saying things they ought not to." (1Timothy 5:13)

Reflection
We all have our own habits. Some are good ones, whereas others are bad ones. It is our duty as Christians to increase our good habits and reduce our bad ones. Good habits will make us better people over time, whereas bad ones will corrupt our character and cause us to do bad things. Faith and religion are supposed to help increase our good habits and help us become like our God. It also keeps us away from bad habits and makes our world a better place.

Lord Jesus, I want to see
Jesus, my Moral Compass and Guide, you never stopped warning God's people about the bad habits of the scribes and Pharisees such as showing off their good deeds or condemning others. You also encouraged them to do more good things for everyone around them. It is easier for me to take up bad habits and more difficult to embrace good ones. With your help and my determination, I will try to accumulate more good habits each day and get rid of the bad ones.

Resolution
Today, I will welcome a good habit or try to eliminate a bad one and try to stick with it.

October 13

<u>Issue:</u> **Integrity**

"...Encourage the young men to be self-controlled. In everything set them an example by doing what is good. In your teaching, show integrity, seriousness, and soundness of speech that cannot be condemned, so that those who oppose you may be ashamed because they have nothing bad to say about us." (Titus 2:6-8)

<u>Reflection</u>

Integrity is often used to describe a person with moral principle, character, honor, and honesty. In the face of corruption and partisanship, a person with integrity will not be swayed or compromise his/her principles. Rather, that person will stand up to defend honor and what is right. Throughout our faith tradition, there have been some distinguished individuals like Abraham, Moses, Peter, and Paul who we call people of integrity. We surely need more people with integrity in our corrupt and dishonest world.

Lord Jesus, I want to see

Jesus, a Person of Integrity and Love, you always knew how to balance love and mercy in your treatment of saintly people and sinners. Yet, you never compromised your principles and honor to get worldly recognition and praise. I might be tempted daily to give up my moral principles, sometimes even my soul, in exchange for worldly things and pleasures. But with your example and inspiration, I will vow to be a person of integrity as a sign of your presence and as a role model for future generations.

<u>Resolution</u>

Today, I will stand up for a moral principle or character in the face of pressure, popularity, or political correctness.

October 14

Issue: **Law**

"You, my brothers and sisters, were called to be free. But, do not use your freedom to indulge the sinful nature; rather, serve one another in love. The entire Law is summed up in a single command: 'Love your neighbor as yourself.' If you keep on biting and devouring each other, watch out or you will be destroyed by each other." (Galatians 5:13-15)

Reflection

Most people do not like laws and regulations. Some would love to live in a world without any law at all. In fact, New Hampshire's state motto is, "Live free or die." But, laws are what hold our world together and have brought justice to our humanity. Our world will turn to chaos without any laws or regulations. Laws help bring order to society, homes, and neighborhoods. The greatest set of laws that helped build future laws for our world was the Ten Commandments of Moses.

Lord Jesus, I want to see

Jesus, the Fulfillment of the Law and Prophets, you came to fulfill God's Law and prophecy. You did not come to throw away all the Laws and establish a lawless world. Most important, you summarized all the Laws into one simple Law of love, Love God and love your neighbors. I might not be fond of laws and rules. But, they bring order to our world and help give me discipline and guidance in my daily life.

Resolution

Today, I will show some respect for law and order by following what I am asked to obey at work, school, church, shopping malls, and everywhere I go.

October 15

Life

"...I have set before you life and death, blessings, and curses. Now choose life, so that you and your children may live and that you may love the Lord your God, listen to His voice, and hold fast to Him. For the Lord is your life, and He will give you many years in the land..." (Deuteronomy 30:19-20)

Reflection

God gives us many gifts from the moment of our birth. But, the most precious and valuable gift that God gives us is the gift of life. God formed us in our mothers' wombs and breathed life into our bodies at the moment of our conception. This gift is worth more than anything on earth, and we realize this when we are about to lose it due to death or a health condition. Sadly, our world has misused, mistreated, and wasted life without any concern at all.

Lord Jesus, I want to see

Jesus, the Author of Life, by entering our world, you wanted to preserve our life and save it from sin and darkness. You tried to save life at every chance possible with your healing hands and loving heart. Often, I take my life for granted and do not realize how precious it is. But with your grace, I will try to give thanks for it regularly and try to take good care of it physically, mentally, and spiritually.

Resolution

Today, I will take time to relax and find some peace for my body and soul.

October 16

Issue: **Missionary**

"When I came to you, brothers and sisters, I did not come with eloquence or superior wisdom as I proclaimed to you the testimony about God. For I resolved to know nothing while I was with you except Jesus Christ and Him crucified... My message and my preaching were not with wise and persuasive words, but with a demonstration of the spirit power, so that your faith might not rest on human wisdom, but on God's power."
(1Corinthians 2:1-5)

Reflection
Missionary is one of those words we do not hear a lot these days, especially in a world of high technology and self-gratification. Yet, we continue to have faithful and generous Christians who care so much about the Good News of Jesus Christ that they dedicate their lives to share it with others around the world and do mission work in God's forsaken places. These missionaries reflect the spirit of the apostles and want to continue the mission of their Lord Jesus by caring for the misfortunate and saving more souls. Our world has changed for the better because of these dedicated and caring missionaries.

Lord Jesus, I want to see
Jesus, Bearer of the Good News, you were the first missionary who went from towns to villages to do mission work for God the Father and were able to call on many people to do the same. I pray that you will inspire me to have a missionary spirit and try to share your Good News with the world around me with joy and enthusiasm.

Resolution
Today, I will reach out to share the love and Good News of Jesus with the world by volunteering at God's kitchen or some charity group.

October 17

"My dear brothers and sisters, take note of this: Everyone should be quick to listen, slow to speak and slow to become angry, for human anger does not bring about the righteous life that God desires. Therefore, get rid of all moral filth and the evil that is so prevalent and humbly accept the word planted in you, which can save you." (James 1:19-21)

Reflection

Morality is not a strong suit for our modern, materialistic, self-gratifying society. For the world would rather hear more about how to get more material possessions and pleasures than to live a moral life. Ironically, most people hate lying, cheating, greed, envy, selfishness, vengeance, and so on. Furthermore, a society without a set of moral principles can easily turn chaotic and violent. Moses knew this firsthand as God's people formed a golden calf and worshipped it. He had to call on God to give them the Ten Commandments and create a basis for future moral laws.

Lord Jesus, I want to see

Jesus, my Moral Compass and Guide, you helped the teachers of the law and religious leaders understand and appreciate the moral laws a little better as they brought many moral cases for you to resolve. You wanted them to consider one more factor in all ethical cases, namely, mercy. I might act like the scribes and Pharisees and judge everyone or every situation harshly. But, you ask us to look at every moral law or case under the lens of mercy, because that is the way we should always behave.

Resolution

Today, I will do something to highlight the importance of moral laws in society, such as trying not to lie or cheat someone.

October 18

Issue: **Pain**

"Dear friends, do not be surprised at the painful trial you are suffering, as though something strange were happening to you. But, rejoice that you participate in the sufferings of Christ, so that you may be overjoyed when His glory is revealed." (1Peter 4: 12-13)

Reflection

If there is one thing we humans hate and want to get rid of, it is pain. None of us likes to endure pain. Nor do we want our loved ones to suffer pain. We do everything possible to reduce pain and perhaps eliminate it altogether. So far, we humans have tried to control pain with medicine. But, we can never get rid of pain completely, for it is part of our human imperfection on earth. Yet, we the faithful believe that pain is part of the purification process to build our character and prepare us for Heaven. Therefore, pain and the Cross are the ways for us to get to Heaven.

Lord Jesus, I want to see

Jesus, my Pain Relief and Comforter, you were always concerned about the length of time that God's people would have to endure pain. Hence, you broke the Sabbath Law and healed victims without any delay. I might question God's love for me or blame God when I must face pain and suffering. But, based on your rescuing stories in the Gospels, I know you never want me to suffer. May I learn to let you suffer with me and for me in my daily life.

Resolution

Today, I will offer any pain to you, Lord, and trust that you will relieve me from it and heal me.

October 19

Issue: **Praise**

"May God give you a Spirit of unity among yourselves as you follow Christ Jesus, so that with one heart and mind you may glorify the God and Father of our Lord Jesus Christ. Accept one another, then, just as Christ accepted you, in order to bring praise to God." (Romans 15:5-7)

Reflection

We all love praise and recognition, but find it difficult to do that for others around us. For it takes courage and humility for someone to give praise and fine compliments to another person. It certainly makes that person feel great and causes everyone to be excited as well. We have an example in the Bible about how God's people gave praise to David after his victory over Goliath, which caused King Saul to become jealous. Clearly, we need to give more praise to more people in our world.

Lord Jesus, I want to see

Jesus, Son of God, you should expect praise for your status and the wonderful works you did for God's people. You did not hesitate to praise John the Baptist for his selfless and God-centered work. This is something I should imitate and do more in our world. I hope I can try to give more praise to others instead of seeking praise for myself.

Resolution

Today, I will give praise and compliments to someone around me who has done some great work lately. I hope to make the world a little better by doing so.

October 20

Pressure

"We do not want you to be uninformed, brothers and sisters, about the hardships we suffered in the province of Asia. We were under great pressure, far beyond our ability to endure, so that we despaired even of life. Indeed, in our hearts we felt the sentence of death. But this happened that we might not rely on ourselves but on God who raises the dead."(2Corinthians 1:8-11)

Reflection

We are constantly under pressure from one thing after another every day. It comes from our job, health, families, friends, relationships, society, culture, tragedies, and so on. But, the greatest pressure we deal with these days comes from our culture and political correctness. We Christians are pressured daily to give up our sacred and ethical beliefs, because people who do not like us decide to put an end to our faith tradition or make fun of it.

Lord Jesus, I want to see

Jesus, my Defender and Advocate, you warned your disciples about all the pressure and mistreatment they would encounter as your disciples. But, you promised them the Holy Spirit would defend and help them through those tough moments. I might feel scared and overwhelmed by all the pressure in my daily life. However, with you by my side, I will have nothing to worry about and will continue to hold high your Cross and follow you to the end.

Resolution

Today, I will identify a pressure that has created anxiety in me lately. I will then bring it to the Lord in prayer to find a solution and reduce the pressure on me.

October 21

Prudence
"Stay away from a foolish person, for you will not find knowledge on one's lips. The wisdom of the prudent is to give thought to their ways, but the folly of fools is deception." (Proverbs 14:7-8)

Reflection
If there is one thing we, especially our leaders, should pray for each day, it is prudence. For this virtue gives us wisdom and guidance to make the right decisions and do the right things. Prudence helps us consider every fact and look at an issue from every possible angle before making a decision. An imprudent person acts rashly and simply on impulse. The result of is often a disaster and a big mess.

Lord Jesus, I want to see
Jesus, the Wisdom of God, you constantly counseled your disciples to act prudently and not let their impulses drive their thoughts and actions. You sought out prudence in moments of prayer and quiet meditation. My life is bombarded with noise and instant gratification. Help me learn to rely on prudence as a sign of your presence for all my decisions and not let anything else drive my thoughts and actions.

Resolution
Today, I will identify an issue or a decision that I must make. Then, I will bring it to the Lord in prayer to see how I should make that decision prudently.

October 22

<u>Issue:</u> **Regret**

"Even if I caused your sorrow by my letter, I do not regret it. Though I did regret it – I see that my letter hurt you, but only for a little while – yet now I am happy, not because you were made sorry, but because your sorrow led you to repentance. For you became sorrowful as God intended and so were not harmed in any way by us. Godly sorrow brings repentance that leads to salvation and leaves no regret, but worldly sorrow brings death."
(2Corinthians 7:8-10)

<u>Reflection</u>

Although we have done our best to weigh our decisions and consider our actions, our lives are full of regrets. We look back on our lives and second guess the decisions we made or our choices. We might also be sorry about the alliances and friendships we formed. Our hearts are full of regret and hurt all the time. The Bible is filled with stories of regret and sorrow, like the story of Kind David and some of the bad decisions he made. But, God can heal and restore us from regrettable decisions or moments.

Lord Jesus, I want to see

Jesus, my Source of Healing and Comfort, you ran into many sinners who regretted their past and wrongdoings. Instead of condemning or rejecting them, you embraced them with mercy and forgave them. I know you forgive me for whatever wrongs I might have done. What I find most difficult for me to do is to forgive myself for all the wrongs I have committed. For this I regret the most. Please heal me.

<u>Resolution</u>

Today, I will think about what I regret and then ask the Lord to help me let go of it and heal me.

October 23

Issue: **Resistance**

"Be self-controlled and alert. Your enemy the Devil prowls around like a roaring lion looking for someone to devour. Resist him, stand firm in faith, because you know that your brothers and sisters throughout the world are undergoing the same kind of sufferings." (1Peter 5:8-9)

Reflection

We Christians are called to resist worldly temptations and all the empty promises of the Power of Darkness. At the same time, we are asked to embrace God's ways and teachings. Unfortunately, many Christians have done the opposite. They often embrace worldly allurements from the Power of Darkness and resist God's teachings instead. This apparent reversal of focus has not only caused much confusion among the Christian community but also created all sorts of hurts and casualties. By resisting God and embracing wrongful things, we do much harm to our soul and spiritual life.

Lord Jesus, I want to see

Jesus, my Hope and Salvation, you had to fight and resist many temptations by the Devil before your Passion and death. You also called on your disciples to resist the hypocritical lifestyle of the scribes and Pharisees. For these religious leaders set a bad example of spirituality by doing the opposite of what they preached. I need to resist worldly allurements and empty promises from the Power of Darkness. Instead, I should embrace God's love and blessings from Heaven.

Resolution

Today, I will resist temptations and bad habits such as swearing, smoking, excessive drinking, pleasures, or any form of the sin of the flesh.

October 24

Respect

"Make it your ambition to lead a quiet life, to mind your own business, and to work with your hand, just as we told you so that your daily life may win the respect of outsiders and so that you will not be dependent on anybody." (1 Thessalonians 4:11-12)

Reflection
Perhaps one of the things all human beings—rich and poor, famous or not, educated and uneducated alike—desire from their fellow men is respect. This same desire is true in all cultures, customs, traditions, and ethnic groups. Without respect, people treat one another horribly and have no consideration for folks in authority. Unfortunately, that is what is occurring in our world today. There is no longer any respect for sacred things, institutions, or responsible positions such as parents, religious leaders, educators, law enforcement, and other positions of authority. The result is constant chaos and violence.

Lord Jesus, I want to see
Jesus, my Lord and God, although you disagreed with the religious leaders and civil authorities on many issues, you always maintained a level of respect and great consideration for them. The same is true for you and the other two persons in the Holy Trinity. I might not be influenced by the virus of the current culture and show respect for you, sacred things, institutions, and responsible positions. With your help and example, I will always show respect to others, especially everyone mentioned above.

Resolution
Today, I will try to be respectful to others or people in responsible positions by the way I treat them.

October 25

<u>Issue:</u> **Revenge**

"Do not repay anyone evil for evil. Be careful to do what is right in the eyes of everybody. If it is possible, as far as it depends on you, live at peace with everyone. Do not take revenge, my friends, but leave room for God's wrath, for it is written: 'It is mine to avenge; I will repay,' says the Lord. On the contrary: 'If your enemy is hungry, feed him; if he is thirsty, give him something to drink…' Do not be overcome by evil, but overcome evil with good." (Romans 12:17-21)

<u>Reflection</u>

Humans have all kinds of emotions, but one of them is quite powerful, deadly, and long-lasting, namely, revenge. This dark emotion has been well-documented in the Bible, has caused all kinds of conflicts, and destroyed many relationships and lives throughout history. In fact, it continues to play out in society and around the world every day. Once it takes hold of our hearts, it will simmer with the help of anger, hatred, and destruction. Only God can remove it from our hearts or take us out of this deadly, vicious circle.

<u>Lord Jesus, I want to see</u>

Jesus, Source of Forgiveness and Reconciliation, you not only called on your disciples to forgive often and avoid vengeance but also practiced it yourself when you were hung high on the Cross. I might harbor this deadly and destructive virus in my heart. With your grace and example, I will learn to forgive and expel this virus so that my heart and the world around me will always be full of peace and love.

<u>Resolution</u>

Today, I will examine my heart to see if I might hold some hatred and vengeance against someone. Then, I will bring it to the Lord in prayer and ask Him to help me forgive.

October 26

Servant

"After a long time the master of those servants returned and settled accounts with them. The person who had received five talents brought the other five. 'Master,' one said, 'you entrusted me with five talents. See, I have gained five more.' The master replied, 'Well done, good and faithful servant! You have been faithful with a few things; I will put you in charge of many things. Come and share your master's happiness!'" (Matthew 25:19-21)

Reflection

Most of us do not like the idea of being a servant for someone. Besides, we all like to have fun, and the idea of service is quite a letdown. However, all the big names in the Bible, including Abraham, Moses, David, John the Baptist, Peter, and Paul were faithful servants of the Lord. These folks answered the calling from the Lord and dedicated their lives to serve Him and God's people. They were honored to fulfill that duty.

Lord Jesus, I want to see

Jesus, the Suffering Servant of God, you constantly reminded your disciples of the following message, "The Son of Man came to serve, not to be served, and to give His life as a ransom for many" (Matthew 20:28) as they argued with each other about who would be the greatest in your Kingdom. Maybe I feel scared or overwhelmed about being your servant. But, there is no one better than you for me to serve. I will put my life at your service and try to produce abundantly for your Kingdom.

Resolution

Today, I will serve the Lord by reaching out to help someone who might be in need around me.

October 27

<u>Issue:</u> **Solutions**

"When you were slaves to sin, you were free from the control of righteousness. What benefit did you reap at that time from the things you are now ashamed of? Those things result in death. But, now that you have been set free from sin and have become slaves to God, the benefit you reap leads to holiness, and the result is eternal life. For the wages of sin is death, but the gift of God is eternal life in Christ Jesus our Lord." (Romans 6:20-23)

<u>Reflection</u>
Many people love to argue and debate problems, but very few are interested in finding solutions. For it is always easier to criticize or blame a problem on someone than to search for a way to solve it ourselves. Solving a problem means committing ourselves to a process and spending our sweat and tears for something greater than ourselves, even if we have to sacrifice ourselves for it. This is how God deals with all the problems of our world, even if He had to sacrifice His only Son, Jesus, to save us.

<u>Lord Jesus, I want to see</u>
Jesus, Son of God and Savior of the world, you brought salvation and solutions for many problems to our world. You challenged your disciples to find a solution to the problem of a hungry crowd and not ignore it or pass it on to someone else. Like the world, I tend to run away from problems and ignore them or let someone else deal with them. But, you want me to face problems head-on at home, work, and church and find merciful and reasonable solutions. Give me the wisdom and courage to follow through.

<u>Resolution</u>
Today, I will look over one of the problems in my life and prayerfully consider a solution for it.

October 28

Issue: **Struggles**

"I urge you, brothers and sisters, by our Lord Jesus Christ and by the love of the Spirit, to join me in my struggle by praying to God for me. Pray that I may be rescued from the unbelievers in Judea and that my service in Jerusalem may be acceptable to the saints there, so that by God's will I may come to you with joy and together with you be refreshed. The God of peace be with you all. Amen." (Romans 15:30-33)

Reflection

Since the moment of our birth, we humans have had to struggle through our entire life for survival. Each day, we struggle through one thing after another to make ends meet or stay healthy and happy. Some of us have to struggle for social justice and equality, whereas others must fight with other personal demons to have a normal life. Some must deal with relationship issues, whereas others try to keep alive a fragile faith and some must keep hope in a tough situation. Our constant struggle is the journey of the Cross for us believers. But, God will not abandon us on this journey.

Lord Jesus, I want to see

Jesus, our Savior and Guide, you struggled to carry the Cross up to Calvary and bore the sufferings of all the afflicted. Yet, you never cursed us and our sins. Rather, you stopped along the way to comfort the women of Jerusalem who wept for you. Sometimes I might feel overwhelmed by my daily struggles and life's burdens. But with your help, I will never give up and continue to walk my journey of the Cross all the way to the end.

Resolution

Today, I will look over one of the problems with which I have struggled and ask the Lord to help me deal with it.

October 29

Issue: **Trust**

"Be merciful to me, O Lord, for people hotly pursue me; all day long they press their attack. My slanderers pursue me all day long; many are attacking me in their pride. When I am afraid, I will trust in you. In God, whose word I praise; in God I trust, I will not be afraid. What can mortal humans do to me?" (Psalms 56:1-4)

Reflection

Trust is one of the issues many of us struggle with in our relationships with others, God, and institutions such as the Church and the government after being hurt by lies and betrayals. Our lack of trust makes us skeptical and question everything around us. Yet without trust, miracles cannot happen and relationships cannot prosper. Even the early disciples realized this problem and once asked Jesus, "Increase our faith."

Lord Jesus, I want to see

Jesus, my Hope and Salvation, you never stopped calling on your disciples to put their trust in you and take a leap of faith like all the desperate souls who came to you for healing. You blessed all your future believers by saying to doubting Thomas, "You came to believe because you have seen me. Blessed are those who have not yet seen and believed." (John 20:29) I might be afraid to get hurt by putting my trust in you or in a relationship. But with your grace, I will take risks and learn to trust you, so that I may experience miracles in my life.

Resolution

Today, I will learn to trust you by putting into your hands one of the problems with which I am dealing and allowing you to help me through it.

October 30

Issue: **Violence**

"Here is a trustworthy saying: 'If anyone sets one's heart on being an overseer, one desires a noble task.' Now, the overseer must be above reproach, the husband of but one wife, temperate, self-controlled, respectable, hospitable, able to teach; not given to drunkenness, not violent but gentle, not quarrelsome, not a lover of money. One must manage one's family well and see that the children would obey with proper respect." (1 Timothy 3:1-4)

Reflection
Most of us have to admit that the level of violence in our society has reached an unprecedented level in human history. People have unloaded violence on other human beings in the name of Allah and the holiest. But, who made these violent people the divine sheriff? In the end, it is pure hatred that has driven these scum-of-the-earth animals to maximize horror and pain on the whole of humanity. Worse yet, these criminals show no respect to the sacred body and intensify the level of violence by blowing themselves up next to their neighbors.

Lord Jesus, I want to see
Jesus, Gentle and Peaceful Shepherd, you never treated your opponents like the scribes and Pharisees violently. You even granted the request of a legion of evil spirits after you drove them out of a possessed man. For you desired peace, love, and mercy in all human communities. I might let our violent culture make me feel callous about various forms of violence around the world. But, you continue to call me and others to be the bearer and promoter of peace wherever we go.

Resolution
Today, I will try to resist any form of violence in action or speech and be a person of peace, even when I am upset.

October 31

Issue: **Waste**
"When they all had enough to eat, Jesus said to His disciples, 'Gather the pieces that are left over. Let nothing be wasted.' So, they gathered them and filled twelve baskets with the pieces of the five barley loaves leftover by those who had eaten." (John 6:12-13)

Reflection
Humans have not been good stewards of the earth and have destroyed and wasted many of earth's natural resources. In the Western world, we have consumed so many of the world's resources and wasted many as well. We just need to look at the amount of food being thrown away every day from all the homes, restaurants, food stores, and so on. Beside food, we have waster all sorts of other resources without any concern. This wasteful attitude has influenced the way we look at a human life and has caused us to throw away the gift of life without a second thought.

Lord Jesus, I want to see
Jesus, Good Steward and Manager of God's Creation, you never wasted anything after your miracle of multiplying the loaves and fishes. Furthermore, you called on your disciples to collect all the left-overs so that nothing went to waste. I might not have paid much attention to the importance of not wasting God's blessings in my life. But, it is time for me to stop my wasting attitude and follow your example by being a good steward of God's blessings.

Resolution
Today, I will not waste time and resources like food and water by carefully watching everything I eat or use.

November

Lord Jesus,
I Want to See...

November 1

<u>Issue:</u> **Admiration**

"Finally, brothers and sisters, whatever is true, whatever is noble, whatever is right, whatever is pure, whatever is lovely, whatever is admirable – if anything is excellent or praiseworthy – think about such things. Whatever you have learned or received or heard from me [Paul], or seen in me – put it into practice. And the God of peace will be with you." (Philippians 4:8-9)

<u>Reflection</u>

We all have certain people in our lives we admire and look up to. These men and women have shown us exemplary, rare qualities that we do not see often in our common society. They might have also demonstrated a unique way of life in our rambunctious culture. For us believers, these admirable folks are our Lord Jesus and the Saints. We Christians look up to them and try to imitate their ways of life. But, it is difficult to find these folks today, and our chaotic world needs more people like them for its young generations to look up to and imitate.

<u>Lord Jesus, I want to see</u>

Jesus, my Hero and Role model, you have so many wonderful qualities that I would like to acquire. You have also shown us how to have a truly happy and peaceful life. Amidst this chaotic and uncertain world, I look up to you for guidance and inspiration. I admire your way of life and want to make it my own. Help me make that dream come true and be like you.

<u>Resolution</u>

Today, I will think of a certain Saint, family member, teacher, or coach I admire and for whom I have great respect. Then, I will name qualities about that person that I would like to imitate.

November 2

Issue: **Advocate**

"O earth, do not cover my blood; may my cry never be laid to rest! Even now my witness is in Heaven; my advocate is on high. My intercessor is my friend as my eyes pour out tears to God; on behalf of a man he pleads for his friend." (Job 16:18-21)

Reflection

When we go to court or in front of a judge, we need an advocate to fend for us and guide us through the tangled mess of the legal system. In our daily life, an advocate is someone who stands up on our behalf under the law and fights for our benefits. Advocates are our extra pair of eyes and ears in this messy and confusing world of ours. We Christians also believe that each of us has been given a guardian angel and a patron saint to be our advocates before God in Heaven. So, the more advocates we have around us, the more benefits we receive.

Lord Jesus, I want to see

Jesus, my Defender and Advocate, you have always been the voice of advocacy for the poor, the misfortunate, the widows, the outcast, and the lowly. For these folks have no one to fend for them. Your whole ministry was about being that voice, and I believe you continue to be the advocate for your Church in Heaven. The world might tell me to care simply for myself. But with your calling, I will use my abilities to be the advocate for the misfortunate and the lowly around me.

Resolution

Today, I will stand up and fend for someone at work, at a store, or on a street when this person is bullied or has no one to help in his/her time of need.

November 3

"But because of God's great love for us, God, who is rich in mercy, made us alive with Christ even when we were dead in transgressions — it is by grace you have been saved. And God raised us up with Christ and seated us with Him in the Heavenly realms in Christ Jesus." (Ephesians 2:4-6)

Reflection
There was a movie that came out in the 1980s called *Alive*. This movie portrayed a group of athletes who were in a plane crash and had to struggle to stay alive for more than a month by eating whatever they could find, including cannibalizing their deceased friends. In the end, some of them were found alive and rescued. Like those athletes before the plane crash, we take our lives for granted. We cannot see how blessed we are to be alive each day until we must face a life-and-death moment. Only then will we realize the value of the gift of life and begin to thank God for it.

Lord Jesus, I want to see
Jesus, the Author of Life, you restored sick people to good health and brought dead people back to life. You brought joy to many people through these experiences and helped them realize how blessed they were to be alive. Like many people, I may take my life for granted and not realize how blessed I am to be alive. Help me learn to thank you daily for my life and make good use of it for the sake of your Kingdom.

Resolution
Today, I will reach out to someone who might be sick or near death and offer to do something nice for that person.

November 4

Almsgiving

"Give generously and do so without a grudging heart; then because of this the Lord your God will bless you in all your work and in everything you put your hand to. There will always be poor people in the land. Therefore, I command you to be openhanded toward your brothers and sisters and toward the poor and needy in your land. (Deuteronomy 15:10-11)

Reflection

We Christians often practice almsgiving during Lent as a sign of self-sacrifice and doing good for our neighbors. In many religions, almsgiving and helping one's neighbors, especially the ones in need, is part of their tenets. Most, if not all, religions teach and require their believers to do good for their fellow men. By practicing almsgiving, we not only try to do good for others but also learn to share God's blessings for us with others around us. Hence, we show them God's love and presence in our lives.

Lord Jesus, I want to see

Jesus, Generous Giver of all Good Gifts, you called on God's people to be thankful and learn to do many good things for one another. Yet, you cautioned them not to brag about or show off their almsgiving and good deeds. Rather, they should do it in secret and let God reward them privately. I might not take the teaching of almsgiving seriously. But with your calling, I will make it an essential part of my faith life.

Resolution

Today, I will practice almsgiving by giving a homeless person or a panhandler something or helping someone in need.

November 5

<u>Issue:</u> **Apocalypse**

"'Teacher,' they asked, 'When will these things happen? And what will be the sign that they are about to take place?' Jesus replied: 'Watch out that you are not deceived. For many will come in my name claiming, 'I am he,' and 'The time is near.' Do not follow them. When you hear of wars and revolutions, do not be frightened. These things must happen first, but the end will not come right away.'" (Luke 21:7-9)

<u>Reflection</u>

Dozens of movies have been produced regarding the apocalypse. Apocalypse usually means the end time and is one of the main foci of many religions. For us Christians, it often means the time to change, convert, and turn one's life around. For unrepentant sinners, it is a horrifying and frightening time. But for the faithful, it is a time of vindication and jubilation. They are ready to see their Lord and judge. Apocalypse might be the end for sinners and the rest of the world. But, it is a new beginning for the faithful.

Lord Jesus, I want to see

Jesus, Judge of the Living and the Dead, you promised your disciples that you will come back to take them to your home at the end of time. You also constantly called on God's people to get themselves prepared for that time. I might not believe in the Apocalypse. But, one thing I should count on is that there will be an end for me. May I keep my eyes fixed on that end and be prepared to meet you when that day comes.

<u>Resolution</u>

Today, I will ask myself, "Am I scared or excited when I hear about the apocalypse?"

November 6

<u>Issue:</u> **Consolation**

"After Job had prayed for his friends, the Lord made him prosperous again and gave him twice as much as he had before. All his brothers and sisters and everyone who had known him before came and ate with him in his house. They comforted and consoled him over all the troubles the Lord had brought upon him, and each one gave him a piece of silver and a gold ring. The Lord blessed the latter part of Job's life more than the first." (Job 42:10-12)

<u>Reflection</u>

The road to Heaven is paved with sweat and tears. That road is part of our journey of faith. God's people have embarked on that journey since the beginning of time and have not stopped shedding tears ever since. They were kicked out of their homes, driven into slavery, and suffered under the cruel hands of their captors. The Lord heard their cries and tried to console them. Still, the lives of God's people are full of tragedies, disappointments, and mishaps. The Lord thus sent prophets and missionaries to comfort them over the years.

Lord Jesus, I want to see

Jesus, my Comforter and Hope, you spent much your ministry time comforting God's people—from losing a loved one or suffering an illness to being away from God due to sin. You also tried to lift up their spirit with your messages of hope, including the Beatitudes. I might feel uncomfortable around someone who is distraught. But with your grace and by your example, I will push myself to console and bring comfort to people who might feel broken or sad as you direct them my way.

<u>Resolution</u>

Today, I will look around for people who might feel down or burdened and try to console and comfort them.

<u>Issue:</u> **Death**

"Then I [John] saw a new Heaven and a new earth, for the first Heaven and the first earth had passed away, and there was no longer any sea. I saw the Holy City, the new Jerusalem, coming down of Heaven from God, prepared as a bride beautifully dressed for her husband. And I heard a loud voice from the throne saying, 'Now the dwelling of God is with the people, and God will live with them... God will wipe every tear from their eyes. There will be no more death or mourning or crying or pain, for the old order of things has passed away." (Revelation 21:1-4)

<u>Reflection</u>

Death is one of the topics most of us do not like to talk about. For it is morbid, depressing, sad, and unappealing. But, death is a fact of life and part of our fragile, imperfect life on earth. If we do not know how to deal with it, death can be a fearful and horrible moment. For our mundane world, death is the end of ourselves—body and soul. But for us believers, death is simply a transition from our imperfect, short life here on earth to the perfect, eternal life in Heaven for us. For we Christians believe that our souls never die, only our bodies do.

<u>Lord Jesus, I want to see</u>

Jesus, the Risen Lord, you died and were buried in the tomb. The discussion of your death caused some discomfort among your disciples. But, God the Father raised you from the dead and brought the hope of the eternal life to all your followers. I might not be too excited to talk about death. But with your help and example, I will slowly get accustomed to it and see it as a way for me to come home to you. Thank you dying to save my soul.

<u>Resolution</u>

Today, I will pray for someone who is dying or facing a terminal illness so that the person may be at peace and be ready to go home with you, Jesus.

November 8

<u>Issue:</u> **Despair**

"We do not want you to be uninformed, brothers and sisters, about the hardships we suffered in the province of Asia. We were under great pressure, far beyond our ability endure, so that we despaired even of life. Indeed, in our hearts we felt the death sentence. But, this happened that we might not rely on ourselves but on God, who raises the dead. God has delivered us from such a deadly peril and will deliver us. On God we have set our hope that God will continue to deliver us, as you help us by your prayers..." (2Corinthians 1:8-11)

<u>Reflection</u>

Perhaps, one of the biggest problems facing our human society in 21st Century is despair. This illness has taken thousands of lives around the world and has turned into a pandemic. Medicine and science do not seem to have the answer or treatment for it. Neither do they know how it originate and develops. Perhaps it begins from little worries and then becomes bigger when the person feels overwhelmed by life's burdens and pressures. Sadly, the person has nowhere to turn for help and soon falls into despair.

<u>Lord Jesus, I want to see</u>

Jesus, my Hope and Salvation, Judas did not turn to you for help after his terrible mistake of selling you for twenty pieces of silver. He soon fell into despair and took his own life. That is usually the tragic end for a soul in despair. May I always come to you for help and guidance when I feel despair or overwhelmed in life. May I also try to reach out to my neighbors who are depressed and help bring them to you for healing and spirit renewal.

<u>Resolution</u>

Today, I will search out people in despair around me and try to do something nice for them. I will say words of encouragement to lift up this person.

November 9

<u>Issue:</u> **Entitlement**

"During the days of Jesus' life on earth, He offered up prayers and petitions with loud cries and tears to the one who could save Him from death...Although He was a Son, He learned obedience from what He suffered and, once made perfect, He became the source of eternal salvation for all who obey God and was designated by God to be high priest in the order of Melchizedek." (Hebrews 5:7-10)

<u>Reflection</u>

When we want something, we must work hard for it. Things do not just land in our lap by accident. Only recently have we heard a lot about the term "entitlement." This term tells us that some people do not work for what they want, but simply claim ownership of it. This is a relatively new phenomenon and is definitely not fair to hard-working folks. In fact, it creates much resentment and fights. It also creates a culture of lazy selfishness, because everything is just about "me" regardless of all the hard work of others.

<u>Lord Jesus, I want to see</u>

Jesus, my Lord and Savior, although you are the Son of God, you never tried to claim your status to receive better treatment in your daily life. Instead, you worked hard for everything and reached out to help the misfortunate and the broken around you. I might be influenced by the co-dependency culture and demand certain things from society for myself without hard work on my part. But with your example, I will take pride in earning everything in this life and certain things in the next one on my own.

<u>Resolution</u>

Today, I will not make people around me do anything for me. Instead, I will take pride in doing everything on my own.

November 10

Issue: **Giving**

"Give; and it will be given to you. A good measure, pressed down, shaken together and running over, will be poured into your lap. For with the measure you use, it will be measured out to you." (Luke 6:38)

Reflection

We might have heard the saying, "It is better to give than to receive." When we give, we learn to be thankful, to share with people around us, and to care for others. Many giving examples in the Bible and our world tell us that the experience makes us feel good, for we are able to help others. The best Biblical example of giving is the poor widow who gave all her livelihood to the Temple. Jesus praised her generosity and faith.

Lord Jesus, I want to see

Jesus, the Generous Giver of all Gifts, you never hesitated to give to others whatever you had. You even gave your own life on the Cross so that all might live. Indeed, "Greater love has no one than this, that one lay down one's life for one's friends." (John 15:13) I might find it difficult to give and share my blessings with others, especially the poor and the misfortunate. With your example and encouragement, I will practice sharing and giving God's blessings for me with others around me. For that is how I can continue your mission and build a caring and generous culture around the world.

Resolution

Today, I will gladly give my blood, time, talents, or treasures to a charity group or someone in need.

November 11

<u>Issue:</u> **Gluttony**

"There are many rebellious people, also mere takers and deceivers, especially those of the circumcision group. They must be silenced, because they are ruining whole households by teaching things they out not to teach – and that for the sake of dishonest gain. Even one of their own prophets has said, 'Cretans are always liars, evil brutes, lazy gluttons.' This testimony is not true. Therefore, rebuke them sharply, so that they will be sound in faith…" (Titus 1:10-13)

<u>Reflection</u>

Gluttony is one of the seven deadly sins. The term is used to describe a person who overeats and consumes food nonstop. A glutton uses food as the way to deal with stress, worries, anxieties, or all kinds of issues in one's life. This is certainly not a healthy thing. For this person simply turns food into an idol and relies on it more than God. This sin and bad habit can easily cause other health and spiritual problems like obesity and laziness.

<u>Lord Jesus, I want to see</u>

Jesus, my Spiritual Coach and Master, you never let food or any mundane things be the god of your life. In fact, you fasted to confront the potential demons and prepare yourself for your Passion and death. I might not give up food for forty days the way you did. But, I certainly will not let food or any worldly thing control my life and salvation.

<u>Resolution</u>

Today, I will give up some food or snack to strengthen my spirit and follow the way of Jesus. For you once said, "One does not live on bread alone, but on every word that comes from the mouth of God." (Matthew 4:4)

November 12

<u>Issue:</u> **Good work**

"But as for you, continue in what you have learned and have become convinced of, because you know those from whom you learned it, and how from infancy you have known the Holy Scriptures, which are able to make you wise for salvation through faith in Christ Jesus. All Scripture is God-breathed and is useful for teaching, rebuking, correcting, and training in righteousness, so that the person of god may thoroughly equipped for every good work." (2Timothy 3:14-17)

<u>Reflection</u>

In a time when everyone seems to focus simply on one's own benefits and well-being, it is rare to hear about good works. People do not care enough to talk about and promote good works in society, communities, and neighborhoods. But, adopting that way of life would help our world reduce evil and bad things, while trying to increase love and kindness among its citizens. This is exactly what our world needs these days. We need people to do more good works for one another and make this world a better place.

<u>Lord Jesus, I want to see</u>

Jesus, Source of Love and Kindness, you did many good works for God's people and showed abundant care for the broken and the misfortunate. Your amazing works touched the lives of many people and brought great transformation to our world. I might feel indifferent about good works or acts of kindness. But, their impact on our world is immeasurable. Help me learn to reach out and do many good works for the world around me.

<u>Resolution</u>

Today, I will do some good works for someone and try to show God's love for the person that way.

November 13

Issue: **Grateful**

"Let the peace of Christ rule in your hearts, since as members of one body you were called to peace. And be grateful. Let the Word of Christ dwell in you richly as you teach and admonish one another with all wisdom, and as you sing psalms, hymns, and spiritual songs with gratitude in your hearts to God. And whatever you do, whether in word or deed, do it in the name of the Lord Jesus, giving thanks to God the Father through Him."
(Colossians 3:15-17)

Reflection
We were taught to say "Thank you" and be grateful to anyone who has helped us. One who has constantly given us a hand is our God. We should show gratitude to our God daily for all the blessings we have received. Having a grateful attitude will help us to be humble and better connected to our benefactors. If our world would be a little more grateful, there would be less complaining or fighting about entitlement.

Lord Jesus, I want to see
Jesus, Source of all Goodness and Blessings, you brought many wonderful things to God's people, including healing to the lepers. Unfortunately, out of ten healed lepers, only one of them returned to give thanks to God. I certainly want to be that grateful leper and please you with my grateful attitude. I do not want to end up like those nine ungrateful lepers and say nothing about the blessings I have received. That is how the world does it every day.

Resolution
Today, I will say "Thank you" to God or someone around me who might have done something nice for me.

November 14

Issue: **Grief**

"Jesus said to them, 'Are you asking one another what I meant when I said, 'in a little while you will see me no more, and then after a little while you will see me?' I tell you the truth, you will weep and mourn while the world rejoices. You will grieve, but your grief will turn to joy... So with you: Now is the time of grief, but I will see you again and you will rejoice and no one will take away your joy.'" (John 16:19-22)

Reflection
Our lives are filled with grief and moments of sadness due to tragedies and mishaps. God's people had their fair share of grief throughout the Bible. Many of us can relate because we've had similar experiences. Most Christians who must deal with grief become humble and trusting in God, whereas some turn bitter and run away from God. I hope I can reach out to someone in grief and bring comfort and hope to that person.

Lord Jesus, I want to see
Jesus, my Peace and Comfort, you were often moved with pity upon seeing a sad or tragic situation and would immediately reach out with help and comfort. You even shared this blessing with listeners in the Beatitudes, "Blessed are the sorrowing; they shall be consoled." (Matthew 5:4) I might have suffered grief lately, and I am advised to count on you for comfort and consolation. I am also called to be the crying shoulder for the grieving and help lift them out of the valley of tears and sorrow.

Resolution
Today, I will see if I can comfort someone around me by being a good listener and bringing a message of hope and peace.

- 322 -

November 15

<u>Issue:</u> **Healing**

"And when the people of the place recognized Jesus, they sent word to all the surrounding country. People brought all their sick to Him and begged Him to let the Sick just touch the edge of His cloak, and all who touched Him were healed." (Matthew 14:35-36)

<u>Reflection</u>

If there is one thing we humans ask God for at all times is healing. We need healing physically, mentally, and spiritually. For we are broken and fragile in many ways. We know how God's people called on Moses to ask God for healing when they were bitten by snakes at an alarming rate during their flight out of Egypt. God came to their rescue and brought them much-needed healing. Our world—more now than ever—needs God's healing in homes, neighborhoods, and societies. For there is so much pain, in addition to our life's burdens, that has been inflicted on humanity by the Power of Darkness.

Lord Jesus, I want to see

Jesus, Healer of Body and Soul, you healed countless folks with physical ailments and disturbed spirits. For you knew how much pain they had to endure. You could not wait to relieve their pain and even performed miracles on the Sabbath. Along with our world, I need your healing in every way; for I am broken, fragile, and hurt in one way or another. However, it is not just healing for which I pray, but also my desire to bring God's healing to our broken world.

<u>Resolution</u>

Today, I will try to bring God's healing to our broken world by visiting a hospital, nursing home, or some sick family member or neighbor.

November 16

<u>Issue:</u> **Home**

"…We sat down and began to speak to the women who had gathered there. One of those listening was a woman named Lydia, a dealer in a purple cloth from the city of Thyatira, who was a worshiper of God. The Lord opened her heart to respond to Paul's message. When she and the members of her household were baptized, she invited us to her home. 'If you consider me a believer in the Lord,' she said, 'Come and stay at my home.' And she persuaded us." (Acts 16:13-15)

<u>Reflection</u>

After being far away on a trip or a journey, we all look forward to being at home. For home is where our heart is and where we truly feel at peace. It is important for us to maintain a peaceful and loving home for our children, grandchildren, and other family members to enjoy and seek refuge from all of life's storms and dangers. However, the true home for us believers is in Heaven. It is very important for us to prepare for it and look forward to it without any fear or sadness. For this is where we will meet our Lord, all the holy figures, and our faithful deceased loved ones.

Lord Jesus, I want to see

Jesus, my Guide and Strength, although you never had a home on earth, you tried to create and restore more homes for God's people. When the rest of the world wanted to shun sinners and bar others from their homes, you came to theirs and shared a meal with them. You wanted even sinners to have a loving and peaceful home. I want you to help me build the same loving home so that it may keep my loved ones from all of life's storms.

<u>Resolution</u>

Today, I will do something constructive and avoid anything destructive to help build a loving and peaceful home for my family.

November 17

Issue: **Hunger**

"Jesus called His disciples to Him and said, 'I have compassion for these people; they have already been with me three days and have nothing to eat. I do not want to send them away hungry, or they may collapse on the way.'" (Matthew 15:32)

Reflection

Even in a modern and advanced world like ours, there are still millions of people who go to bed hungry every night. Worse yet, our world is desperately hungry for spiritual nourishment. Just look at the countless number of violent and random killings of innocent lives around the world every day. People have lost any sense of respect for other human lives and morality. Their souls are starved from lack of spiritual guidance such that they cannot tell right from wrong.

Lord Jesus, I want to see

Jesus, Source of Nourishment and Life, every time you fed the physical bodies of God's people, you always tried to point them to the spiritual life and nourishment. For without proper care and nurturing, our souls will be starved to death or make the wrong decisions. I feel cranky and foggy when my body is hungry. Similarly, I make wrong choices and decisions when my spirit is starved. But, by connecting to you, I will never be hungry.

Resolution

Today, I will take extra time to care and nourish my soul with spiritual food. I will also try to feed the hungry and the poor around me.

November 18

Issue: **Lamp**

"Be dressed ready for service and keep your lamps burning, like people waiting for their master to return from a wedding banquet, so that when he comes and knocks they can immediately open the door for him. It will be good for those servants whose master finds them watching when he comes. I tell you, he will dress himself to serve, will have them recline at the table and will come and wait on them" (Luke 12:35-37)

Reflection

We use lamps to bring light into our homes and show us the way. Without lamps, our lives would be filled with darkness and many fears. We would not know where to go and might run into each other and get hurt. After many years of sin and darkness, we Christians believe that our God has brought light into our world again with the help of the lamp Jesus. Indeed, that lamp has brought light into our world and has shown us the way. Anyone who follows that lamp will find life and other wonderful blessings.

Lord Jesus, I want to see

Jesus, the Divine Lamp in a Dark World, you helped brighten up many lives with your Good News and acts of kindness. You opened the eyes of the blind and showed them the way to true happiness and peace. I might be blinded by worldly stuff and lost in this confusing world. But with you as my lamp, I will see and find the way to true happiness and peace.

Resolution

Today, I will light up the lamp of Jesus for the world around me by doing an act of kindness for someone in need.

November 19

Listening

"My dear brothers and sisters, take note of this: Everyone should be quick to listen, slow to speak and slow to become angry, for one's anger does not bring about the righteous life that God desires. Therefore, get rid of all moral filth and the evil that is so prevalent and humbly accept the word planted in you, which can save you." (James 1:19-21)

Reflection

Listening is a skill with which we are not born. It takes time and much training for us to be a good listener. A good listener makes a wonderful friend and a great partner for life. This person shows us care, concern, attention, understanding, and respect. Certainly, it takes a good listener to hear God speaking to us in the course of a day. For God often talks to us in a whisper amidst this noisy world of ours.

Lord Jesus, I want to see

Jesus, the Word of God made flesh, although you were the voice of God on earth and a great preacher, you were also a wonderful listener. You paid attention to every detail of people's lives and all the emotions that went on in their hearts as you met people from all walks of life. I might not listen well to you daily or others around me, for that matter. But with your help and my constant practice, I will work hard to be a good listener to you and everyone around me.

Resolution

Today, I will focus completely on the people with whom I might talk and listen well for their concerns and ideas.

November 20

<u>Issue:</u> **Patience**

"Be patient then, brothers and sisters, until the Lord's coming. See how the farmer waits for the land to yield its valuable crop and how patient he is for the autumn and spring rains. You too, be patient and stand firm, because the Lord's coming is near." (James 5:7-8)

<u>Reflection</u>

Patience is one of the great virtues that has helped God's people through many years of slavery and hardship before finding the Promised Land and new life. Like most of us, they wanted their prayers answered immediately. But, it often takes a long while and much patience for prayers to be answered. A patient person shows humility, endurance, persistence, and trust in God.

<u>Lord Jesus, I want to see</u>

Jesus, Maranatha God-with-us, you waited for three days in the tomb before being raised from the dead. As you prepared to return to God the Father and Heaven, you asked your disciples to wait patiently for your Second Coming and not let their hearts to be troubled by daily crosses. I might want God to answer my prayers right away. But, as the saying goes, "Good things come to those who patiently wait." I will walk humbly and wait patiently for your Second Coming, as well as God's answers to my prayers.

<u>Resolution</u>

Today, I will try to be patient in taking care of my daily business and in dealing with people throughout the day.

November 21

Issue: **Preparation**

"We speak of God's secret Wisdom, a Wisdom that has been hidden and that God destined for our glory before time began...However, as it is written: 'No eye has seen, no ear has heard, no mind has conceived what God has prepared for those who love Him' – but God has revealed it to us by His Spirit." (1Corinthians 2:7-9)

Reflection

There is no greater feeling than knowing that we are well-prepared for an upcoming event. For us Christians, the important event for which we want to be completely prepared is the moment we will be summoned before the Almighty Judge of the living and the dead. We do not want to be caught unprepared and not have our act together before that Judge. We Christians prepare for that final day by following God's Commandments and completing the Lord's mission that he left for us.

Lord Jesus, I want to see

Jesus, the long-awaited Messiah, you often cautioned your disciples about Judgment Day, "Be prepared! Be alert! You do not know when the time will come." (Mark 13:33) In fact, your entire ministry was about calling attention to that important day and being ready for it. Like the rest of the world, I might think I am invincible and pay no attention to the day you, Lord, might call me home while I'm busy doing worldly things. However, with your guidance, I will take that day and its preparation seriously.

Resolution

Today, I will do one thing, like forgiving someone and letting go of past hurts, to prepare myself for my Judgment Day.

November 22

Issue: **Selfishness**

"But if you harbor bitter envy and selfish ambition in your hearts, do not boast about it. Such 'wisdom' does not come down from Heaven, but is earthly, unspiritual, of the devil. For where you have envy and selfish ambition, there you find disorder and every evil practice." (James 3:14-16)

Reflection

Most of us do not like selfish folks, and yet the rest of the world acts selfishly toward one another every day. Many rich or powerful folks care simply for their fortunes and ambitions without any concern for the poor and the lowly. Big companies continue to accumulate great wealth at high records, while many workers still get laid off or paid dirt cheap wages. God condemned this selfish way of life over and over in the Bible. We humans must change if we want a better world and more blessings from God.

Lord Jesus, I want to see

Jesus, Caring and Generous God, you not only shared your time and miracles with God's people, especially the poor and the misfortunate, but also your own life on the Cross for us. You kept calling everyone not to be selfish with God's blessings and to try to take care of one another. I might be bitten by that selfish bug and care simply about my own welfare. However, with your challenge and example, I will learn to share God's blessings for me with others and be concerned for the welfare of others around me.

Resolution

Today, I will try to share part of myself with others by reaching out to help people in need around me.

November 23

<u>Issue:</u> **Sloth**

"God is not unjust; God will not forget your work and the love you have shown God as you have helped God's people and continue to help them. We want each of you to show this same diligence to the very end, in order to make your hope sure. We do not want you to become lazy, but to imitate those who through faith and patience inherit what has been promised." (Hebrews 6:10-12)

<u>Reflection</u>

Sloth is one of the seven deadly sins that can corrupt and destroy one's soul completely. A slothful or lazy person does not take care of him/herself and does not maintain a healthy and balanced lifestyle. This person cannot complete his/her duties and daily responsibilities. Finally, this person does not care about the well-being of others or the world at large. Basically, a slothful person does very little work and wastes all God's blessings for him/her without any concern at all.

Lord Jesus, I want to see

Jesus, my Source of Encouragement and Motivation, you were sent to us with a mission and were able to compel many people to labor. You worked tirelessly for that mission from sunrise to sunset and sometimes did not have any time to rest. I might be affected by the sloth virus and not work hard for your mission. Or, I might bury all of God's gifts and blessings for me and not live up to my potential. With your example and encouragement, I will take care of my duties at home, work, and church with much pride.

<u>Resolution</u>

Today, I will try to do all the chores that my family has asked me to do, and then I will volunteer myself at church or a charity organization.

November 24

Issue: **Stewardship**

"The Lord said, 'Who then is the faithful and wise steward, whom the Master puts in charge of his servants to give them their food allowance at the proper time? It will be good for that steward whom the Master finds doing so when he returns. I tell you the Truth; he will put the steward in charge of all his possessions." (Luke 12:42-44)

Reflection
When we hear the term stewardship, some of us might think of the folks who help serve us on a plane flight. But, the term "steward" has been used in the Bible extensively to refer to us working in the vineyard of God. For God has entrusted to us—

God's stewards—various gifts, and it is up to us to make good use of them and produce abundantly for the vineyard of God. Anyone who produces more will be rewarded more on the day of harvest. Meanwhile, anyone who does not produce anything will have everything taken away.

Lord Jesus, I want to see
Jesus, Master of the Harvest, you called us to be your stewards in the vineyard of God. You encouraged us and all God's people to make good use of God's blessings by serving God and one another. I might not realize what all my gifts are or how to use them wisely. With your guidance, I will learn each day how to maximize God's gifts and produce more for the vineyard of God.

Resolution
Today, I will try to be a good steward by reviewing what I have been given such as time, talent, and resources. Then, I will use some of those gifts to help someone or bring someone a laugh.

November 25

Issue: **Sympathy**

"Finally, all of you, live in harmony with one another; be sympathetic, love as brothers and sisters, be compassionate and humble. Do not repay evil with evil, or insult with insult, but with blessing because to this you were called so that you may inherit a blessing." (1Peter 3:8-9)

Reflection

We live in a cut-throat society. There is no room to err or make any mistakes. If we do err, we pay a dear price for it. People, especially our leaders, are usually not sympathetic to our plight or difficult situations. No one takes time to listen to someone who is in pain. People have felt disconnected from their leaders. The poor and lowly have been left to fend for themselves. The number of folks who feel lonely and hopeless has increased exponentially. It is time for our world to show more compassion and care for one another.

Lord Jesus, I want to see

Jesus, my Compassionate and Loving God, you never ignored or passed a troublesome person without stopping to help. You were always moved and sympathetic to sad situations. I might be numb and indifferent toward all the heart-breaking circumstances around me. But, you have shown me the importance of showing compassion to one another. Help me to have your sympathetic heart—the heart of God.

Resolution

Today, I will try to be sympathetic to someone or a situation and then bring some comfort and help.

November 26

<u>Issue:</u> **Tears**

"I wrote as I did so that when I came I should not be distressed by those who ought to make me rejoice. I had confidence in all of you, that you would all share my joy. For I wrote you out of great distress and anguish of heart and with many tears, not to grieve you but to let you know the depth of my love for you." (2Corinthians 2:3-4)

<u>Reflection</u>

Some of us might find it difficult and embarrassing to shed tears, for it can be a sign of weakness. Tears also mean that we have failed and given up. The Bible is full of stories about tears and sadness, for God's people had to endure all sorts of hardships, suffering, tragedies, and losses. As God witnessed these terrible things, we are told that God cried for God's people. So, tears are not a sign of weakness, but compassion.

<u>Lord Jesus, I want to see</u>

Jesus, a Sign of God's Compassionate Heart, you cried at least once upon witnessing the death of a widow's son. You could not hide your compassion and care for the misfortunate, and the crowd knew it. For one reason or another, I might not want to shed tears upon seeing a sad situation. But, it is all right to cry and show sad emotions. For I know you will be there to wipe my tears and bring me comfort when I cry.

<u>Resolution</u>

Today, I will try to face a past hurt or some sad and heart-wrenching situation. Then, I will shed tears if the sad emotion moves me to that point.

November 27

Issue: **Thanksgiving**

"Let the peace of Christ rule in your hearts, since as members of one body you were called to peace. And be thankful...And whatever you do, whether in word or deed, do it all in the name of the Lord Jesus, giving thanks to God the Father through Him." (Colossians 3:15-17)

Reflection

Whenever we hear the term thanksgiving, we automatically connect it to the fun family event in November and the turkey dinner with pumpkin pie for desert. But, the root of the term calls us to give thanks. Certainly, it takes more than just one day for us to do that. In fact, we should give thanks every day of our lives. We should thank God for many things: our families, friends, health, lives, jobs, basic necessities, our sharp mind, caring hearts, humble faith, and the list can go on. The more we give thanks, the more humble we become and the closer we grow to God.

Lord Jesus, I want to see

Jesus, my Source of Blessings and Security, you often prayed about giving thanks for everything around you, including your disciples and the revelation of God the Father to them. You reminded God's people to appreciate God's blessings as we learned in His healing story of the ten lepers. I might not be accustomed to showing gratitude to God and others around me. However, with your example and encouragement, I will try to do that more often every day of my life.

Resolution

Today, I will give thanks to you for something in my life and say "Thank you" to someone when I receive something.

November 28

<u>Issue:</u> **Tradition**
"So then, just as you received Christ Jesus as Lord; continue to live in Him, rooted and built up in Him, strengthened in the faith as you were taught, and overflowing with thankfulness. See to it that no one takes you captive through hollow and deceptive philosophy, which depends on human tradition and the basic principles of this world rather than on Christ." *(Colossians 2:6-8)*

<u>Reflection</u>
The term tradition is important not only in a healthy society but also in all thriving institutions. For tradition gives us a set of standards to move forward into the future. It also provides a great foundation on which an institution can build its beliefs and gather its supporters. Unfortunately, our current culture does not seem to appreciate the values of tradition, nor does it care about the importance of standards for the sake of comparison. Therefore, everything nowadays is uncertain and shallow.

<u>Lord Jesus, I want to see</u>
Jesus, the Fulfillment of Ancient Prophecies and Tradition, many thought you came to abolish all the laws and prophets and establish your own tradition. But, you reminded them that your presence was to fulfill past prophecies and complete ancient tradition. Like our modern culture, I might not see any value in traditions and may want to throw them all out and begin a new one. However, I must realize that without tradition I have nothing to hold onto and nothing on which to base my beliefs.

<u>Resolution</u>
Today, I will remember a tradition in my family, culture, or faith that my ancestors often did on occasions of the year.

November 29

Issue: **Volunteer**

"Do everything without complaining or arguing, so that you may become blameless and pure, children of God without fault in a crooked and depraved generation in which you shine like stars in the Universe… I am being poured out like a drink offering on the sacrifice and service coming from your faith. I am glad and rejoice with all of you." (Philippians 2:14-17)

Reflection
Volunteering is definitely under used and under-valued in our society. However, we cannot imagine what our world would be like without volunteers. A volunteer brings us care, love, generosity, gratitude, sharing, community, and much more. A volunteer answers the call of a worthy cause and steps up to help with a community's needs. This generous act comes from a caring heart, and our society must do more to promote and show its appreciation for these heroes.

Lord Jesus, I want to see
Jesus, the Greatest Volunteer of All Time, you voluntarily entered our world to serve us without any fanfare or recognition. You worked tirelessly for the salvation of the world and gave us a great model of humble service. I might not see the importance of volunteers in a successful society. However, I must admit that these great heroes certainly show us how to live as a family of God and act as brothers and sisters in Christ. I need to share myself and be a volunteer.

Resolution
Today, I will sign up for charity work at church, work, or in my neighborhood and volunteer my time and talent.

November 30

Issue: **Worry**

"Therefore I [Jesus] tell you, do not worry about your life, what you will eat or drink; or about your body, what you will wear. Is not life more important than food, and the body more important than clothes? ...For the pagans run after all those things, and your Heavenly Father knows that you need them. But, seek first His Kingdom and His righteousness, and all these things will be given to you as well." (Matthew 6:25-33)

Reflection

None of us is free from worries; our lives are full of worries and anxieties. We worry about our families, friends, health, jobs, necessities, retirement, and so on. Martha worried about being a good host for Jesus. Other folks in the Bible were concerned about what to eat or wear. For many of us these days, terrorism and jobs are at the top of our list of worries. But, our Lord wants us to entrust all our worries to Him and let Him take care of them for us. He knows what is best for us.

Lord Jesus, I want to see

Jesus, my Comfort and Hope, you once said, "Come to me all who are weary and find life burdensome. And I will refresh you." (Matthew 11:28) Many with their worries and life's problems responded to your admonition and came in great numbers during your ministry. I need to do the same and come to you with all my worries so that you can find answers and lift me up.

Resolution

Today, I will recall one thing that has made me worried a lot lately and bring it to the Lord in prayer. Only then can He help me find a solution.

December

Lord Jesus,
I Want to See...

December 1

<u>Issue:</u> **Angel**
"See that you do not look down on one of these little ones. For I tell you, their angels in Heaven always see the face of my Father in Heaven."
(Matthew 18:10)

<u>Reflection</u>
Angels play an important role in our Christian faith and in our popular culture. We can find images of angels in different sizes and shapes in a shopping mall or a local store. The Bible also gives us many examples of human encounters with angels. Jacob wrestled with an angel in a tent in the Old Testament. The Archangel Gabriel appeared to Mary to announce her conception of Jesus. Later, an angel showed up in Joseph's dream to warn him about King Herod and the flight of the Holy Family to Egypt. Angels are an important and endearing figure in the life of Christian believers and our human culture.

<u>Lord Jesus, I want to see</u>
Jesus, my Advocate and Protector, you addressed the subject of angels on several occasions and once talked specifically about the guardian angels of the children waiting on God in Heaven. You believed in angels and most people do, too. Every day, many people have encountered angels or been rescued by them through the help of kind and courageous folks. With your help, I can strive to be an angel to everyone around me by being their protector, guide, comforter, and role model.

<u>Resolution</u>
Today, I will be an angel for someone in need by doing something kind and generous for that person.

December 2

Issue: **Bearer of the Good News**
"How beautiful on the mountains are the feet of those who bring Good News, who proclaim peace, who bring glad tidings, who proclaim salvation, who say to Zion, 'Your God reigns!'" (Isaiah 52:7)

Reflection
Being the bearer of the Good News is often attributed to prophets, preachers, missionaries, and so on. For these folks are committed to bringing the Good News to God's forsaken places and sharing it with their residents. The messages of the Good News are in contrast to the ones of the prophets of doom, who often predicted destruction, calamities, and the downfall of the Kingdom due to its sins. The Bearers of the Good News did the opposite and talked to God's people about God's love, mercy, forgiveness, and other blessings. Naturally, everyone should welcome the Bearers of the Good News.

Lord Jesus, I want to see
Jesus, the Author and Messenger of the Good News, you came to share with God's people the Good News and lift them up from the valley of tears and sadness. You brought hope with your preaching and restored people to a new life with your healing and forgiveness. I might like to be a prophet of doom and condemn sinners with severe punishment. But, I am called to be the Bearer of the Good News and do everything in my power to lift up people around me, especially the broken, with hope and love.

Resolution
Today, I will try to be the Bearer of the Good News by bringing comfort or hope to someone feeling down.

December 3

Issue: **Charitable**
"You, my brothers and sisters, were called to be free. But, do not use your freedom to indulge the sinful nature; rather, serve one another in love. The entire Law is summed up in a single command: 'Love your neighbor as yourself.' If you keep on biting and devouring each other, watch out or you will be destroyed by each other." (Galatians 5:13-15)

Reflection
As we approach the year end, we will see many charitable groups asking us for contributions. Since Biblical times, God's people have been charitable and generous to the poor and the needy. The Bible includes countless examples of wonderful and charitable folks and their caring hearts for their fellow men. But, the most popular one is the story of the Good Samaritan. Since then, we Christians have continued that great tradition and challenged one another to be more charitable in our words and actions.

Lord Jesus, I want to see
Jesus, the Source of Goodness and Blessings, you often ran into with religious leaders over rules and regulations like the one concerning the Sabbath. Time and again, you stress the importance of being charitable to other human beings over rules. I might be too rigid and uptight regarding Church laws and judgments on sinners. Then, you challenge me to be charitable in my treatment of others, especially sinners.

Resolution
Today, I will try to be charitable in my words and actions with people around me, even if I'm in a bad mood or am having a bad day.

December 4

Prophetic

"Christ commanded us to preach to the people and to testify that He is the one whom God appointed as judge of the living and the dead. All the prophets testify about Him that everyone who believes in Him receives forgiveness of sins through His name." (Acts 10:42-43)

Reflection
The term prophetic is used a lot in the Bible and often refers to someone with the ability to predict or something in the future. Prophets Zechariah and Annas, for example, spoke prophetically about the upcoming Passion and death of Baby Jesus when he was presented in the Temple. We, the faithful, believe that God will pass on prophetic messages to God's representatives here on earth to warn us about something or let us know about something serious that's approaching.

Lord Jesus, I want to see
Jesus, the Voice of God Among Us, you certainly made many prophecies, including the one regarding the destruction of the Jerusalem Temple and another concerning your own death and resurrection. Both prophesies came true. But, there is one prophetic message on which you want me to focus wholeheartedly, namely, the prophesy about the Last Day and the eternal life in Heaven. I pray that I will be well-prepared for that prophecy.

Resolution
Today, I will try to recall some of God's prophecies in our human history and learn how they have come true.

December 5

<u>Issue:</u> **Darkness**

"For God did not send God's Son into the world to condemn it, but to save it through Him... This is the verdict: Light has come into the world, but people loved darkness instead of light because their deeds were evil. Everyone who does evil hates the light, and will not come into the light for fear that one's deeds will be exposed. But whoever lives by the truth comes into the light, so that it may be seen plainly that what one has done has been done through God." (John 3:17-21)

<u>Reflection</u>

Our world is surely still in darkness. We see that because all kinds of evil things still happen around the globe and in our country every day. People still act mean and treat one another badly for all kinds of reasons. Sin continues to flex its muscles and dominate virtues. Hatred and violent killing seems to be the battle cry and mantra of many groups in society these days. Injustices and oppression do not seem to let up. Our world looks depressing at times!

Lord Jesus, I want to see

Jesus, the Light of the World, you tried to shine the light of truth and love into our dark and broken world. Your positive and hopeful spirit moved St. Paul to give us this encouraging message, "Where there is sin and darkness, grace and mercy abounds even more." (Romans 5:20) I might be enmeshed in darkness and far away from God's grace. But with your love and mercy for me, I will come back to you and help bring your light to our dark world.

<u>Resolution</u>

Today, I will try not to be mean or do evil things to anyone. Instead, I will perform an act of kindness or mercy for that person.

December 6

Issue: **Deafness**

"At that very time Jesus cured many who had diseases, sicknesses, and evil spirits, and gave sight to many who were blind. So, He replied to the messengers, 'Go back and report to John what you have seen and heard: The blind receive sight, the lame walk, those who have leprosy are cured, the deaf hear, the dead are raised, and the Good News is preached to the poor." (Luke 7:21-22)

Reflection

Not being able to hear is more than just an annoyance. It is a big setback. If we have ever seen two people with hard-of-hearing problem talking to each other, they seem to scream at each other, or they must use sign language in order to speak. Either way, they miss a lot on each other's messages. Our world seems to be deaf to God's messages. All the noise in the world gets turned up and drowns out God's important messages. God can no longer talk to the world and it slowly tunes God out of its life.

Lord Jesus, I want to see

Jesus, the Voice of God, you not only preached God's messages to the world but also helped the deaf hear. You also regularly reminded God's people, "Let those who have ears ought to hear." (Matthew 11:15) Like the world, I often let other noise drown out God's voice speaking to me in my daily life. I need you, Lord, to heal my hearing and put on me your divine hearing aid so that I can hear your messages for me loudly and clearly every day.

Resolution

Today, I will listen carefully to God's messages for me by paying attention to what other people tell me throughout the day.

December 7

Issue: **Disguises**

"A malicious person disguises oneself with one's lips, but in one's heart one harbors deceit. Though one's speech is charming, do not believe that person, for seven abominations fill one's heart. One's malice may be concealed by deception, but one's wickedness will be exposed in the assembly."
(Proverbs 26:24-26)

Reflection

Many people these days love to live in disguise. They try to hide behind social status and other worldly values to make them look good and feel good. Society encourages people to put on masks and make others believe that is "the real you." These masks not only mislead people but also cause them to become pretentious. Over time these disguises keep people from getting to know their neighbors well or acknowledging the changes they need to make to get themselves to become better citizens.

Lord Jesus, I want to see

Jesus, the Real and Gentle Face of God, you definitely object to any form of disguise and often called out the religious leaders for hiding themselves behind the look of holiness and pretense. You certainly want your disciples to be themselves and not try to be someone else. I might want to look a certain way in front of the public. But, I must realize that no one wants to find out that I fooled them by putting on a disguise.

Resolution

Today, I will recall some of my weaknesses and try to embrace them without shame instead of putting on the disguise of being a perfect, wonderful person.

December 8

<u>Issue:</u> **Dreams**

"I will pour out my spirit on all people. Your sons and daughters will prophesy, your old men will dream dreams, your young men will see visions. Even on my servants, I will pour out my spirit in those days. I will show wonders in the Heavens and on the earth… And everyone who calls on the name of the Lord will be saved…" (Joel 2:28-32)

<u>Reflection</u>
Every night we go to sleep, we dream; often however, we cannot remember our dreams. Every day we wake up, but often our dreams do not come true. Everyone also dreams and hopes for something. Dreams are what keep us alive and motivate us to overcome our daily crosses and hurdles. God's people dreamed of the Promised Land, which kept them going through their horrible days of slavery, war, and destruction. We Christians need to start dreaming about Heaven and spiritual things if we want to make it through our earthly life.

<u>Lord Jesus, I want to see</u>
Jesus, my Dreams and Hopes, your incarnation made the ancient dream of God's people for a Savior come true. However, you did not stop there. Rather, you encouraged God's people to dream more and dream big by focusing on Heaven and the eternal life. With your guidance, I will start dreaming about Heaven and my home in that place with you after my time here on earth.

<u>Resolution</u>
Today, I will think of a world where there is only peace and love, with no more fighting and hurting one another. That is one of my dreams.

December 9

Issue: **Eyes**

"Two blind men were sitting by the roadside, and when they heard that Jesus was going by, they shouted, 'Lord, Son of David, have mercy on us!' …Jesus stopped and called them. 'What do you want me to do for you?' He asked. 'Lord,' they answered, 'We want our sight.' Jesus had compassion on then and touched their eyes. Immediately, they received their sight and followed Him." (Matthew 20:29-34)

Reflection

Someone once said, "The eyes are windows to the soul." If your eyes have a problem or cannot see for some reason, our soul might become dark or be affected in a major way. Among our five senses, the eyes play an important role in connecting with our interior as someone can look into our eyes and see if we are telling the truth. If we do not safeguard our eyes and prevent al bad and evil things from entering through them, our souls will be infected and corrupted over time. Our world is suffering from this problem.

Lord Jesus, I want to see

Jesus, my Healer and Age-Old Physician, you opened the eyes of the blind and let them see a new world. You also relentlessly helped many people have a good spiritual vision and connected them to their souls and the whole spiritual world. I might be blind or lose my spiritual vision and not be able to see you in my daily life and the wonderful blessings of the spiritual world. With your help, I will regain my spiritual vision slowly.

Resolution

Today, I will spend time gazing on you on the Cross and let you open my spiritual vision to gain a better perspective.

December 10

Issue: **Foresight**

"Understand then, that those who believe are children of Abraham. The Scripture foresaw that God would justify the Gentiles by faith, and announced the Gospel in advance to Abraham: 'All nations will be blessed through you.' So, those who have faith are blessed along with Abraham, the man of faith." (Galatians 3:7-9)

Reflection

Foresight is often used to describe a visionary, prophet, or special saintly person. The Bible and Christian tradition give us ample examples of some of the individuals with this extraordinary ability. John in the Book of Revelation tells us what he foresaw about the Last Day and the next world. Joseph was sold by his brothers, but had the ability to foresee the future, and the Egyptian King Pharaoh exploited him for the good of his kingdom. If we could foresee like these people, we certainly would know the future and what is coming. That would be a great gift.

Lord Jesus, I want to see

Jesus, the Greatest Prophet of All Times, time and again you showed us how you foresaw Heaven and the spiritual world. You also wanted to pass on to us this extraordinary ability so that we can be well-prepared for the next life. I might have some doubts about foresight or not see the value of the ability to foresee the future. However, your admonition convinces me that this ability will give me an advantage over the Devil and the Power of Darkness.

Resolution

Today, I will focus on acquiring the ability to foresee the future by thinking about future things and spending time in prayerful reflection.

December 11

Issue: **Generosity**

"Remember this: whoever sows sparingly will also reap sparingly, and whoever sows generously will also reap generously. Each person should give what one has decided in one's heart to give, not reluctantly or under compulsion, for God loves a cheerful giver. And God is able to make all grace abound to you, so that in all things at all times, having all that you need, you will abound in every good work." (2Corinthians 9:6-8)

Reflection

Generous folks are God's helping hands that bring our present world a bit closer to Heaven and make our journey on earth a bit easier to walk. A generous spirit is what helps make God's love a reality and drives away the dark and evil spirits of our world. The Bible is surely full of generous folks, including the Good Samaritans and the poor widow who gave her whole livelihood to the Temple donation box. Our world would be darker and meaner if there are fewer generous folks.

Lord Jesus, I want to see

Jesus, Source of Blessings and Goodness, you rarely took time off for yourself but preferred to give everything you had to the world around you, especially the poor and the misfortunate. You also encouraged your disciples to be generous with God's blessings to others. Their generosity will be repaid handsomely. I might be selfish and stingy with others around me, much like the rest of the world. However, with your example and encouragement, I will learn to give more of myself to others, especially those in need.

Resolution

Today, I will share some of my time, talent, and treasures with a charity group or someone who might need help.

December 12

<u>Issue:</u> **Happiness**
"A person can do nothing better than to eat and drink and find satisfaction in one's work. This too, I see, is from the hand of God, for without God, who can eat or find enjoyment? To the person who pleases God, God gives wisdom, knowledge, and happiness, but to the sinner God gives the task of gathering and storing up wealth to hand it over to the one who pleases God..." (Ecclesiastes 2:24-26)

<u>Reflection</u>
Everyone in this world—young and old, rich and poor, men and women—agree on one thing, namely, we all want to be happy. But, each person has his/her own way to achieve happiness. Most of God's people in the Old Testament wanted to get to the Promised Land, whereas some wanted to sit by a pot of meat in Egypt. The hungry would be happy if they could be fed. The leper would find happiness if cleansed, the deaf if their ears opened, the blind if their sight restored, the sick if their health healed. We Christians will be happy if we make it to Heaven.

<u>Lord Jesus, I want to see</u>
Jesus, my Source of Peace and Happiness, after your miracle of loaves and fishes, the crowd came to you for earthly happiness and worldly possessions. But, you pointed them to a good spiritual life and Heaven. I might make the same mistake and assume happiness can be found in the things of this world. But, your wisdom tells me that true happiness can only be found in you and a good spiritual life. Only with you will I be truly happy.

<u>Resolution</u>
Today, I will search for happiness by doing something nice for someone and sharing God's love with the world.

December 13

Issue: **Heaven**

"For as I have often told you before and now say again even with tears, many live as enemies of the Cross of Christ...Their mind is on earthly things. But, our citizenship is in Heaven. And we eagerly await a savior from there, the Lord Jesus Christ, who by the power that enables Him to bring everything under His control, will transform our lowly bodies so that they will be like glorious body." (Philippians 3:18-21)

Reflection

Most people these days know about Hell and mention it often in their daily conversations. Perhaps they are not even afraid to go to Hell. Unfortunately, many people do not talk about Heaven today or care enough about it and desire to spend eternity there. Imagine if God's people rarely mentioned the Promised Land; they never would have wanted to be there or end up there. We Christians need to talk about Heaven often and keep that favorite destination before us at all times.

Lord Jesus, I want to see

Jesus, Son of God, you left Heaven to enter our world and offered your life on the Cross for our salvation. As you returned to Heaven to prepare a place in your Father's home for your faithful followers, you promised to return and bring us along. I cannot be happier than to end up with you and the Heavenly hosts in Heaven after this life! Help me keep my eyes focused on that goal and do everything possible to achieve it.

Resolution

Today, I will talk to someone about Heaven and the eternal life and help this person think seriously about that destination.

December 14

Issue: **Hope**
"Never be lacking in zeal, but keep your spiritual fervor, serving the Lord. Be joyful in hope, patient in affliction, faithful in prayer. Share with God's people who are in need. Practice hospitality. Bless those persecute you; bless and do not curse. Rejoice with those who rejoice; mourn with those who mourn. Live in harmony with one another..." (Romans 12:11-16)

Reflection
Throughout our human history, hope has been the sunshine that brings light and warmth to a dark and cold place. It gives a breath of fresh air to a dying person and a reason for all of us to wake up every morning. Without hope, God's people would never have made it through those horrible days of slavery. Without hope, the early disciples would never have left the upper room or would never have gone out to tell the world about the risen Christ. Hope is like God's helping hand that lifts us out of a tough situation and continues to move us forward.

Lord Jesus, I want to see
Jesus, my Joy and Hope, you brought hope and new life to so many people during your short ministry on earth. You also sent out your disciples on the same mission and commanded them to give hope to the world. I might put others down and have a negative attitude or a grim outlook of the world. However, your hopeful viewpoint of the world encourages me to go out to bring smiles and lift up as many people as I can.

Resolution
Today, I will speak words of hope and encouragement to someone who might be down in the dumps and make that person feel good.

December 15

<u>Issue:</u> **Humility**

"Do nothing out of selfish ambition or vain conceit, but in humility consider others better than yourselves. Each of you should look not only to your own interests, but also to the interests of others. Your attitude should be the same as that of Christ Jesus." (Philippians 2:3-5)

<u>Reflection</u>

Humility is a very difficult virtue for us to practice and acquire in this day and age. For our society encourages people to brag about many things on social media and take credit for themselves in every way possible. Our prideful culture even makes it difficult for people to apologize for their mistakes. In fact, many horrible things in the world would not happen if the perpetrators knew how to act humbly. The Prince of Darkness would not be created if Lucifer had served God faithfully and humbly. Judas would still be alive if he had been humble enough to admit his wrong, just as Peter did.

<u>Lord Jesus, I want to see</u>

Jesus, Son of God and of Mary, you humbled yourself to take on our human form, even though your home was in Heaven. Your humble birth in a manger certainly was not fit for the King of the Universe. I am moved by your humble attitude and example of good Christian living. I need to practice this virtue daily and come to possess it for myself so that your wonderful glory may shine through me.

<u>Resolution</u>

Today, I will humbly do something at home, work, or church without seeking recognition or praise.

December 16

<u>Issue:</u> **Image of God**

"He [Jesus Christ] is the image of the invisible God, the first born over all creation. For by Him all things were created: things in Heaven and on earth, visible and invisible, whether thrones or powers or rules or authorities; all things were created by Him and for Him. He is before all things, and in him all things hold together." (Colossians 1:15-17)

<u>Reflection</u>
The phrase "the image of God" is part of the spiritual language and is seen in the Bible and many theological and spiritual books. It basically tells us that we were created out of God's love and in the likeness of God. When we look at ourselves, we can see the image of God. The same thing is true when we look at our neighbor—we see the image of God. Hence, we must treat our neighbors with love and respect, just as we treat God.

Lord Jesus, I want to see
Jesus, Son of God, you are the image of the invisible God. For years, our God was invisible to our human eyes. But, with your presence, we have seen God for the very first time. Indeed, you assured your disciples that they had seen God the Father through you, when they insisted you show them God the Father. I am honored to be made in the image of God. I am grateful to have a glimpse of our God having seen you. I need to invite more people to see God by showing you to them.

<u>Resolution</u>
Today, I will help someone meet God by showing this person an act of love and kindness.

December 17

"I always thank my God as I remember you in my prayers because I hear about your faith in the Lord Jesus and your love for all the saints. I pray that you may be active in sharing your faith, so that you will have a full understanding of every good thing we have in Christ. You love has given me great joy and encouragement because you, brothers and sisters, have refreshed the hearts of the saints." (Philemon 4-7)

Reflection

Whenever we hear about joy, we often think about moments like Christmas, the birth of a child, winning something, finding something that was lost or is valuable, completing a task, or making it to the finish line. This is certainly a wonderful feeling to have and one of the fruits of the Holy Spirit. If our lives are full of joy, we are very close to Heaven. We Christians are called to share the joy of following Christ with the world.

Lord Jesus, I want to see

Jesus, my Joy and Hope, you came to show us the joy of Heaven and the eternal life. You also let your disciples see how real joy looks compared to the fleeting joy of this world. I might try to chase that fleeting joy day in and day out like the rest of the world. But, real joy must be rooted in the spiritual world, because it has a real purpose. Anyone who finds joy will always be content and at peace amidst the daily chaos and turmoil of this world.

Resolution

Today, I will search for real joy by continuing Jesus' mission and serving the poor and the misfortunate around me at God's kitchen.

December 18

Issue: **Light**

"You are the light of the world. A city on a hill cannot be hidden. Neither do people light a lamp and put it under a bowl. Instead, they put on its stand, and it gives light to everyone in the house. In the same way, let your light shine before all, that they may see your good deeds and praise your Father in Heaven." (Matthew 5:14-16)

Reflection

We cannot imagine what our lives would be like without light. A cloudy, gloomy day surely affects our mood and how we feel and act that day. A life in darkness would make us fearful and cause us to run into each other. Realizing this problem, God said, "Let there be light," and there was light at the moment of Creation. The source of that light comes from the sun, which continues to brighten our days with the dawn of every morning. Light not only shows us the way but also brings life into our dark world.

Lord Jesus, I want to see

Jesus, Light of the World, you came to bring us spiritual light and guide us in our dark world. After many years of waiting for it, your light brought excitement and new life to God's people, including the blind, the hopeless, the possessed, the leper, the hungry, the poor, the sinful, and many others. For some reason, I have been far away from your light. But, having seen that light can do in our world, I would like to be near it from now on.

Resolution

Today, I will shine the spiritual light of Jesus to some dark place where someone might be experiencing sadness or hopelessness and help that person feel at peace and hopeful.

December 19

<u>Issue:</u> **Long**
"God can testify how I long for all of you with the affection of Jesus Christ. And this is my prayer: that your love may abound more and more in knowledge and depth of insight, so that you may be able to discern what is best and may be pure and blameless until the day of Christ, filled with the fruit of righteousness that comes through Jesus Christ – to the glory and praise of God." (Philippians 1:8-11)

<u>Reflection</u>
God's people longed for a Savior and a return trip to their homeland after being away from slavery. The blind, the leper, the possessed, the hopeless, and the sinful all longed for a new life. Some of us long for a loving family and a good job, whereas our children mostly hope to have good friends and wonderful Christmas gifts. The point is that we all long for all sorts of things in life. We Christians, besides some earthly wishes, want to pine for the eternal life in Heaven after this life.

Lord Jesus, I want to see
Jesus, my Answer and Hope, you longed to gather all of God's people back to the fold and give them a new life, including the eternal life. Throughout your ministry, you continued to express that hope to your disciples and wanted them to help you make it come true. I have longed for various things in my life. But, there is one very important thing on which you want me to keep my eyes focused at all times— the eternal life in Heaven.

<u>Resolution</u>
Today, I will focus on my longing for the eternal life a little more seriously by thinking about it constantly and looking for ways to make it come true.

December 20

<u>Issue:</u> **Messiah**
"Andrew, Simon Peter's brother, was one of the two who heard what John had said and who had followed Jesus. The first thing Andrew did was to find his brother Simon and tell him 'We have found the Messiah (that is, the Christ)'. And he brought him to Jesus. Jesus looked at him and said, 'You are Simon son of John. You will be called Cephas.' (which means Peter)." (John 1:40-41)

<u>Reflection</u>
God's people were driven into slavery for years and lost everything, including their homes, country, possessions, and dignity. They prayed that the Lord would finally give them a Messiah to defeat the Romans and lead them back to the glorious days of King David. This Messiah would be their political leader who would restore their dignity and fight for their interests. Many prophets and sacred writings discussed this Messiah and long anticipated His coming.

Lord Jesus, I want to see
Jesus Christ, although God's people did not recognize you as the Messiah during your ministry on earth, you performed all the works of a Messiah for God's people. You healed the sick, fed the hungry, drove out demons, and lifted up the hopeless with your Good News. I might not feel as enthusiastic about the Messiah as God's people did. But, I still need a Messiah to protect me from the Power of Darkness and guide me on this earthly journey.

<u>Resolution</u>
Today, I will give thanks to God for Jesus as my Messiah to save me and watch over me.

December 21

<u>Issue:</u> **Miracle**
"They devoted themselves to the Apostles' teaching and to the fellowship, to the breaking of bread, and to prayer. Everyone was filled with awe, and many wonders and miraculous signs were done by the apostles. All the believers were together and had everything in common." (Acts 2:42-44)

<u>Reflection</u>
For a nonbeliever, miracles happen few and far between. But, for us believers, miracles happen daily and all around us. We believers recognize these extraordinary events easily and see God's hands in them all. Christians also believe that miracles are a sign of God's love and presence in our lives. God simply extends His hand to help us in times of need by having miracles happen around us. The Bible and Christian tradition give us many examples of miracles that have happened throughout human history.

<u>Lord Jesus, I want to see</u>
Jesus, the Miracle Worker, your life and ministry made miracles happen often and easily in our world. Your miracles helped shine light into darkness and brought hope and new life to a miserable situation. I certainly want to welcome more miracles around me. But, I must create an environment that allows and fosters miracles by being a faithful, trusting, and loving Christian.

<u>Resolution</u>
Today, I will point out a miracle that has happened to me recently and then give thanks to God for it.

December 22

"I have become the servant of Christ by the commission God gave me to present to you the Word of God in its fullness – the mystery that has been kept hidden for ages and generations, but is now disclosed to the saints. To them, God has chosen to make known among the Gentiles the glorious riches of this mystery, which is Christ in you, the hope of glory." (Colossians 1:25-27)

Reflection

Our life is a mystery. God is a mystery. Jesus' conception and resurrection is a mystery. This term is used to summarize something that is indescribable. Religion tends to accept mysterious things as the core of its beliefs, whereas science wants to uncover and explain all mysteries. These two powerhouses seem to be at opposing ends with each other when it comes to mystery. No wonder they are often tangled up with each other in the eyes of the public. Many people have even wondered if religion and science can co-exist in this world.

Lord Jesus, I want to see

Jesus, the Mystery of God's Love and Salvation, your life is a total mystery, because the Bible adds it to the mystery of the journey that God's people underwent in the Old Testament. I feel joyful and relieved when I begin to understand a mystery and make some sense of it. Yet, life would be dull and boring if there are no mysteries.

Resolution

Today, I will recall a mystery that has fascinated me over the years and now remain content with it without any concern.

December 23

Issue: **Peace**

"Do not repay anyone evil for evil. Be careful to do what is right in the eyes of everybody. If it is possible as far as it depends on you, live at peace with everyone. Do not take revenge, my friends, but leave room for God's wrath, for it is written: 'It is mine to avenge; I will repay,' says the Lord... Do not be overcome by evil, but overcome evil with good." (Romans 12:17-21)

Reflection

If there is one thing our world is desperately in need now more than ever, it is peace. If we must ask for one thing for our daily life, it is certainly peace. In fact, our longevity will be reduced tremendously if we have no peace inside and outside ourselves. For our human history is full of wars, fighting, and killing. The ultimate reward at the end of our life on earth is peace; hence, we hear and see this farewell wish—R.I.P.

Lord Jesus, I want to see

Jesus, Prince of Peace, after your resurrection, you appeared to your disciples and greeted them, "Peace be with you!" You also sent them out to continue your mission and suggested they greet every household with the message of peace. In your eyes, peace seemed like the crucial element of our daily life or the air that we breathe. I pray that I will always appreciate this precious gift above everything else and try to bring it wherever I go.

Resolution

Today, I will try to promote peace in the world by rejecting any form of violence, even when I am upset.

December 24

<u>Issue:</u> **Promised Land**

"Then Joseph said to his brothers, 'I am about to die. But, God will surely come to your aid and take you up out of this land to the land God promised on oath to Abraham, Isaac, and Jacob.' And Joseph made the sons of Israel swear an oath and said, 'God will surely come to your aid, and then you must carry my bones up from this place.'" (Genesis 50:24-25)

<u>Reflection</u>

The Promised Land is used in the Bible to describe a paradise-like place that God promised to His people since the days of Abraham. It provided many good things, like milk and honey, for them. This land was the best place for God's people to grow and plant a fruitful harvest and also the safest place for them to build their homes and raise their families. For God watches over this land and protects God's people and everything in it.

<u>Lord Jesus, I want to see</u>

Jesus, the Protector and Caretaker of God's People, you continued to guide and show your people the way to Heaven during your ministry. Like the Good Shepherd, you fed them and healed their wounds, while trying to search for the lost to bring home. I thank God I have you as my shepherd to lead me to the green pasture of the Promised Land. I cannot wait to be on that land and enjoy the blessings of Heaven that you promised to your faithful ones.

<u>Resolution</u>

Today, I will prepare myself for the Promised Land by making sure I have followed your Commandments.

December 25

Issue: **Christmas**

"This is how the birth of Jesus Christ came about: His mother Mary was pledged to be married to Joseph, but before they came together, she was found to be with child through the Holy Spirit... All this took place to fulfill what the Lord had said through the prophet: 'The virgin will be with child and will give birth to a son, and they will call Him Immanuel' – which means, 'God with us.'" (Matthew 1:18-23)

Reflection
Christmas is certainly the most joyous and exciting time for the whole world. People of other faiths and traditions cannot help but want to join in with Christians to celebrate the wonder and awe of the season. The whole world tries to prepare for Christmas by lighting its homes and decorating its front yards with lights. Certainly, this is a special time for us Christians. After many years of praying and asking for a Savior, our God finally answered and sent us God's Son Jesus with His birth at Christmas.

Lord Jesus, I want to see
Jesus, the Immanuel, your birth at Christmas is what God's people have been praying and hoping for many years. Now that hope has become a reality. You have certainly brought hope and joy to God's people. That is exactly what Christmas is all about. Perhaps I have caused pain and sadness around me. But with the example of Christmas, I will learn to bring hope and joy to the world, just as you have done for us.

Resolution
Today, I will try to bring someone around me hope or joy by giving that person a positive compliment or sharing uplifting words.

December 26

<u>Issue:</u> **Refuge**

"David said: 'The Lord is my rock, my fortress and my deliverer; my God is my rock, in whom I take refuge, my shield and the horn of my salvation. He is my stronghold, my refuge and my Savior – from violent people you save me. I call to the Lord, who is worthy of praise, and I am saved from my enemies.'" *(2Samuel 22:2-4)*

<u>Reflection</u>

For us to survive a day anywhere on earth, we need a refuge. God's people lost their refuge by being driven into slavery, and they felt like fish out of water. For us Christians, God is our refuge through all kinds of situations. A refuge is a shelter that shields us from the elements and protects us from anything dangerous and harmful. The Power of Darkness and bad habits are some of the harmful things from which God our refuge will protect us.

<u>Lord Jesus, I want to see</u>

Jesus, my Shelter and Fortress, you once expressed your life of poverty as follows, "The birds have nests. Foxes have dens. But, the Son of Man has no place to lay his head." Clearly, you did not have a refuge. However, you became a refuge for God's people as they all flocked to you for help and salvation. I certainly need you to be my refuge in this life and look forward to a sturdy and long-lasting refuge prepared for me in Heaven.

<u>Resolution</u>

Today, I will look at my home and give thanks to God for my humble refuge. Without it, I would be out in the elements and exposed to all sorts of danger.

December 27

Rejoice

"Rejoice in the Lord always. I will say it again: Rejoice! Let your gentleness be evident to all. The Lord is near. Do not be anxious about anything, but in everything, by prayer and petition, with thanksgiving, present your request to God. And the peace of God, which transcends all understanding, will guard your hearts and minds in Christ Jesus." (Philippians 4:4-7)

Reflection

God's people rejoiced when they were freed from slavery, when they found the Promised Land, and when they were healed from poisonous snakes. The Bible shares with us many examples of rejoicing. One of the best moments is the birth of our Lord Jesus. His birth brought joy not only to the Heavenly hosts but also the shepherds in the field. They were glad to hear about this incredible news and anxious to meet Baby Jesus.

Lord Jesus, I want to see

Jesus, my source of Joy and Hope, as the Good Shepherd, you rejoice when you find a lost sheep and bring it home to the fold. Certainly, we cannot forget the amazing moment when the disciples saw the risen Christ again. For they all rejoiced. I might not have experienced that joyful moment yet, but I surely have had occasions that bring me rejoicing. I hope I will see the risen Lord and rejoice with Him in Heaven.

Resolution

Today, I will rejoice with my family and friends by celebrating a special event and spending time with them.

December 28

Issue: **Silence**

"I said, 'I will watch my ways and keep my tongue from sin; I will put a muzzle on my mouth as long as the wicked are in my presence.' But, when I was silent and still, not even saying anything good, my anguish increased. My heart grew hot within me, and as I meditated, the fire burned; then I spoke my tongue: 'Show me, O Lord, my life's end and the number of my days; let me know how fleeting my life is.'" (Psalms 39:1-4)

Reflection

Something our modern world is very afraid of is silence. For our world is filled with noise, and everyone feels very uncomfortable if there no sound for several minutes. People try to fill dead air with trivial talk. People can go to church and observe people around us dealing with silence before and after the service. Only when we remain in silence will God and other people be able to communicate with us.

Lord Jesus, I want to see

Jesus, the Voice of God in Our Midst, you often found yourself in a quiet place for prayer. You also spent forty days and nights in the silent setting of the desert. Like the rest of the world, I might be fearful of silence, But, I know that you entered our world on a silent night and often communicate with us in moments of silence. Help me embrace silence without any fear.

Resolution

Today, I will spend some prayer time remaining in silence without reading or saying anything and see if I feel uncomfortable.

December 29

<u>Issue:</u> **Singing**
"Be careful then how you live – not as unwise but as wise, making the most of every opportunity, because the days are evil. Therefore, do not be foolish, but understand what the Lord's will is... Speak to one another with psalms, hymns, and spiritual songs. Sing and make music in your heart to the Lord, always giving thanks to God the Father for everything in the name of our Lord Jesus Christ." (Ephesians 5:15-20)

<u>Reflection</u>
St. Augustine once said, "Singing is praying twice." Singing is certainly one of the important elements in any worship setting. We can travel to the ends of the earth and still find singing and music in worship and culture. In fact, singing and music are ways we humans can be connected to one another regardless of culture, customs, and language barriers. It is also the best way for us to join ourselves to God. For singing and music take us right out of this world.

<u>Lord Jesus, I want to see</u>
Jesus, the Starting Note in my Life Song, you began the singing and new song that brought joy, hope, and new life to our world at the moment of your birth. Since then, this singing and new song has caught on around the world and continued to touch many lives. I might not have a good voice or enjoy singing. But with your encouragement, I will keep singing and giving praise to you for the rest of my life.

<u>Resolution</u>
Today, I will sing *Amazing Grace* or some song to give praise to you and thank you for all the blessings you have given me.

December 30

<u>Issue:</u> **Welcome**

"Jesus took a little child and had the child stand among them. Taking the child in his arms, He said to them, 'Whoever welcomes one of these little children in my name welcomes me; and whoever welcomes me does not welcome me but the One who sent me.'" (Mark 9:36-37)

<u>Reflection</u>

One of the topics the Bible talks about is the importance of being welcoming and hospitable. Jesus called on God's people to welcome the poor, the lame, the misfortunate, and especially children, to their banquets, even though these folks have no way to repay us and invite us back. When we welcome and show someone hospitality, we not only try to be friendly and warm but are also kind and caring to that person. Jesus surely wants us to practice this virtue often.

<u>Lord Jesus, I want to see</u>

Jesus, Kind and Gracious Host, you never made anyone feel rejected during your ministry on earth. Rather, you constantly reached out and welcomed folks from all walks of life. I might be influenced by our divided society and only befriend certain groups of people. But, you call me to welcome and embrace everyone so that I will be welcomed at the Gate of Heaven someday.

<u>Resolution</u>

Today, I will try to reach out and welcome people with a warm handshake and a kind smile.

December 31

<u>Issue:</u> **Wish**

"…If anyone does not remain in me, one is like a branch that is thrown away and withers; such branches are picked up, thrown into the fire and burned. If you remain in me and words remain in you, ask whatever you wish, and it will be given you. This is my Father's glory, that you bear much fruit, showing yourselves to be my disciples." (John 15:6-8)

<u>Reflection</u>
On our birthdays, we are asked to make a wish while blowing out the candles on our cake. Standing in front of a wishing well, we are invited to think of a wish before throwing in a coin. God's people in the Old Testament wished to make it to the Promised Land, whereas people in the New Testament wished to have a Messiah. We humans all have our own wishes and dreams. For we all lack something as a human being. Wishing helps make up for whatever is lacking within us and in our world.

Lord Jesus, I want to see
Jesus, Source of all Goodness and Blessings, you had your own wishes, namely, hoping that your disciples would be united as one in love and the whole world would turn back to God and be saved. I surely have my own wishes and pray that you, Lord, will make them come true for me. But, the best wish of mine is to be able to enjoy the eternal life and see you face to face in the Kingdom of Heaven.

<u>Resolution</u>
Today, I will think of a wish and bring it to you, Lord, in prayer to ask for your blessing and ask you to make it come true for me.

Index to Issues

Contrite: February
Controversy: July
Convenient: June
Conversation: August
Conversion: February
Cooperating: August
Correction: February
Corrupt: April
Cost: March
Counsel: May
Courage: January
Courteous: July
Create: September
Criticize: September
Cross: March
Cursing: August
Danger: June
Dark Night of Soul: March
Darkness: December
Dead End: March
Deafness: December
Death: November
Deceitful: June
Decent: October
Decisions: January
Dedicated: June
Delightful: August
Demons: March
Deny: August
Desert: March
Desirable: January
Despair: November
Despise: June
Destroy: July
Detachment: February
Determined: September
Devil: February
Devoted: May

Difference: May
Diligence: September
Direction: January
Disappointment: July
Disaster: August
Discern: May
Discord: February
Disguises: December
Dissension: May
Distraction: June
Distress: October
Divine: December
Doubt: June
Dove: January
Dreams: December
Duty: July
Ears: January
Easter: April
Encouraging: October
Endurance: June
Enlighten: October
Enriched: June
Enterprising: September
Entice: June
Entitlement: November
Eternity: January
Evil: February
Example: September
Excitement: April
Excuse: June
Expect: October
Experience: June
Exploit: August
Eyes: December
Failure: May
Fairness: June
Fasting: March
Fault: February

Favor: August

Fear of Lord: March

Feed: August

Feel: October

Feet: May

Fidelity: May

Fight: July

Flexibility: August

Focused: September

Follow: January

Forbear: April

Foresight: December

Forgiving: March

Freedom: July

Freewill: July

Friendship: June

Friendly: September

Fruitful: May

Fulfilling: April

Fun: June

Gate: April

Generosity: December

Gentle: June

Giving: November

Gladness: June

Glory: April

Gluttony: November

God's Will: July

Good Soil: August

Good work: November

Gracious: August

Grateful: November

Grief: November

Guidance: August

Habit (Good): October

Hand: August

Happiness: December

Harm: August

Harmony: August

Hate: August

Head: January

Healing: November

Heart: August

Heaven: December

Hell: March

Helping Hand: August

Hero: July

Holiness: April

Home: November

Honest: June

Honorable: July

Hope: December

Hospitality: September

Humility: December

Humor: August

Hunger: November

Hurt: August

Hypocrisy: February

Idolatry: April

Ignorance: January

Image of God: December

Indifference: January

Influential: May

Inquisitive: February

Inspired: April

Instrument of God: Sep

Integrity: October

Intercede: April

Jealous: July

Jesus: January

Journey: May

Joy: December

Judge: April

Justice: July

Kindness: September

Kneel: March

Knowledge: September
Lack: August
Lamp: November
Laugh: July
Law: October
Learn: September
Licentious: July
Lies: February
Life: October
Lift up: May
Light: December
Listening: November
Lonely: July
Longing: December
Lost: March
Loud: July
Love: March
Loyal: May
Lust: April
Materialism: September
Mean: July
Meaning: September
Mercy: March
Messiah: December
Miracle: December
Missionary: October
Morality: October
Motivate: September
Mountain: March
Mouth: May
Mystery: December
Neighbor: August
Noisy: July
Obedience: February
Outcast: April
Pain: October
Passion: April
Patience: November

Peace: December
Persecution: May
Persevere: September
Pleasure: August
Pledge: January
Praise: October
Prayerful: March
Predestined: April
Prejudice: July
Preparation: November
Pressure: October
Problem: September
Promise: July
Promised Land: December
Prophetic: December
Protection: July
Prudence: October
Purpose: May
Reach out: May
Reasonable: September
Reconcile: March
Reflective: September
Refresh: August
Refuge: December
Regret: October
Rejection: March
Rejoice: December
Relief: August
Repent: March
Resentful: July
Resistance: October
Respect: October
Responsible: September
Rest: January
Restore: April
Retribution: October
Reveal: January
Revenge: October

Reverence: April
Reward: April
Right: February
Rock: April
Role Model: September
Rude: July
Sabbath: Feb
Sacred: May
Sacrifice: March
Salt: May
Satisfied: June
Save: March
Search: January
Security: September
Self-Control: July
Self-Examination: February
Selfishness: November
Serenity: September
Servant: October
Shame: April
Sign: August
Silence: December
Sin: February
Sincere: June
Singing: December
Slander: August
Sloth: November
Snake: February
Soil: August
Solidarity: September
Solutions: October
Sorrowful: March
Soul: July
Sow: January
Special: March
Spirit: May
Spiritual: January
Steadfast: September

Stewardship: November
Strength: September
Strive: August
Struggles: October
Stubborn: February
Suffering: April
Sunshine: February
Sympathy: November
Tears: November
Temperance: August
Temple: February
Temptation: March
Terror: September
Thanksgiving: November
Thoughtful: September
Tolerance: July
Tomorrow: April
Tradition: November
Treasure: August
Trust: October
Truth: January
Understand: May
Unity: July
Victory: March
Vineyard: June
Violence: October
Virtuous: January
Vocation: January
Volunteer: November
Waste: October
Weakness: February
Welcome: December
Willingness: August
Wisdom: January
Wish: December
Witness: May
Worry: November
Wrong: February